The News Formula

A Concise Guide to News Writing and Reporting

The
News
Formula

A Concise Guide to
News Writing and Reporting

Catherine C. Mitchell
Mark D. West

University of North Carolina, Asheville

St. Martin's Press
New York

Editor: Suzanne Phelps Weir
Managing editor: Patricia Mansfield Phelan
Project editing: Jennifer Valentine
Production supervisor: Scott Lavelle
Art director: Lucy Krikorian
Text design: Levavi & Levavi
Cover design: Patricia McFadden
Cover photo: Charles Thatcher/Tony Stone Images

Library of Congress Catalog Card Number: 95-67064

Manufactured in the United States of America.

0 9 8 7 6
f e d c b a

For information, write:
St. Martin's Press, Inc.
175 Fifth Avenue
New York, NY 10010

ISBN: 0-312-09710-7

Contents

Preface

Movies like *All the President's Men* and television talk shows that feature journalists have created a public impression that writing for newspapers is an art and a sacred calling. News writing professionals, however, know that writing for newspapers starts with good craftsmanship—and then sometimes moves on to art.

In reality, a traditional formula guides news writers who work on deadline. Newspaper reporters and editors have developed this formula to meet the needs they see in their readership and to fit the pressures that news writers face.

✦ THE NEWS FORMULA

The News Formula: A Concise Guide to News Writing and Reporting aims to demystify the craft of news writing by presenting an outline of the news formula. In a short text, the book summarizes the traditional wisdom on news writing that any seasoned editor would pass on to a junior reporter.

This book rests on a description of two ideas that all news writers and editors know and use: the five Ws and the inverted pyramid. Together these two concepts form the news formula—an interlocking system of assumptions that dictate what information goes into a news story, and where in the news story a specific piece of information goes. The news formula gives reporters a way to analyze the information in their notes and tells them how to organize and structure this information in their news stories.

Although the news formula is a creation of American newspapers, the basic methods for gathering information and the principles for translating it for an audience apply to almost all writing for the media. The broadcaster follows the same approach to gathering information and analyzing its importance, but tends to use a briefer, punchier vocabulary. Anyone who wishes to practice successful public relations must also know the news formula. Most publicists send written articles to newspapers, radio, and television, and press releases that arrive in already usable form have a much higher chance of making it into the news. All writers face the primary task of getting the attention of their audience and then holding that attention long enough for the audience to read, hear, and see the message.

The News Formula addresses beginning journalism students enrolled in their first course in news writing. The book explains, simply and quickly, how to write a news story. It assumes that people learn to write by writing, not by reading about writing. It also assumes that what beginning writers need most is a skilled and compassionate reader/editor to give them detailed critical comments about their writing. This book sketches the basic principles of news writing and then gets out of the way, allowing students early in the semester to stop reading about writing and turn their focus to the central part of a news writing course, the actual composition of news stories.

Because the book aims at an efficient presentation of information, it may appear simplistic to some. It does not, however, attempt to present an overly simplified body of material for weak students to plod through over the course of a semester. Instead, the simplicity supports the cramming of a significant amount of information into a book that's a "quick read."

The book aims to serve a classroom setting in which students begin the semester by writing complete news stories in basic prose. As the semester progresses through the process of receiving critical feedback from the professor and then writing more articles, students begin to develop a writing style that starts to move from basic craftsmanship to art.

◆ THREE MAIN PARTS

The book contains three parts:

1. Writing the News
2. Gathering the News
3. The News Business

In a weekend, students can read Part One and obtain the fundamental guidance necessary to begin writing complete news stories. This part aims to present the basics of news writing quickly, so that students can move on to the really important part of a beginning course in news writing—doing the writing itself.

Students can read the other two sections later in the semester after they have mastered the basics of the news formula. Part Two, "Gathering the News," discusses ways in which reporters find news—the way they cover news events, the types of news events they cover, and the strategies they use in covering them. Part Three discusses journalism as a business, and the way a working reporter functions as a professional, relating in a businesslike way with editors, sources, other journalists, and the law.

✦ THE STRUCTURE OF THIS BOOK

This book uses a "how-to" structure to help students move through the material quickly. Since the book has the basic goal of getting students started quickly at writing, the how-to structure encourages them to skim, stopping only at the details they seek. Headings, subtitles, and end-of-chapter summaries should help skimming readers quickly understand the rules that make up the news formula and let them begin writing news articles. In the interest of brevity, the text avoids long examples of published news stories, since students can easily obtain these on the news racks every day.

Reading published articles in conjunction with *The News Formula* will give students an understanding of the realities of news writing. By definition, newspaper work lacks perfection. Writers on deadline work from instinct and do not have time to polish their words. Almost every published article will reveal a writer who has broken some rule outlined in this book.

For instance, the passive voice, though a very weak construction, litters the pages of American newspapers. Also, stories often begin with trick leads in which writers confuse readers by delaying the presentation of important information until late, sometimes very late, in the story.

Reading and critiquing real articles published under deadline should help beginners see the importance of craftsmanship in news writing. Reading these articles should also show students that most news stories follow the basic formula outlined in this book.

Many of the exercises at the ends of chapters draw on articles that students will find in newspapers. Therefore, the authors recommend that the instructor use a newspaper as an additional text.

✦ INSTRUCTOR'S MANUAL

Both of the authors use the workshop method to teach news writing as described in the Instructor's Manual. The manual also includes three detailed syllabi, one for a workshop course in news writing that uses the exercises in this book, a second course that uses longer real-world assignments, and a third course that uses predominantly fictional in-class assignments.

✦ OTHER BOOKS

This book does not claim to be the definitive work on news writing. It only aims to sketch a quick introduction to the news formula. William Zinsser's *On Writing Well* and Strunk and White's *Elements of Style,* both excellent works, quickly and efficiently tell writers how to improve style and voice—but no other text briefly explains the structure of news stories.

Many other excellent texts discuss news writing at more length. These texts support a teaching method that moves students into the writing of complete news stories at a more leisurely pace; students spend a great deal of time analyzing data and writing leads before they begin writing entire articles. Our assumption, however, is that the readers of this book don't have that sort of time. *The News Formula* supports a quick-start approach to the teaching of news writing.

Finally, a section entitled "Recommended Reading," at the end of the text, outlines other excellent books about news writing that students may want to consult.

✦ FINAL THOUGHTS

Learning the news formula allows beginners to write news stories that will work for readers and editors alike, but mastering the news formula only starts a student moving toward becoming a fine news writer and an excellent news gatherer. After mastering the formula, most seasoned news writers dispense with it in the same way that a composer dispenses with playing scales when writing a concerto. Entertaining writing does not come from tossing out the formula, however, any more than the artistry of a composer comes from putting wrong notes or extra measures in a sonata.

Great writing comes from knowing the formula so well that a reporter writes beyond it, not without it. As the first step toward excellent writing, a beginner must write with the news formula. This book shows how to start becoming a competent news writer. After beginners have mastered the craft of news writing, they need to do much more refining before their level of craftsmanship allows their writing to approach art.

✦ ACKNOWLEDGMENTS

We would like to thank the following professional colleagues who took the time to read and comment on the manuscript of this book: Avi Bass, Northern Illinois University; J. Laurence Day, University of West Florida; James L. Highland, Western Kentucky University; Gwyneth B. Howard, Essex Community College; Hugh Merrill, University of Florida; Pam Narney, Nova Community College; Ted Nugent, University of Maryland–Baltimore County; Mary-jo Popovici, Monroe Community College; Shirley B. Quate, Indiana University–Indianapolis; Garrett W. Ray, Colorado State University; Howard Seeman, Humboldt State University; and Nancy E. Stetson, College of Marin.

We really would like to thank everyone at St. Martin's Press for working with us on this project; Suzanne Phelps Weir, in particular, and Jennifer Valentine helped us immensely.

Catherine C. Mitchell
Mark D. West

The News Formula

A Concise Guide to News Writing and Reporting

PART ONE

Writing
the News

CHAPTER 1

The Contract
─────────────────────── ▄

With the Reader

When readers buy a newspaper, they bring with them a set of expectations about what they are going to get. They expect stories dealing with certain sorts of subject matter, written in one of a very few specific formats, about things that have happened recently. Readers don't want these expectations frustrated, and they will abandon newspapers that don't fulfill their expectations.

Often, reporters think in terms of a contract with their readers. The reader agrees to buy the newspaper and thus provide an income for the reporter. In return, the reporter agrees to provide information the reader wants or needs, in a format that makes the important information available to the reader in a hurry. As with any other contract, violators of this contract imperil themselves. The police won't arrest reporters for misunderstanding or failing to consider the needs of their readers. The readers will just stop reading.

Editors have a contract with the reader, too. An editor has an incredible amount of news copy available—enough to fill several newspapers every day without any repetition. Unfortunately, it is the amount of advertising that determines the size of a particular edition, not the amount of news available. Because the news must fit into the holes left by the advertising, editors always have news left over.

Beyond this, most readers have only a limited amount of time to devote to news stories. Studies have shown that most people read only the first few paragraphs of stories. That makes it imperative that the important information in the story come in the first paragraphs.

If a newspaper's staff wants people to read its stories, the language must be clear, concise, and simple. At the first unfamiliar word, the first too-complex sentence, readers simply stop reading. Perhaps readers should follow complex grammar and story structure, but they don't—and newspapers should not try to educate them.

Further, for many people the modern newspaper has ceased to be a major source of spot news. In a crisis, people turn to television, because there they do not have to wait long for the information. Newspapers, to compete, must provide the sorts of in-depth coverage that television can't, because of its time constraints. Yet newspapers also must acknowledge the reader's need for short and concise articles that get the information across as quickly as possible. The reporter must remember these sometimes competing needs for thoroughness, in-depth coverage, and simplicity.

Knowing what is and isn't worth reporting distinguishes the merely good reporters and editors from the great ones. In the newspaper business, people compliment fine reporters by saying they have a "good news sense" or a "nose for news." Deciding on the **newsworthiness** of an event means deciding whether readers will think the information was worth what they paid for it. Making a decision about the newsworthiness of an event tells a reporter not only whether to bother to write the story, but also how to start the story and how to structure it.

The most important step in determining newsworthiness is to know the readers. They, even more than editors or publishers, are the final court in which a news writer's work is judged. If, in their opinion, a writer provides the information they want in a format they like, he or she is a success. If not, that writer fails. In defining news, then, the touchstone of all considerations is the reader.

✦ NEWSPAPER AUDIENCES

As we've emphasized throughout this text, news writing is product-oriented. The focus of attention is always on a newspaper story as a consumer good—a good that must fulfill the desires of consumers if it is to succeed. A news writer, then, has to understand the needs of those who will consume the news product.

The audience—the group of readers who subscribe to a specific publication—is thus a crucial reference point in making a judgment of newsworthiness. A reporter must, therefore, have a good picture of what the audience considers important. Most newspapers define their audience geographically. The audiences for the Richmond (Va.) *Herald* and the Charlotte (N.C.) *Observer*, for example, are very similar except that they live in different areas. Some newspapers have audiences defined by ethnicity or religion; others, like *The Christian Science Monitor*, have broad geographic ranges but cover the news from a particular perspective. No matter what the paper, though, determining the newsworthiness of an event—or, for that matter, determining what specific items should make up the lead of the story—hinges on an understanding of the audience.

Getting to know the audience of a publication isn't hard, but it does take time. The reporter working for a general-interest publication usually lives in the community in which a newspaper is published, and in this case knowing one's readers is analogous to knowing one's neighbors. With newspapers that have a special-interest audience, the topical thrust of the publication is, by definition, of interest to the audience.

In any event, what stories are covered, and how stories are written, are determined by what the audience thinks is news.

✦ THE CRITERIA OF NEWSWORTHINESS

A standard classification lists six criteria of what makes a story newsworthy. Four are audience-specific and differ by audience and locale; these are **impact, proximity, prominence,** and **unusualness.** Two are universal, holding true for audiences in different locations; these are **timeliness** and **conflict.** All of these criteria focus on the needs of the audience, because all consideration of what is and what isn't news focuses on the needs and interests of the reader.

Impact

To be newsworthy an event must have some impact on readers. The more seriously the event affects readers, or the greater the change it might generate in their lives, the more interested they will be in it.

Judging the effect an event will have on readers can be difficult; the important issue is not how the event will affect the reporter, but how it will impact the audience. Sometimes the audience may not understand how or why an event has significance for it; in this circumstance, an important aspect of the story is explaining how it will affect people's lives.

Occasionally, a story appears with a lead like:

> The Sylvan Corporation, a Detroit manufacturer of air-conditioner components, has announced plans to build a plant in the Boswell area. The plant will manufacture vacuum control components for new domestic automobiles.

This lead is fine, as far as it goes. But it could readily be improved by emphasizing the impact of the event on the average reader.

> The Sylvan Corporation, a Detroit manufacturer of air-conditioner components, has announced plans to build a plant in the Boswell area. The plant is expected to employ approximately 400 people and generate about a million dollars in tax revenues a year for Delphos County.

Similarly, good reporters don't just report that the county plans to build a new $15 million jail. They also explain how much impact this $15 million expenditure will have on the property taxes on a typical home, or what this will mean for the future of law enforcement in the region.

Often, newspapers rewrite copy from national sources to add a local-impact angle. A story might come off the wire like this:

> Representatives of the state Educational Services Division announced today that plans for closing older school buildings in Kansas would be accelerated. Savings of up to $300 million per year are expected, according to Lynne Douglas, secretary of educational services.
>
> "We understand that people might object to the school closings, but, from our perspective, it's necessary," said Douglas. "Our mandate is to give the taxpayers the best schools possible for their dollars, not to preserve schools because of local sentiment."

Such a story has a generic feel. It could run in any newspaper in Kansas, because it deals with generalities about the state rather than with specifics that affect individual people. The story with an improved local-impact angle might read:

> Representatives of the state Educational Services Division announced today that plans for closing older school buildings, including Jesse L. Croom Middle School in Cheney Crossing, would be accelerated. Savings of up to $300 million per year are expected, according to Lynne Douglas, secretary of educational services.
>
> "They want to close Croom Middle School and send all the kids over to West Central just to save a buck or two," said Tami Tenille, a spokesperson for an organization called Save Our Schools, or SOS. "We think a better way to save money would be to fire Lynne Douglas."

Feature stories are often just news stories in which the lead focuses on the impact of an event on a single individual.

> Today, Shenita Simpson has about a five-minute bus ride to Croom Middle School. Next year, if Lynne Douglas has her way, Shenita will ride about 45

minutes to West Central, and Croom School will be empty for the first time in 47 years.

Representatives of the state Educational Services Division announced today that plans for closing older school buildings, including Jesse L. Croom Middle School in Cheney Crossing, would be accelerated. Savings of up to $300 million per year are expected, according to Lynne Douglas, secretary of educational services.

If readers don't see the impact an event will have on them, the news story won't interest them. If readers are made to understand the ways in which events will change their lives, they'll find a story fascinating.

Proximity

The second audience-related criterion of newsworthiness is proximity. All other things being equal, the closer to home an event is, the more newsworthy it is. An earthquake in a far-off land, for example, isn't nearly as interesting as a local one. Proximity affects impact as well; clearly, an event that happens far away is less likely to have an effect locally than something that happens nearby.

This is why local newspaper staffers will almost always try to inject some local angle when they rewrite wire copy. The old joke about a newspaper headline that reads "Moon Explodes; No Dakotans Killed" contains more than a little truth.

In general, though, the stories that a reporter is likely to cover always have proximity. The trick is to play that angle prominently, rather than burying it. A lead like the following will catch no one's attention.

> In a nationally televised press conference, Bernhard Lowe, chief executive officer of Lowe Holdings, PLC, announced a restructuring that will result in the closing of several national retail chains.

The lead works much better when a local angle is employed:

> In a nationally televised press conference, Bernhard Lowe, chief executive officer of Lowe Holdings, PLC, announced a restructuring that will result in the closing of the local Levine Brothers appliance store as well as several national retail chains.

Prominence

The third criterion, prominence, is name recognition. Readers care more about the doings of famous people than about events in the lives of ordinary people. Defining fame is not as obvious as it may seem, though—the definition depends on the audience. The local mayor, the president, and certain actors and musicians are all prominent, but readers in Omaha, Neb., really don't care about the mayor of Eugene, Ore. When things happen to prominent people, the events are often newsworthy, though the same event might be of little interest if it involved only ordinary people.

As an example, consider the president's health. People catch the flu every day, and the press runs routine flu epidemic stories. But when President George Bush came down with the flu at a state dinner in Japan, the story dominated all media. Similarly, most people have problems in their marriages without much public notice, but the relationship between the Prince and Princess of Wales is a staple of magazines and newspapers because "Di" and "Charlie" are prominent people.

Unusualness or Novelty

The final audience-centered criterion of newsworthiness is unusualness or novelty. A cliché of the newspaper business is that it's not news when a dog bites a man, because dogs bite men every day. It's definitely news when a man bites a dog, however, because men seldom bite dogs. Judgments of unusualness are linked directly to the lives and expectations of the audience. In some community weeklies, for example, trips taken by local people are given routine coverage—but trips to exotic locales, such as New Zealand, get detailed coverage, precisely because to the readers of those newspapers these trips are unusual. Larger publications cover only vacations that are extraordinarily grand or exotic—as when Malcolm Forbes rented the Concorde to fly guests to his birthday bash in Tangiers. Things that might be everyday occurrences in another part of the world may be very unusual for local readers. A story about a foreign recipe that calls for dog steaks might warrant play in an American newspaper—although such an article shows a lack of understanding about other cultures.

Timeliness

An old newsroom adage is that even the most crucial news event has approximately the same life span as raw fish. As with fish, there is no such thing as news that is too fresh. To help readers fulfill their need for surveillance—timely information—a newspaper reports events in the very first edition that comes out after the event has happened. A story that can sit for a month isn't, by definition, a news story.

Readers want as much warning about upcoming events as possible. So the more recently an event has occurred, the more newsworthy it is. The importance of timeliness shows up in the word *news* itself. Embedded in "news" is "new." The term *news* comes from early German publications, so many of which used "new" (or, in German, "neue") as part of their titles that the word entered both German and English as a term for the type of timely information those publications contained.

Conflict

Another element that readers look for in a newspaper is conflict. The German philosopher Hegel taught that the truth emerges from the conflict between opposing viewpoints. This idea forms the basis for the structure of American government, with its competing powers of the Senate, the House, and the administration. The American legal system, with two competing sides in every lawsuit, follows the same principle. Fiction inevitably involves conflict, whether between people, armies, or lovers. For example, Vladimir Propp studied thousands of folktales from many countries and found that almost all the stories dealt with conflict of some sort. Some theorists have argued for a psychological or even physical basis for the universal belief in the importance of conflict.

Whatever the cause, though, people want to read stories containing conflict. News stories that describe crimes, political disputes, or even the romantic troubles of the rich and famous all involve conflict.

✦ THE MOST NEWSWORTHY STORY

A survey once asked a group of editors to name the most important story of their lifetimes. The most common answer was the Japanese attack on Pearl Harbor. Second most frequently mentioned was the assassination of President John F. Kennedy. Both of these stories involved many different news criteria.

The Pearl Harbor story had high levels of the four audience-specific characteristics of the newsworthy story. It involved proximity for a national audience because the Japanese attacked U.S. territory. The event involved prominent people: The president—the first citizen—called for a declaration of war in a moving speech to a joint session of Congress. The event was unusual, since the United States goes to war only rarely, and an armed attack on U.S. territory is even more exceptional. And, as everyone guessed then and saw later, the attack was the first blow in a war that affected everyone in the nation.

The story was also high in the two universal criteria of newsworthiness. Most papers came out with special extra editions immediately upon the declaration of war because they wanted to make the information as timely as the printing technology of the age would permit. And of course, a declaration of war has a powerful and obvious conflict angle.

✦ DECIDING ABOUT NEWSWORTHINESS

Most stories, though, aren't about declarations of war. Most are about far more mundane topics. Unfortunately, no simple calculation will tell if a story high in proximity but low in unusualness is more newsworthy than a story that is high in unusualness but low in proximity. The news sense that reporters and editors speak of with such respect isn't a sixth sense that can draw a good reporter to a crime scene before the crime occurs. Instead, reporters with a nose for news can quickly assess whether a particular event may, with a little digging, yield a newsworthy element that will fascinate readers.

Each day, an editor handles hundreds of stories. Some will have a strong local angle. Some will be about very unusual events. Some will be breaking news—news so timely that the wire services send bulletins as the events unfold. Most, though, will contain some combination of audience impact, timeliness, and unusualness. The editor must decide which stories to run and how much prominence to give to these stories. Do the readers care more about a plane crash in Venezuela, a space shuttle mission, or the mayor's drunk driving arrest?

The individual reporter must pick out the most important aspect of a news story, because this information must go into the first paragraph of the story. Often this selection is a simple matter. Most reporters cover perfectly straightforward events in which only one element makes sense in the lead. The more interesting stories, though, often involve several important factors. Then the reporter, with the readers in mind, must pick the most important angle and feature that angle in the lead.

The main criterion in picking the aspect of a story to use for the lead has to be the needs and interests of the audience. Timeliness and conflict, after all, are easy enough to identify, but deciding what the audience will rate as worthwhile news is a more difficult matter.

✦ THE CONTRACT WITH THE READER

The definitions of newsworthiness offered here may sound like pandering to the reader. Is it right for newspapers to cede the decision about which stories will see print? If the readers don't think a story is important, should it see print? Who should decide what's important? Do reporters know enough to take that responsibility? Should publishers or editors, with their political and social biases, make the decision? Should the government? Reporters and editors are the ones who make the final decision about publication, but a newspaper that ignores its readers' news needs puts its survival at risk.

When people buy a Stephen King novel, they expect a tale of occult horror. If instead they found the story of Mopsy the Bunny's first day at school, they would feel cheated. Readers and authors have a contract, an unwritten but real set of agreements about what a given piece of writing will contain. A novel entitled *Love's Windswept Flame,* for example, had better contain some romantic clinches.

The same unwritten contract exists between a newspaper and its readers. The readers agree to pay for the time and expense and intellectual effort of a newspaper staff, if that staff quickly and efficiently gives readers information they can use.

Creativity or art is not a part of this basic contract. People buy newspapers for information. They see creative, fanciful presentation as an embellishment if it improves the effectiveness of the communication of information—but creativity is icing on the cake, not the cake itself. Creativity or art that interferes with clear communication violates the unwritten contract between newspapers and their readers. People do buy newspapers for entertainment. They may like the editorial page—the home of columnists who are the most creative writers on the paper—but for many readers this is secondary. The majority of readers want information that will fulfill their needs for surveillance of their town, their nation, and their planet.

✦ READERS' NEEDS

A major area of study in modern sociology is **functionalism**—the examination of the functions that firms, institutions, and products serve in society. Many functionalists approach the role of media in American society by discussing the uses and gratifications of the audience. They look at the reasons people use newspapers, and at the needs that newspapers serve. Researchers have concluded that newspapers serve three main functions. They help fulfill readers' needs for surveillance, entertainment, and social interaction.

Surveillance

Many people use the media primarily to fulfill what sociologists call **surveillance** needs. People read newspapers to get information that will help them predict events that may affect their lives. They want and need to know what to expect of the future so that they can plan their activities, both personal and corporate. For instance, after seeing an article entitled "Home Loan Interest Rates Drop," they may decide to buy house paint. Dropping interest rates would make it easier to sell the family house, and a gleaming new paint job would make the house even more marketable. On the other hand, an article about a hurricane heading toward town can inspire a run on the grocery store for milk and bread. No matter how readers use an article, though, they want timely information about events that may affect them.

Newspaper advertising also serves a surveillance function. It comes as a bitter shock to many beginning reporters, but many newspaper buyers have almost no interest in the news. These people buy newspapers for the advertising alone. They want to find out what movies are showing at which theaters, what store has a sale on toaster ovens, and who has a kitten to give away. Whether the information concerns products or politics, it must be accurate and current. Old news, or false news, serves little surveillance purpose.

Entertainment

People also buy newspapers for entertainment. People enjoy reading newspapers. They like the mental stimulation provided by the comics, the columns, the crossword puzzle. Newspapers cater to this need for entertainment by providing non-news material like comics pages, advice columns, and sports pages. The score in the Atlanta Braves game isn't something a reader needs to know for personal safety or for political or economic reasons, yet many people want to know about the game, and buy newspapers for that reason.

The entertainment function of newspapers helps explain why people read those lurid supermarket tabloids. Reading an article like "Savage Parakeet Ate My Child" wouldn't serve any surveillance function. People with good sense will not board up their windows and stay indoors after reading such an article. They read those tabloids for entertainment, and then talk about the articles with friends. Such articles serve entertainment and social functions, not surveillance.

Feature articles—stories that focus on human interest—primarily entertain. So do most columns, the comics, the sports pages, and opinion pages. Feature and sports articles often follow the same writing rules that apply to news stories. By this book's working definition of news, though, the information in these stories often isn't timely and doesn't serve a surveillance function.

Social Interaction

The final function that the newspaper fulfills is, oddly enough, social. Many routine daily conversations center on information that people have gleaned from the media. People often disagree about politics, religion, and their outlook on life. Few subjects are interesting enough to fuel a conversation and yet noncontroversial enough to discuss without getting into an argument. The newspaper, television, and radio provide such safe but interesting topics. When someone asks a coworker about the Braves game, and uses information from the sports pages in conversation, the newspaper is serving a social function.

Even the most factual article, perhaps an article clearly designed to serve a surveillance function such as "Common Market Stalls on Tariff Talks," might provide entertainment or a conversational topic for some.

◆ STORY FUNCTIONS

No story fulfills only one function. Even a story about international trade negotiations might be amusing or interesting to some, and might spark a conversation. Articles intended for pure entertainment, like the endless Elvis sightings in the tabloids, may somehow inform. If nothing else, they inform readers about some people's exceptional gullibility.

The primary function of the story, though, determines its structure and format. Most people read the newspaper primarily to fulfill the surveillance function. Newspapers usually segregate nonsurveillance material into separate sections, such as features and sports sections. The stories that matter to people's lives, the stories that contain the information they buy a newspaper to read, are surveillance stories. Newspaper writers call these stories hard news. In these hard news stories, the writer tries to provide facts for hurried readers. Newspaper people believe that a simple and clear writing style, coupled with a straightforward and logical structure, will do this in the most effective way.

This book focuses on how to write news stories whose main function is telling readers about events that will affect their lives. To serve readers' need for surveillance, newspaper stories must be accurate in all respects. They must be concise and clear, because readers are, after all, scanning the newspaper for material that will help them. Stories must conform to certain rules of structure and style—because readers and editors expect it.

In short, the form of the news (or surveillance) story established during the American Civil War survives today because it dictates a way to compress the news quickly. The most important information comes at the beginning of the story, with less important information presented later. A discussion of how to write according to that format occupies most of the rest of this book.

SUMMARY

- Newspapers have a contract with readers to give them newsworthy information.
- Readers' interests determine the news.
- Events that will impact readers are news.
- Events that occur in close proximity to readers are news.
- Things that happen to prominent people are news.
- Information or events that are unusual or novel are news.
- The most recent or timely information is the most newsworthy.
- Stories that involve conflict are news.
- Most big stories involve all these elements.

IN-CLASS EXERCISES

1. What is the audience of your local newspaper? How did you determine the demographic composition of that audience? Is the audience for the newspaper the same as the population of your city, county, or state? What makes you think so?

2. Examine the first five news pages of your local newspaper. For each story, answer the following questions: Who is impacted by it? Does it have a local angle? How is it novel? How is it timely? Who is in conflict in the story? Do all news stories have all of the news values?

3. Find a story in your local daily newspaper that you believe has significant impact on a majority of the newspaper's readers. Describe that impact. Would the story have the same impact in a city in another state? Why or why not?

4. What kind of story would you consider novel? Why? Would such a story seem novel to the average reader of your local paper? Why or why not?

5. Go to the library and locate a special-interest publication. Who is the average reader of that publication? Write out this publication's "contract with the reader."

6. Locate a paper from another city, and find an article about a subject that is also covered in your local newspaper. How do the articles differ, and in what ways are they the same?

7. Look at the *New York Times*. How does this newspaper's treatment of stories differ from that in your local newspaper? Why? What is the contract with the reader of the *New York Times?*

OUT-OF-CLASS EXERCISE

Obtain a press release from a local agency or group, and get a copy of your local newspaper. Does the event described in the press release have each of the elements of newsworthiness? Describe them. Would the average reader of your local paper consider the article newsworthy?

CHAPTER 2

Accuracy and

Fairness

This chapter deals with the topic of what readers want and need in a modern newspaper. In a world where there's a varied array of news sources, they want the news in a hurry. And in a world where there are multiple sources of information, many of which are trying to sell them something, they want accurate news without editorializing or sermonizing from the reporter. They want news that grabs them, news packaged so they can tell in an instant if they want to read further. They want balanced news reporting that does not push any predetermined point of view.

✦ NEWS OVERLOAD

In the information age, new technologies for gathering and transmission flood readers with news. The Sunday edition of a major metropolitan daily like the *Atlanta Constitution* may be 200 or 250 pages long. Even in the smallest hamlets, residents can choose from four or five national newspapers, several state and local papers, three news magazines, and more than 40 television channels (some devoted exclusively to news).

Consumers respond to this flood of information with behaviors called "scanning" or "bursting." Cable television studies have shown that most television viewers watch several shows at once, "bursting" back and forth between them with remote channel controls. Researchers watching the eye motions of newspaper readers have concluded that the average newspaper reader flicks over the page, scanning only the first paragraph or headline of most stories, reading only short snippets of a few. Rarely does the reader turn a page to complete a story that skips or jumps to another page. Hardly ever do readers finish a story. At best, most readers scan only a headline or the first paragraph of most stories.

Under less favorable circumstances—for instance, when readers have trouble with a difficult word or a clumsy phrase—they read even less. Readers in a hurry do not turn to a dictionary to figure out an unfamiliar word. They just stop reading.

Sometimes pundits charge the newspaper audience with lacking education because readers will not sit still for stylistic experiments and complex words. These complainers miss the problem. Today's audience has a lot to read in a very limited amount of time. They have to scan. In that context, a reader's resistance to stylistic complexities in a newspaper makes sense.

If a writer makes a reader waste time by presenting complex or grammatically difficult material, the reader will throw down the newspaper and pick up a novel or turn on the television or do the dishes. If a writer buries the important facts of the story in the middle, readers will never see this information because they will not read that far. If a writer includes judgmental language or biased words and phrases, readers will notice. Especially if they disagree with the writer's viewpoint, readers will resent the intrusion of opinion, and they will stop reading.

People have had access to multiple media sources of information for a long time. Between World War I and World War II, New Yorkers could read more than a dozen newspapers covering their city alone. Yet today, with the widespread availability of out-of-town papers and the increase of electronic media news coverage with cable and satellite technologies, more and more readers have begun to scan. Some researchers actually blame this tendency on television itself, which trains teenagers to zap around, looking for something that excites or interests them. Newspaper readers with these consumption habits will not patiently read through a story.

Since editors know that their readers suffer from news overload, they have developed a method for packaging news stories for the immediate use of the consumer. In this book we call this method **the news formula.**

✦ STORY STRUCTURE

An important part of the news formula for structuring the traditional news story is the **inverted pyramid.** In the inverted pyramid the most important information goes first in the story, with the first paragraph containing as much of the important information as possible. The remaining paragraphs contain material that elaborates on or develops ideas presented in the first paragraph. The writer presents all this as clearly, concisely, and accurately as possible.

Other ways of writing a news story are possible. The *Wall Street Journal*, for example, often uses a format in which the story initially focuses on an individual. The story then takes a global view of the problem, event, or issue highlighted by the example of the individual in the first section of the story. At the end, the story returns for a concluding look at the individual described in the lead, as discussed in Chapter 10. Countless other variations are possible.

Yet the standard news formula, the inverted pyramid, remains the accepted way to write a news story for most general circulation newspapers in the United States. Every writer for every newspaper in the country uses the formula most of the time; every editor will accept it, and every reader will understand it. This standard formula does not win prizes for creative writing; it will not make editors clap their hands in delight—but it will work.

◆ SUMMARY AND SYNTHESIS

An important aspect of the news formula is the idea that a hard news article should synthesize and summarize. To write a good news story, a reporter must observe everything, scanning for material that seems important. An article that goes into too much detail, or that forces readers to search for crucial information, makes it much more difficult for them to decide whether the story is important. When this happens, they are much less likely to read the story, and much more likely to misunderstand or misconstrue it.

So newspaper writers must condense the welter of quotes, impressions, and facts surrounding an event to make a coherent narrative of reasonable length. They have to do this without changing any of the facts along the way. Sometimes, of course, this can be difficult. At press briefings, government officials, in an honest attempt to inform, will tend to stun reporters with a blizzard of facts. At a trial, motions and countermotions, conflicting testimony from all sides, and a mountain of other information often obscure what really happened instead of clarifying the event. Even at an event as simple as an automobile accident, the statements of eyewitnesses often differ, and usually need condensation anyway.

So the news story must digest and summarize information, often reducing it to its bare bones. Because no reporter should count on readers to finish an entire story, the writer must summarize the most important facts of the story and present them immediately. In the next few paragraphs, the writer may give a particularly telling quote and summarize other less important facts. In the remainder of the story, summary paragraphs alternate with quotations. This is an outline of the inverted pyramid format, the standard format for news stories.

✦ THE PERILS OF SUMMARIZING

The task of summarizing probably causes more trouble for news writers than any other aspect of the news story. Almost everyone knows, and everyone should know, that when a writer uses quotation marks, the words within the quotes must reflect exactly what the source said. A similar standard of accuracy applies to summaries of information. If, in a summary paragraph, a reporter says that someone said something, then the summary has to be accurate.

Most lawsuits against newspapers arise from summary material. This was the point of contention in a recent court case pitting Janet Malcolm, a writer for *The New Yorker,* against Jeffrey M. Masson, a psychiatrist who revealed what he claimed were unsavory details of Sigmund Freud's intellectual past. In this case, Masson argued that Malcolm's summaries and reconstructions of quotations had misrepresented him. The writer had used a tape recorder, but could not locate all of the material she had quoted or summarized. This left the courts with the complex task of first deciding what Masson had really said, and then deciding whether the reporter had accurately transcribed and summarized it. Having a tape recording of what was said always helps, but even then, a reporter must take extreme care in summarizing.

The most crucial part of summarizing is the first or "lead" paragraph. It has to tell the bare bones of the story to satisfy the needs of the skimming reader, and so it has to paraphrase. Some editors label any lead that fails to summarize the entire story a **trick lead.** These were much in vogue during the years of **"yellow journalism."** Trick leads try to trick the reader into continuing with the story instead of honestly summarizing the event so that the reader can decide whether to go further.

An example, given by newspaper writer H. Allen Smith, is the following horror from a Colorado newspaper:

Drip, drip, drip. Oh God! If only the sun would shine!

Can you guess what this story is about? Forty days of rain, right? No, it was about a woman who killed herself, and about the suspicion of her family that she had done so because of an unrelenting spell of bad weather. An even worse example is:

Sex, sex, sex. Now that I have your attention, what about the decline in stock prices?

Such trash is the staple of high school newspapers, where it passes for cleverness.

✦ NEWS AS A COMMODITY

Newspapers package and sell news—a commodity, a product, an item for sale in the marketplace. In capitalist societies, the marketplace decides the value of any commodity, including the news. People, in effect, vote for the value of items with their dollars. Their purchasing decisions have the same effect on goods that their votes at the ballot box have on politicians. A free market assumes that people will buy what they think they want or need. Newspapers, and by extension news stories, follow this rule. Since newspapers sell news, they must fulfill consumer wants and needs just like any other business in the marketplace.

Often, reporters fresh from college see news writing as a sacred mission, a calling to right all injustice. Most experienced reporters and editors believe in this sacred mission, too, but they temper their belief with cynicism.

They know they cannot easily wipe out all injustice. A story will not sell if it attacks a situation that most readers consider just fine. Reporters must resist the temptation to report the news through the haze of their personal, political, moral, or social agenda. Most readers have no use for editorializing or biased journalism. They want the facts. Average readers don't want opinion. If they decide a newspaper does not present the facts, without bias, they will stop buying it.

An early 20th-century newspaper publisher, E. W. Scripps, summarized the marketplace approach this way: "The newspaper's first duty is to make a profit, so that it can continue to publish."

✦ ERRORS DESTROY TRUST

People buy the news to help them plan their actions and make sense of their lives. Any sort of inaccuracy or error in a news story damages the people who based decisions on that inaccurate news.

Even small errors, like misspelling someone's name, matter. Substituting "Steven" for "Stephen," for example, might seem like a trivial error, but it would seem anything but trivial to someone who unexpectedly found himself named by the newspaper as a murder suspect. The newspaper's attorney would not think it a minor thing, either.

Mistakes like this have a second effect, not as dramatic as a lawsuit but in the long run equally detrimental. When readers see a factual error in a newspaper, the fragile trust they have in that paper suffers. No interview subject will ever again trust a reporter who fails to get down correctly such a basic thing as the spelling of a name. Enough errors, and sources and readers will decide that they cannot trust the paper. Then they will not grant interviews and will not bother to read the paper.

Even the most trivial mistakes, then, are serious because of their effects on the faith readers put in individual reporters and in the newspaper where they work. The credibility of a newspaper builds slowly over years. Although intangible, it represents a newspaper's most valuable asset, because it is what makes people buy the newspaper.

When a newspaper is bought out by another publisher, most of the purchase price goes to pay for an item called *goodwill.* The purchase price of any newspaper far exceeds the cost of the word processors and printing presses owned by the company. It is easy to replace these pieces of equipment. The goodwill of the readers, and their dedication to continue buying the publication, makes a newspaper a thriving business.

✦ OPINION

Similarly, any display of bias, any injection of the news writer's feelings or opinions into a news story, hurts the contract between a newspaper and its readers. When an author expresses any sort of opinion, no matter how mild or insignificant, it becomes extremely difficult for readers to trust the fairness of the story.

Opinion can sneak into a news story subtly as well as overtly. Most readers would condemn the following:

"I'm against it," Senator Smith stupidly responded.

Equally laden with opinion, though, is a headline that reads:

Teen Killed in Tragic Plane Crash

All readers will agree on rating this event as tragic. A newspaper does not have to tell readers how to feel about an event. The facts will compel their feelings more efficiently than any editorial exhortation. Nor should a newspaper tell readers what to think. Newspapers present facts, ordered in such a manner that readers can quickly and easily assimilate the information for which they have paid. Readers of the newspaper demand for themselves the right to figure out what the news means and how they feel about it.

In the ideal news story, the author disappears behind the story, becoming invisible to the reader. In a good movie, viewers forget that Harrison Ford is acting the part of a man on the run, and that they are sitting in a local theater with a bag of popcorn. When a movie works, viewers suspend their disbelief and begin to think they are really seeing a man on the run. All the technique needed to act in a movie, to produce a movie, all the skills of the grips and editors and actors vanish, leaving only the viewer really there at the event.

Similarly, in a well-written news story, the skill of producing coherent sentences and paragraphs, the ability to coax sources to reveal information, the talents of the typesetters and designers all disappear. When a news story works, readers have the impression that they saw the events described in the story just as they happened.

A reporter who interjects any editorial opinion into a story behaves like an actor who winks at the camera, or asks, "Can I do that line over?" A reporter can intrude into the story by saying, "Then this reporter went in person to the Johnson house," but this jars a reader. It's like seeing the sprocket holes projected onto the movie screen. The skilled reporter is one who vanishes, leaving the reader as a participant in the events of the story.

✦ THE MARKETPLACE OF IDEAS

What, then, are reporters to do when a public official tells a lie or gives out misleading facts?

The newspaper should report the statement, without any editorial comment, without cunning uses of quotation marks, without any hint of the reporter's feelings about truth or falsehood. If the statement libels someone, of course, the newspaper must be cautious, but in the vast majority of cases in which the reporter disagrees with something a source says, he or she should simply report the statement and let readers decide about its truth for themselves. Even if reporters have strong opinions, they should not attempt to force them on readers. The public does not want and does not pay for reporters' opinions; the public expects and demands the right to make up its own mind.

The system of mass communication in Western societies rests on the notion of the "marketplace of ideas." John Milton, the first exponent of the idea, felt that the public should hear, accurately and faithfully, what their leaders are saying. Over time, with false starts and periods of error, Milton held, the public will figure out what is true and what is false.

The reporter who subverts this process by editorializing or by injecting opinion into a story short-circuits the system society uses to make decisions. These reporters assert that their opinions are somehow better than those of the public, that they are smarter than the citizenry as a whole, and that they deserve the privilege of telling the public what to think.

Sometimes this policy of presenting only facts, without any comment, makes the news difficult to read. Someone accuses a public official of some misdeed, the official then denies it, and others support either the accuser or the accused. The newspaper story leaves loose ends. It does not resolve all claims and counterclaims—but the ambiguity in newspaper coverage reflects reality. Life can be confusing and difficult. Over time, the people will decide what the truth is. The right to do so represents an important part of the system of governance in the United States. When a newspaper injects opinions into news stories, it cheats its readers of their right to reach their own conclusions.

One term that is sometimes applied to the press in America—the **Fourth Estate**—comes from this role of a newspaper in providing facts to its readers. In the United States the press functions as an unofficial part of the governing process—as important as Congress, the judiciary, or the presidency (the first three estates). In a huge country—huge both geographically and in population—voters cannot observe in person all the doings of Congress, the president, and other elected and appointed officials. Yet the American system of government needs an informed populace. People can make good choices in the voting booth only if they know something about the people running for office.

In the United States, the press serves the function of informing voters about the activities of their government. Without the press, American society would lose a critical linkage between policy-makers and the people.

Worse, with a press that editorializes or slants stories in line with the biases of its reporters, the linkage only seems to exist. In reality, the public does not have all the facts. The standard of fairness, difficult as it may be to meet in practice, does not come just from tradition or custom; it represents a civic duty of reporters.

SUMMARY

- Faced with a glut of information, readers scan news articles and read only a few in depth.

- The inverted pyramid structure makes it possible for scanners to get the essentials of a story quickly, while enabling the more interested readers to get the details.
- Summary, a necessary part of the inverted pyramid format, requires extreme caution, because summarizing can create inaccuracies.
- Newspapers sell a commodity—news. Readers can and do choose not to buy some kinds of news.
- Readers will buy the commodity that they trust. They will buy the newspaper that gives them accurate, unbiased information.
- In the United States, the press serves as an unofficial part of the governing process, giving voters information they need to assess how well their government is functioning. To make this assessment, they need accurate and unbiased information.

IN-CLASS EXERCISES

1. During the course of a day, list all the news media to which you are exposed. To which do you pay the most attention? The least? Why?

2. How many news channels do you get on your television? Examine a copy of a complete television guide. How many news channels does it list? For each local news service, describe the intended audience. How do its members differ from one another?

3. Select five stories from your local newspaper. For each, describe how they do or do not fit the inverted pyramid.

4. Locate in a newspaper a news story and an editorial on the same topic. Write a paragraph describing the differences in tone, structure, language, and content.

5. Using your library, find out how much money was made last year in the news business. How does that compare to the motion picture industry? What has happened to the number of newspapers in the United States between 1950 and 1990? Why do you think that has happened? What does it mean?

6. Select five stories covered by your local television station. For each, describe how they do or do not fit the inverted pyramid. Do they differ in this respect from those in Exercise 3? Why or why not?

7. For five stories from the front page of your local newspaper, identify the institutional source of the story—local reporters, a U.S. news agency, a foreign news agency. Do you think the differences in the stories are attributable to differences in the sources of these stories? Why or why not?

OUT-OF-CLASS EXERCISE

Locate a press release from a local agency or group, or from your university. Using as a model a newspaper story that employs the inverted pyramid, write up the information in the press release as a news story. If the story you selected from the local paper uses summary in a paragraph, you should use summary. If the story uses a quote in a paragraph, do so as well.

CHAPTER 3

The Lead

—— ▄

The **lead**—the opening sentence—is by far the most important item in any news story. An intriguing lead hooks readers into the story, but a boring lead pushes readers away. Reporters who write leads that work are valuable to newspapers, because they play a critical role in making a newspaper salable.

Editors often call the lead for a news formula story the **summary lead,** because they expect the lead to summarize the essential elements in the story. In essence, the summary lead is a preview of what will come in the rest of the story. Readers who glance at a well-written lead can tell immediately whether or not they are interested in reading further. Poorly written leads either confuse the reader about what is to follow or mislead the reader. In either case, the badly constructed lead violates the contract with readers, frustrating and irritating them.

Reporters know that a good lead makes the rest of a story very easy to write, while a weak one means that a reporter will have to work hard in writing the rest of the story. If the lead summarizes the story well, then writing the rest of the piece requires merely expanding and fleshing out the central idea by providing more information.

Since a good lead is truly crucial, writers often spend as much time creating this one sentence as they do producing the rest of an article. Many beginning news writers spend a good bit of time fiddling with this one beginning sentence, sharpening and polishing it.

Sometimes even the best writers can stew for a while and not come up with an appealing lead. If that happens, do not panic. Just write the rest of the story. By the end of the story, the focus will appear. Then just go back and tack a lead onto the top. The resulting story probably will not win a writing award, but it will see print.

◆ THE FIVE Ws

So what are the most important and compelling parts of a news story? How does a reporter decide what to put in the crucial lead sentence? The **five Ws,** probably the best-known part of the news formula, give writers answers to these questions.

The writer asks five questions: Who? What? When? Where? and Why? The answers to these questions form the building blocks of the lead. In their notes, writers will have lots of possible answers to these questions. The strongest answers compel and interest the reader. To find these strongest answers, a writer evaluates each item in terms of the news values. The most newsworthy item should go in the lead.

Beginning reporters often find their lead by writing the five Ws in a column on a piece of scratch paper and filling in the answers.

- Who? Who is making the event happen? Who is the event happening to?
- What? What is the event? What is happening?
- When? When is it happening? If the event is forthcoming, exactly when will it occur? If the event has already occurred, on what day did it happen?
- Where? Where did or will this take place? This type of information has to be much more precise in a story announcing a future event than in a story about an event that has already occurred. Readers planning to attend an event need very specific information about time and place.
- Why? What made or is making this event happen? Who's sponsoring it? Why is it where it is? Why is it when it is?

Usually a reporter cannot answer all of these questions, and so some of the areas on the scratch sheet normally remain blank.

Consider a story about a car wreck in which a car was traveling at high speed, spun out of control, and rolled down an embankment. The driver died. The passenger is in intensive care; the hospital lists his condition as critical.

A first-time reporter's scratch sheet might look like this:

- Who? Driver, Sam Smith, and passenger, Fred Westover
- What? Killed and injured

- When? Monday at 11:52 p.m.
- Where? High Top Mountain Rd. 100 yards north of the intersection with Low Top Mountain Rd.
- Why? Car going too fast for curves, according to Phil Montalban, Hwy Ptrl.

With answers to each of the five Ws, one can draft a sentence. Following this process may seem mechanical at first, but it soon becomes natural.

First, write down the answer to *who*. *Who* is always a noun, and can therefore be the subject of the sentence. *What,* as in *what happened,* is usually a verb and becomes the verb of the sentence. *When* (yesterday, Monday, Jan. 14 at 11:52 p.m.) always modifies the verb. A writer should place the *when* element near the verb. A prepositional phrase usually tells *where.* The *why* comes up in a subordinate section of the sentence.

Following this order, then, the scratch sheet would yield this lead:

> The driver [who] died [what] and a passenger [who] suffered severe injuries [what] late Monday night [when] in a one-car accident on High Top Mountain Rd. [where].

Notice that not everything from the scratch sheet made it into this lead sentence. Obviously, stuffing complete answers to the five Ws into one sentence would create an impossibly long and ponderous string of words. This is why lead writing often involves some doodling, as the writer tries different combinations of information in order to make a grammatical sentence that conveys the most important information about the story.

Grammatically, the most difficult part of the lead to construct is the *why.* The other elements of the lead naturally fit into a simple declarative sentence, but inclusion of the *why,* which usually falls into a subordinate clause, is often a cause of grammatical trouble.

An example of the *why* falling into a subordinate clause is:

> Mayor Sue Anthony resigned today after a local court found her guilty of accepting payoffs from contractors employed by the city.

Sometimes, leads that include the *why* element become quite complex, in which case using a second sentence for the *why* makes sense.

> Mayor Sue Anthony resigned today in a tearful press conference held on the steps of Lowell Hall. Anthony was found guilty of accepting payoffs from contractors employed by the city.

✦ GUIDELINES FOR A GOOD LEAD

Writing a good lead resembles writing a poem or doing a crossword puzzle. The first words that come to mind are often clichés or are imprecise; clichés, after all, are clichés because they're the first phrases that come to mind. Trying this word and that word, writing and rewriting, the reporter generally experiments for a while before finding the best combination to create a strong beginning.

Editors have developed some advice that can help you in this juggling process.

Start with a compelling noun. Editors want a writer to grab the reader by putting the fascinating information at the start of the sentence and throwing in the boring data at the back of the sentence. To write a lead, search through the answers to the five Ws. Pick the most interesting or compelling word and use this as the first word of the lead.

Usually this most fascinating word will come from the *who* or the *what* sections. Notice that the sample lead concerning the car crash puts death and injury at the start of the sentence and the location of the accident at the end of the sentence.

Keep it short. The best lead sentences run about 20 words. A 30-word lead will still work, but anything over that length gets ponderous. The sample auto accident lead has 21 words, but the first draft of the sentence ran 41 words. Here's the first draft:

> The driver died and a passenger suffered severe injuries late Monday night when the car in which they were riding flipped and rolled down an embankment off High Top Mountain Rd. just north of the intersection with Low Top Mountain Rd.

This lead provides a lot more information, but it forces too much at the reader all at once. Instead of trying to write an all-inclusive lead, a reporter should write a short, punchy lead sentence and save the rest of the information to reveal as the story unfolds.

Do not lead with a prepositional phrase. A prepositional phrase adds extra information to a sentence, but the real pop and push come from the main noun and verb. Since the first words in a lead must grab the reader, use the most compelling information as a noun that will be the subject of the sentence. Avoid writing a lead like this:

> In a one-car accident Monday night on High Top Mountain Rd., the driver died and the passenger suffered severe injuries.

Do not start a lead with a person's name. Unless the person is Elvis or the president, many readers will not recognize the name anyway. For example, the car wreck story could have begun:

> Sam Smith died and Fred Westover suffered severe injuries in a one-car accident Monday night on High Top Mountain Rd.

Sometimes a reporter really does think it crucial to include a name in the lead. In that case, instead of making the name the first word in a sentence, put an intriguing modifier or phrase in front of the name. For example:

> Historian Carole Levin will discuss her new book on Elizabeth I Saturday in Forrest Auditorium.

Do not start a lead with either the when *or the* where *element.* The *when* and *where* elements usually provide important but secondary information. Don't write a lead like this:

> Monday night on High Top Mountain Rd., the driver died and a passenger suffered severe injuries in a one-car accident.

Do not lead with a source's name. The most deadly of leads begins with the source the reporter used to gather the information. For example:

> According to the Highway Patrol, the driver died and a passenger suffered severe injuries late Monday night in a one-car accident on High Top Mountain Rd.

Sometimes, especially when writing a speech story, one just can't get all the five Ws into the lead. A writer doesn't have to answer all the five Ws in the first sentence. In some cases it makes more sense to think of the lead as the first two sentences. However, the first sentence must always include three of the five Ws: the time element (when), the news element (what), and the main actor (who). The other Ws can appear in the second sentence if necessary.

✦ BURYING A LEAD

Besides libeling someone, misspelling a name, or missing a deadline, the sin that most infuriates newspaper editors is a **buried lead.** Burying a lead means putting the most important or newsworthy information deep in the article instead of in the lead.

A reporter should not lead with the obvious. The city council meets every week. It would be news if the city council didn't hold one of its regularly scheduled meetings. So editors do not like an article to lead:

The city council met Tuesday.

The classic buried lead starts a speech story. The junior reporter leads with:

Maria Granger spoke today at Millspaugh Auditorium on global warming.

An advance story in yesterday's paper should already have announced Granger's speech. Today, after the speech, the newspaper should do more than just announce the topic she spoke about. Instead, it should report the most compelling thing she had to say about global warming. A more interesting lead is:

Global warming is creating a disaster of epic proportions, a spokesperson for an international environmental organization said yesterday.

This lead contains a good indication of what will follow in the story, but it also defers giving names until later.

Sometimes a reporter has to abandon a perfectly good lead because of new information that becomes available. In the auto accident story, just as the reporter was ending the interview with the state trooper, the trooper might say, "Oh, by the way, I don't know anything about the money they found in the trunk."

At this point, the reporter knows that the story has completely changed.

"What? What money?"

"When the tow company got the wreck to the garage, they opened up the trunk and found all this money. It was all stacked up real neat, and wrapped with those little labels the bank puts on it."

"How much was there?"

"Well, it was around half a million dollars."

The little car wreck story has just changed dramatically. Auto accidents are routine news. People die in them regularly. Very rarely does the tow truck operator find $500,000 in the trunk.

Here are the five Ws for the new story:

• Who? Workers at Leakey's Garage
• What? Found about $500,000
• When? Tuesday morning

- Where? In the trunk of a wrecked car
- Why? Nobody knows

Here's the new lead:

> Some $500,000 in cash greeted workers at Leakey's Garage Tuesday when they opened the trunk of a wrecked car.

This sets up a much more interesting story. Reporters who lead with death and injury but bury $500,000 in the bottom of their stories can expect nasty encounters with their editors.

Buried leads infuriate editors for two reasons. First, a story with a buried lead needs thorough rewriting, which is a burden on the copy desk. Second, a buried lead says that the reporter lacks news sense, and doesn't understand what is news and what isn't.

Knowing what makes a good lead is perhaps the most important part of the contract reporters have with their readers. Buried leads violate that contract, forcing readers to waste their time reading material that really does not interest them. Editors can forgive the lack of almost any other skill, but knowing how to lead is the most critical skill a reporter develops.

✦ FROM INTERVIEW TO LEAD

The writer must remember that people do not naturally organize their thoughts about an event in order of importance. Usually, sources will arrange the information about an event in time sequence, leading to interviews that look like this:

> Well, this woman—Caroline Sabetti, 34, of 112 Wilshire Park—was driving down Klymer Street, in front of Morris Jewelers, at about 4:30 yesterday afternoon.
>
> Evidently she fell asleep at the wheel. She was going about ten miles an hour, and ran into the front window of the jewelry store.
>
> She was going slowly enough that her car just went through the window and then rolled up to the front counter, and stopped there.
>
> You won't believe this, but the woman didn't wake up until the police arrived and shook her. She said she was just really sleepy.

Here, the source has arranged the story in a chronological order. The reporter's worksheet would look like this:

- Who: Caroline Sabetti, 112 Wilshire Park
- Where: Morris Jewelers, Klymer Street

- When: about 4:30 pm
- What: fell asleep while driving, ran into front window of jewelry store and into store but didn't awaken until police arrived.

A first-draft lead sentence might look like this:

- (Who) A local woman
- (What) fell asleep while driving in front of Morris Jewelers on Klymer Street and ran
- (Where) into front window of jewelry store and into store but didn't awaken until police arrived
- (Why) said she was really sleepy
- (When) about 4:30 pm

The final lead paragraph, with a little work, is:

> A local woman drove her car through the front window of a Klymer St. jewelry store at 4:30 p.m. yesterday.
> The driver, Caroline Sabetti, of 112 Wilshire Park, told police she fell asleep at the wheel.

Reporters should listen carefully during interviews, jotting down the five Ws as sources reveal them. Often, reporters draw a line down the middle of their page of notes, jotting down verbatim notes on the right and sketching in the five Ws on the left. No matter what method the reporter uses, though, the important issue is being sure that no interview concludes without each of the five W questions being answered.

✦ PRESS RELEASES

A common first assignment for reporters is rewriting **press releases** into news stories. Press releases are a useful source of information on events, but a newspaper cannot use them verbatim. The general manager of the local shopping mall can write up the basics of the story, but this person has usually not studied journalism.

Consider the following press release:

> Fun, frolic, and festivity will be the order of the day when Whozit, the mascot of the Newark Stars basketball team, makes his first appearance in the Newton area!
> At the grand opening of the West Newton Mall, Whozit will delight young and old with his madcap antics. You've seen him on TV—disrupting the basketball games, running off with the ball, kissing umpires, snitching food from

bystanders. Well, of course it's all in fun, and that fun comes to Newton this Saturday, June 10. Be there—or miss the fun!

Besides using overheated prose, this press release clearly contains lots of opinions about how the event will go, and it does not follow the news formula. To turn it into a news story, then, the reporter constructs the five Ws, as follows:

- Who: Whozit, mascot of Newark Stars
- What: makes appearance at opening of mall
- When: this Saturday, June 10
- Where: West Newton Mall
- Why: promotion?

Note the question mark in the *why* entry; the reporter isn't sure why Whozit is appearing.

The constructed lead would be:

- (Who) Whozit, mascot of the Newark Stars basketball team,
- (What) will make an appearance
- (Where) at the opening of the West Newton Mall
- (When) this Saturday, June 10,
- (Why) for promotional purposes.

Since the *why* angle is speculation, it is dropped in the final draft, and with a little polishing, the lead is: •

> Whozit, mascot of the Newark Stars basketball team, will help open the West Newton Mall this Saturday.

The trick in writing a news story based on a press release is to separate fact from puffery. Perhaps Whozit "will delight young and old with his madcap antics," but that's advertising. Often a writer has to hunt down the facts in the press release—but the writer can usually find enough information to make a workable news story.

✦ TRICK LEADS

A common failing of beginning reporters is the trick lead—a lead that attempts to trick readers into continuing with a story by withholding critical information until later. An example might be:

It wouldn't be unusual for most workers to commute three miles to work. It wouldn't be unusual for that commute to be through rush-hour traffic, and, in this day of energy conservation, the commute might even be on foot.

That's what Bobo does every day, rain or shine.

What makes Bobo's commute unusual is that Bobo is a dog, working for the Milton Crossing police department.

Here, a critical piece of information—Bobo is a dog—is deferred until after the lead. Such stories irritate readers, who must trudge through fluff trying to figure out what the story is about. Some newspaper editors call this type of story an Uncle Bat because it hinges on the revelation of crucial information—"But my uncle was a bat, and flew out of the room!"—far later than the news formula demands.

A more subtle example is:

Country singing star Hal Phillips won't be singing at Pete Hamlin's new night club this weekend. Neither will Paula Sanchez and the Latin Lights. But the best local talent will appear, Hamlin says, and listeners may hear the next Hal Phillips there.

Again, this lead defers critical information. Naming the people who won't appear tells the reader little about who is going to perform.

Whenever possible, the reporter should try to honor the contract with the reader by presenting the most important information in the lead, avoiding tricks that aim to lure readers into the story.

✦ A WARNING

In general, beginning news writers should stick to the five W lead, because it is easy to construct and works for any type of story. Many newspaper editors condemn these leads as pedestrian and uncreative, and indeed there are more creative ways to approach the news. Even so, editors will rarely reject a solid news formula story with a five W lead. The five W lead, though often pedestrian, efficiently presents the heart of the story.

Editors expect newspaper reporters to begin their careers by producing five W leads in their copy. Reporters tackle more creative approaches to writing after their work shows that they understand the intermeshing assumptions of the news formula. Five W leads are to the best newspaper writing what crawling is to dancing. Columnists, feature writers, and editorial writers produce the really creative work in a newspaper, but they all mastered the five Ws long before they earned the freedom to take more creative approaches.

SUMMARY

- It is normal for a beginning news writer to stew for a while over the production of one 20-word lead sentence.
- Answering the questions Who? What? When? Where? and Why? produces the information necessary for a lead sentence.
- Take the first words in the lead sentence from the Who? or What? elements of the five Ws.
- Don't bury leads.
- The five Ws are a formula for teaching beginners the craft of journalism. Once reporters have mastered this formula, they move on to more creative ways to write leads.

IN-CLASS EXERCISES

1. Find a story in your newspaper that you think has a buried lead. What makes you think that? Rewrite the lead of the story so that it isn't buried.

2. Find a newspaper story that uses a compelling noun as a hook for the lead. What is that compelling noun, and why is it important?

3. Find a newspaper story that uses a trick lead. Why do you think it is a trick lead? How would you correct it, and why would you make the change?

4. In a newspaper, locate a lead that you think is well-constructed. What makes you think so? What makes the lead you selected particularly good?

5. Select a news story from the newspaper. From the lead, make up a five Ws scratch sheet. Now, without looking at the old lead, construct a new one. Compare your lead to the one in the newspaper. Which do you prefer, and why?

6. Record a story on your local television station. Does it use a trick lead? Is the lead buried? Why do you think so?

7. Select a news story from a local television news show and videotape it. From the story, make up a five Ws scratch sheet. Now construct a new lead. Compare your lead to the one on the television news show. Which do you prefer, and why?

OUT-OF-CLASS EXERCISE

From a local agency or your university's public information office, get a press release. Call one of the people involved, and interview that person briefly. Now, construct a scratch sheet, as described earlier, using the five Ws. From this, make a first draft of a lead; from this, create a finished lead.

CHAPTER 4

The Inverted
Pyramid

A reporter who has covered a major traffic pileup involving 20 cars returns to the newsroom on deadline with a stack of information—information gleaned from interviews with highway patrol officers, rescue workers, and citizens stalled in traffic. The writer must boil this hodgepodge down to an interesting story of 1,000 to 1,500 words, which will appear in the newspaper as 16 to 24 inches of copy. Sometimes, at this stage, the beginning news writer panics. What goes first? What goes in the middle, and where should the story end?

The inverted pyramid provides a format for the news story that helps the reporter on deadline organize material quickly and begin writing. It does not dictate how to write a news story, but it does give important information about how to organize the story. The history of the inverted pyramid makes it easy to remember and understand. Many people who know nothing else about news writing know about the inverted pyramid.

The inverted pyramid tells the reporter how to structure the story by suggesting where to put each fact about an event. In traditional expository writing, the author must do a good bit of organizational work before writing: devising a thesis statement, outlining supporting arguments, deciding on a conclusion. The inverted pyramid eliminates all this worry about structure, because this crucial part of the news formula provides a single, easy-to-remember rule explaining where in the story each element should appear.

The inverted pyramid concept uses a visual device to outline how to write a news formula story. Think about the Great Pyramid of the Pharaoh Cheops. Now turn it upside down so that the structure balances on its tip. The fat, weighty matter sits at the top of the structure and the slender, trivial matter rests at the bottom. A writer structures a news formula story in the same way. At the top of the story goes the most important, interesting, or dynamic information, the information most likely to intrigue or fascinate a reader. These first six to eight paragraphs form a sort of mini-article containing the heart of the story. After these paragraphs, scanning readers with only a passing interest can move on to other articles and still feel they have gotten the essence of the information.

The body of the story, the real detail in the article, follows this mini-article. Here the writer gives all the facts to the reader who has a strong interest in the subject. Though the writer aims at this point at the motivated reader, the newspaper still assumes that a reader may quit the article and move on to a new topic at any point. Therefore, in this central section, the writer brings up new details in descending order of importance or interest to the reader.

The end of the story addresses only the most dedicated readers, the very few people who really care about the topic. The end contains the least important information. The inverted pyramid structure, then, means: Put the most compelling and interesting information at the top of the story and the relatively boring and useless information at the bottom of the story.

✦ WHERE THE INVERTED PYRAMID CAME FROM

Before the American Civil War, news writers used the organizational structure of an essay in composing news articles. First they wrote an introduction, then they provided supporting material, and they led up to final conclusions. Articles used dazzling language, flowery imagery, and literary devices like allegory and personification. Stories were told as stories, rather than as events.

During the Civil War, reporters covering the battlefield used the telegraph to file their articles. Hundreds of reporters representing papers from all over the United States, the Confederacy, and foreign nations competed for the few available telegraph lines.

Often only one telegraph line was available in the small towns near where crucial battles took place, and retreating or advancing armies might cut a line at any moment. Reporters had to write and transmit their news reports putting the most important information first. That way, if troops cut the line or an advancing army made further transmission inadvisable, the newspaper could at least publish something. Further information would follow, again in order of its importance, when the line was available again. The news writing style of the past, giving lengthy descriptions of scene and atmosphere, fell by the wayside, replaced by terse and concise descriptions based on factual observation.

Also, the war itself generated a huge volume of information. The activities of armies as they moved close to the populous capitals of both sides were of vital interest to almost everyone. News of battles, of negotiation, of diplomacy, of suffering and privation endured by both sides competed for space in newspapers made smaller by wartime shortages of paper and ink. Thus, editors hastily edited incoming news reports to fit in the available space. Since the most important information was, by the new convention, at the top of the story, newspapers edited by chopping the story from the bottom upwards.

By the end of the war, the American public had learned to like the new format for news, and the American press never again changed the way in which it wrote stories. The European press, which was always far more centralized, never had the kinds of experiences that the U.S. press did. Consequently, to this day European newspapers use a news writing formula far closer to the essay style than to the inverted pyramid used in the United States.

✦ SUMMARY PARAGRAPHS

The inverted pyramid dictates that the first five to eight paragraphs after the lead—the **summary paragraphs**—establish the main facts of the story. They round out the story and set up the structure of the rest of the article. These paragraphs answer essential questions raised by the information in the lead. To return to the traffic pileup, suppose the reporter wrote the following lead:

> A one-car accident blocked Highway 1 for two hours Wednesday, backing up more than 100 vehicles in both directions.

This lead grabs readers' attention and immediately raises questions. Did anyone die? Did anyone survive? Why was traffic backed up for so long? Why didn't the highway patrol open at least one lane for traffic? How did the accident happen? Why did the accident happen?

The entire summary or lead-in section, which runs from five to eight paragraphs, begins to give partial answers to these questions. This short lead-in gives readers the gist of the story. After reading this far, people without a big interest in the topic can move on with the assurance that they understand the basics of the story. The more interested readers can keep on reading with the assurance that they will get still more new information in the following paragraphs.

The summary section on the traffic pileup might look like this:

> The driver of the car, Brian Anderson, 16, of Fort Jones St., died at Memorial Hospital Wednesday evening. Memorial lists passenger Samuel Hemingway, 16, of Wilson Ave., in guarded condition.
>
> The highway patrol says the accident occurred when the car Anderson was driving skidded on wet pavement 100 feet north of the intersection with Aston Rd. The car rolled over several times and landed on its side in the middle of the roadway.
>
> "The shoulders were too narrow there on the roadway so we couldn't flag cars around," reported Highway Patrol Officer Ned Bigby.
>
> Rescuers had to call out the West Fredericksville Volunteer Fire Department's Jaws of Life squad to work to free the driver trapped in the car.
>
> "We didn't dare try to move that car with the boy trapped in there," said Bigby. "We might have hurt him even more."

Those five paragraphs complete the basic information for the article.

✦ THE FOLLOW PARAGRAPH

A frequently encountered aspect of the news formula is the **follow paragraph,** called such because it closely follows the lead in the summary section. The follow paragraph is the quotation from the story that best sets up the conflict angle of the story, or most succinctly explains what's happening. In the example story given above, the third paragraph ("The shoulders . . .") is the follow paragraph. This quotation is often called the **bright quote.**

✦ COMPLETING THE STORY

After the summary paragraphs, the rest of a news formula story addresses the really interested readers who want details on the topic. The writing of this longest section of the article usually goes very quickly.

To write the summary paragraphs, a reporter carefully analyzes and assesses the importance of the material. With these initial paragraphs completed, a writer usually has a clear idea of where to go with the rest of the story. To complete the article at this point, the writer just fills in the obvious holes left in the summary paragraphs, and answers the striking questions raised there.

✦ STRUCTURING THE BODY

Reporters build the **body** of a news formula story—the part that follows the summary—in topical sections that appear in the order of their importance. To come up with a structure for the body of the story, look back over the summary paragraphs. On a scratch sheet make a list of four or five nouns that describe the main ideas in the story. These ideas become subject headings.

In the traffic accident example, the story can still answer questions like: Why didn't the backed-up cars just detour? Who are the injured people? Who are their families? Just how did the accident happen? Who were all the people in the traffic jam? How did they cope? What are the "Jaws of Life"? Why did the rescue take so long?

A reporter might boil these down to the following topic headings:

- Accident details
- Casualties
- Backed-up cars
- Rescue procedures

With these ideas in mind, the reporter could sort through the notes, assigning all the information to subject headings and then evaluating the material under each heading in terms of the criteria of news values outlined in Chapter 1. In this weighing process, the writer plans the structure of an inverted pyramid story, arranging the sections from most important to least important and including them in the story in that order.

A reporter might reorder the topics like this:

1. Casualties. Death, particularly of a teenager, is always a tragedy.
2. Backed-up cars. A traffic jam involving that many vehicles for that long is highly unusual.
3. Accident details. To fulfill their surveillance needs people want to know how an accident happened, but since the details of a traffic accident are usually fairly routine, these would go near the bottom of this story.
4. Rescue procedures. The standard rescue procedures of a local agency are also by definition routine and would also go near the bottom of this particular story. Some future investigative piece might want to examine whether such time-consuming procedures might need changing.

✦ STRUCTURING THE TOPICAL SECTIONS

Each **topical section** within the body of the story runs four to six paragraphs long. Newspaper editors do not have a set of precepts for writing these topical sections; however, the **"idea, then evidence"** system works well. This system involves pairing an idea presented by the news writer with quotations from news sources.

Ideally, these paired idea-and-evidence paragraphs appear in **"action–reaction"** pairs. In these, the summary paragraph and quotations are followed by a conflicting summary and quotations, as in these paragraphs:

> The Insula Company claims that its products are safe for use in all settings, said a spokesman.
>
> "We don't know of any legitimate scientific research demonstrating our products aren't safe," said Reynard Call, public information officer of Insula. "If anyone has such data, we'd like to see it."
>
> But activists associated with "Clean Up Our World" (CUOW) claim that such evidence is readily available.
>
> "A simple computer database search showed over 100 articles about the relationship between the types of phenols present in Insula products and disease," said Ravi Patel, a CUOW leader. "It's a disgrace, pure and simple."

To use the system, begin each topical section with the statement of an idea or an opinion. To write this **topical sentence,** take the topical noun that formed the conceptual label for the section and elaborate on that noun to make a sentence. To avoid the accusation of editorializing, be sure to include appropriate attribution to a source at the end of the sentence.

In the best use of the "idea, then evidence" approach, the topical sentence should be a paraphrase and not a direct quote. Since the writer has an organizational goal in bringing up this idea at this point in the story, only rarely will a direct quote from someone work. This topical sentence signals the reader about the direction the writer wants to take with the story. The concept or idea or opinion in the topical sentence should come from someone connected with the story.

After this topical introduction, the writer completes the section by writing three to five paragraphs of facts, direct quotes, and paraphrases to elaborate on the topic. As much as possible, the writer reports this information in descending order of importance.

The backed-up cars section of the traffic pileup story might go like this:

Traffic backed up for several miles in each direction on the narrow, twisting section of Highway 1 that is the only connection between the communities of Winston and Abbeyville, said Officer Bigby of the Highway Patrol.

"They just about had to sit there," said Bigby. "Their only other choice was to backtrack and go 50 miles out of their way through Ft. Smith."

Some people read, others did paperwork, some just sat in the sun. "The guy behind me had a chess set," said Aaron Wilshire of Winston. "That's how we passed the time."

"Nobody much groused about the delay," said Bigby. "After all, they knew what was at stake."

✦ ON ENDING

At the end of each topical section, the reporter does not write a concluding paragraph that refers back to the introduction of the section. Each sentence in a news story should add new information. News writers never stop and summarize what they have already said.

Some writers have difficulty with this principle. Every traditional teacher of expository writing insists that good work must include an introduction and a conclusion. In news, because of the requirements of the inverted pyramid, the most important information, the summary (information that, in a standard composition, would normally go in the conclusion), always goes at the top.

A news writer who has completed a topical section simply goes on to the next most important section. After the last topical section, the story stops without a summary.

Some reporters, knowing the ways of copy editors, deliberately end their news formula stories with another topical section. They add three paragraphs of nonessential information just for the editor to cut. A copy editor expects news stories to use the news formula structure. If the layout slot assigned to a story turns out to be too short, the editor does not change the layout, but instead lops off pieces of the story from the bottom to make it fit the hole on the page. Writing something for the editor to cut makes defensive sense to some.

Many beginning reporters do a great job of objective reporting until they get to the last sentence. They can write a straightforward lead like:

Pop singer Madonna will give a concert at the Civic Center Saturday at 8 p.m.

At the end, though, beginners feel called on to add a concluding paragraph. Often they stick on an ending sentence like:

This concert promises to be the musical event of the 90s in our town, and everybody who's anybody will be there.

An important point, then: Never end a news formula story with a pithy summary of the essence of the piece. Very few readers will get that far, and besides, the last paragraph seldom makes it into the newspaper because editors cut most stories. When the story has reported all the information that seems necessary, a reporter should just stop writing. Let the story die without a eulogy at the end.

✦ AN EXAMPLE

Here's an example of the construction of a typical story, from notes to finished product. Imagine a story about a holdup. The reporter took the following notes:

Officer Kraeber (Milton) → call at 11:57 pm to office by Harriet Wilenski, saw lights off at Rufus' QuikStop at 1118 Miller Road. Two squad cars reported, found Helen Bonner, clerk, tied up and cash register gone. She advised two men entered store, turned off lights, held her at gunpoint, couldn't get register open, tied her up, ran off lugging cash register. Police responded at 1:48 am.

"It's unusual, although not unheard of, for thieves to take an entire cash register. These new models can't be opened without knowing a security code, and so they just run off with the whole thing. We don't have any leads yet, although the caller reported that there was an old red Jeep sitting in front of the store. Ms. Bonner was unhurt, although she's at St. Luke's Hospital getting checked out. We don't think we took an unusual amount of time to respond to this call. Had we known a person was tied up, we'd have been much quicker, I assure you."

Wilenski → "I saw lights bobbing around in the store, and I knew right off that somebody was robbing it. It seemed strange, too, that the lights were off. I didn't know until later that that poor woman was trussed up in there like a Thanksgiving turkey, or I'd have gone over and cut her loose. That store has been robbed twice in the last six months. They really ought to do something about it. But the police just don't care, since we're in a poor part of town. If this were Forest Hills, they'd have been out here in five minutes instead of two hours."

Bonner (Helen J., 22, part-time student at Liberty Technical Institute, 44 Lefevre Street) → "When the lights went out, I knew I was in trouble. But at least they didn't hurt me. The store can get more money, but I can't get another me. I guess I was in there for about two hours before the police arrived. Nobody knew I was in there, and so the police took their time. Then, even after the police came in, they didn't know I was there since the robbers had gagged me. So I kept making what noise I could—a little squeak, really—and finally one of the officers came over to see what the racket was. It was pretty funny, really; I heard the police talking, and one of them said he was going to let the cat out. I realized that they thought I was a cat, meowing." Sue? → "I don't think this was the store's fault. They take all the precautions they can, but there's not much they can do when people come into the store with guns." Money? → "They got out of there with about $700. The register itself probably cost $1000, and I have no idea how much fixing the lights is going to cost. I was afraid at first, but calmed down a little after the thieves left."

The story starts with a summary lead, which should include the most important information. Since breaking-and-entering robberies happen more often than robberies where the robbers tie up the cashier, that element needs to go in the lead. A second unusual angle to the story is that the robbers left with the whole register. The story could begin with:

Police last night found a convenience-store clerk bound and gagged but unharmed following a robbery at Rufus' QuikStop on Miller Rd. The clerk said the two robbers took the entire cash register when they could not open it in the store.

Since the story has not yet included any specific information about the clerk, that goes next.

Helen J. Bonner, 22, a clerk at the QuikStop and a part-time student at Liberty Technical Institute, spent almost two hours bound and gagged on the store's floor before police found her.

The follow paragraph comes next with a bright quote. Since the story has so far focused on Bonner, the writer gives her best quote.

"Nobody knew I was in there, and so the police took their time," Bonner said from St. Luke's Hospital, where she is under observation. "Then, even after the police came in, they didn't know I was there since the robbers had gagged me.

"So I kept making what noise I could—a little squeak, really—and finally one of the officers came over to see what the racket was."

Having written the summary paragraphs, the writer can turn to the "idea, then evidence" sections of the story. First, the writer establishes the facts of the story, beginning with the Bonner quote. That quote should go higher than the Wilenski quote because the testimony of an eyewitness is more interesting than that of a bystander, no matter how outspoken. Summary first:

> Bonner said that she was afraid when the robbery began, but once the thieves left, she calmed down a little.

Then evidence:

> "When the lights went out, I knew I was in trouble," Bonner said. "But at least they didn't hurt me. The store can get more money, but I can't get another me. I guess I was in there for about two hours before the police arrived. Nobody knew I was in there, and so the police took their time."

Since conflict angles always play high as well, the story continues with a discussion of previous holdups of the QuikStop. First, the idea:

> Local residents say robbers have repeatedly hit the QuikStop. Residents complained of slow police response.

Now, the evidence:

> "That store has been robbed twice in the last six months," said Harriet Wilenski, who called the police after seeing bobbing lights in the store. "They really ought to do something about it. But the police just don't care, since we're in a poor part of town. If this were Forest Hills, they'd have been out here in five minutes instead of two hours."

To be fair the writer must let the police respond to that accusation. First, idea:

> A police spokesperson rated the length of time between Wilenski's call and officers' response normal.

Then quote:

> "We don't think we took an unusual amount of time to respond to this call," said Milton Kraeber, a police officer who responded. "Had we known a person was tied up, we'd have been much quicker, I assure you."

Now the story concludes with more details about the robbery.

First, idea:

Police are investigating the robbery, but have no suspects at press time.

Now, quote:

"We don't have any leads yet, although the caller reported that there was an old red Jeep sitting in front of the store," said Kraeber.

Next comes some **backfill**—material taken from the newspaper's file of earlier stories.

In one robbery five months ago, thieves took more than $3,000 worth of equipment. In a second robbery three months ago, three men ransacked the store while a clerk stood at gunpoint. Police have made no arrests in either case.

Now the writer uses the remaining quotes, still in the "idea, then evidence" format.

Bonner said she does not believe that the owners of the QuikStop bear any responsibility for the robbery.

"I don't think this was the store's fault," said Bonner. "They take all the precautions they can, but there's not much they can do when people come into the store with guns."

The cash register contained about $700. "The register itself probably cost $1,000," said Bonner.

Now the story ends with the last bit of unused information.

"It's unusual, although not unheard of, for thieves to take an entire cash register," Officer Kraeber said. "These new models can't be opened without knowing a security code, and so they just run off with the whole thing."

And there's the story. With all the quotes in place, the writer has finished. Notice that the story has no summary at the end, no conclusion or final paragraph. With all the material included, the story just ends without ceremony.

Essentially, then, the news story has three parts:

1. The lead paragraph, which summarizes the news event, including the most important information about the story.
2. A follow paragraph, which contains the brightest quotes.
3. "Idea, then evidence" paragraph pairs, which use up all the additional information about the story.

Writers structure news articles differently from the way they structure an essay, a letter, a short story, or any other piece of writing because doing so serves an important purpose—bringing information, quickly, to the attention of the people who are paying for it. While fiction writers assume that the reader has time for elaborate stage-setting and description, news writers know that their audience reads on the run, and so they take time only for the facts, presented without elaboration or opinion.

SUMMARY

- The inverted pyramid helps the reporter on deadline who must organize material quickly.
- The summary paragraphs, the five to eight paragraphs after the lead, establish the main facts of the story and set up the structure of the rest of the article.
- Reporters build the body of a news formula story in topical sections that appear in the story in the order of their importance.
- Begin each topical section with a paraphrase of an idea. Complete the section with information that elaborates on that idea.
- Never end a news story with a conclusion. When the story contains all the pertinent information, just stop writing.

IN-CLASS EXERCISES

1. Find a news article that you think has a good inverted pyramid structure. Why do you think this is a well-constructed story?

2. Find an article that you think does not have a good inverted pyramid structure. Why do you think this is not a well-constructed story?

3. Find a story written using action–reaction pairs in the body of the story. Why was the story constructed this way? How do the action–reaction pairs serve to emphasize the conflict angle of the story?

4. Find a story with an effective follow paragraph. Why did you select this story? Could another quotation paragraph from the story have been used to equal effect? Why or why not?

5. Find a story that has a concluding paragraph rather than just an ending. Do you like this story? Why or why not? Would the story have worked as well had it been edited to a shorter length?

6. Find a story that does not use a follow paragraph. Rewrite it so that it has one. Which version do you like better, and why?

7. Find a story that has a buried conflict angle, and rewrite it so that the conflict angle is overt. Which version do you like better, and why?

OUT-OF-CLASS EXERCISE

From a local agency or campus public information office, get a press release. Interview briefly some of the people involved. Then, write a news formula news story from this information.

CHAPTER 5

Quotations

In the most general sense, quotations are the basis of all news stories. Reporters should seldom, if ever, bring their own ideas or attitudes to stories. Instead, a reporter should let the people who make the news speak through the story. A good news story consists almost entirely of information from sources, much of it paraphrased, some of it quoted directly. In addition, good quotations bring life to a newspaper story by letting the people who make the news use their own voices to relate what happened.

Used properly, quotes can turn a boring story into an exciting one. They can transport readers into the heart of the story, letting them feel what the people who made the news felt. Used improperly, though, quotes can lead to incensed calls to editors from sources who trusted a reporter enough to give an interview and who now feel that the reporter betrayed their trust. Thus, all reporters should concern themselves first with the accuracy of quotations. But if accuracy posed the only issue, stenographers could replace reporters. Since the news formula emphasizes brevity, reporters have to select those quotations that best tell a story or highlight a point—yet most sources often use humdrum language, even when offering important information that needs to get into the story. That is why reporters sometimes paraphrase quotations. Paraphrases relate what sources said with total accuracy, but in the voice of the reporter. Occasionally a single word or phrase from an interview may seem compelling, while the source may have used pedestrian language the rest of the time. In that case, the reporter can pull out the interesting phrase or word, and use it in a format called the **orphan quote,** as in:

> Leslie said that the charges against the construction firm were "hogwash."

Although it may appear to be the one attribute of the news formula that would come easily to the beginner, quotes can actually present a formidable challenge to news writers.

◆ PARAGRAPH LENGTH

The news formula, with its emphasis on brevity, requires that a writer present quotations differently from the way they are presented in most other forms of writing. In standard English composition, for example, a paragraph denotes a structural entity with a topic sentence, then supporting sentences, all of which have a conceptual relationship. A quotation in a novel might appear as follows:

> Derrick turned to face the judge. "Mr. Mason has it right, Your Honor. I was at the McGruder place last night, and I did leave the note for Amy. But I swear I didn't have anything to do with turning the gas on, and I swear I didn't kill Amy. She wasn't there when I arrived, and she wasn't there when I left."

In a news formula story, though, paragraph structure does not itself convey meaning because editors keep paragraphs short for reasons of graphics. When a story appears in print, the copy will run in long, narrow columns. The traditional paragraph design taught in English classes, however, assumes that the copy will appear in a book in columns as wide as the page. When a newspaper typesets book-length paragraphs in very narrow columns, the paragraphs run unusually long. Such long paragraphs intimidate readers, because they create the optical illusion of a great deal of verbiage. Therefore, newspapers limit paragraphs to two or three sentences. This translates to no more than five lines of copy measured in the traditional typewriter paper width and the default computer program width for business correspondence.

Such short paragraphs mean that the traditional paragraph structure—introduction of an idea, expansion of the idea, and then summary—does not work in news writing. Since the look of a newspaper paragraph comes from typesetting aesthetics, and not from logical or conceptual structuring, the news writer should not worry about breaking up ideas across paragraphs. Newspaper writers do hook ideas together conceptually, but they take five or six connecting paragraphs to do what one traditional paragraph written in a composition class would do.

Thus, the paragraph of dialogue might look like this, when submitted as a news story.

> The defendant in a sensational murder trial today admitted on the stand that he did go to the site of the slaying.
>
> "I was at the McGruder place last night, and I did leave the note for Amy," said Derrick Broughton, 31, son of mining magnate Wilbur Broughton.
>
> "But I swear I didn't have anything to do with turning the gas on, and I swear I didn't kill Amy. She wasn't there when I arrived, and she wasn't there when I left," Broughton said.

✦ ATTRIBUTION

The book-format paragraph and the news formula paragraphs above also differ in how often they mention the speaker. The newspaper story makes much more frequent mention of the speaker. In the above example, the reader learns that Broughton is speaking in the third paragraph even though the second paragraph has already pointed that out. The newspaper term **attribution** refers to the part of the sentence that names the person who said the words appearing in quotation marks. At some convenient place, the writer interrupts the quotation to insert a phrase telling the readers who did the talking.

Good news writing demands attribution because this mechanism lets the reporter maintain a stance of objectivity. In the attribution, the reporter tells the reader, "I know the information in that quotation is opinion, but you have to understand that it's not necessarily my opinion. It's the opinion of this person I interviewed." Attribution, therefore, litters news stories, but it should appear only once in each paragraph, because only one person should speak in each paragraph.

Attribution is especially important in paraphrased quotations, because a reader will presume that any material without attribution to someone else represents the words and views of the author of the article. Consider:

> "We could never have continued our evangelical efforts had it not been for the financial help of Mrs. Poitier," Leavis said.
>
> Mrs. Poitier's generous support will be remembered by hundreds touched by the Open-Hand Ministry.

The reader of this passage would rightly assume that the second paragraph is in the voice of—and hence represents the opinion of—the author of the article, and not that of Leavis. In failing to attribute the second paragraph, the reporter has inadvertently given the appearance of bias. The paragraphs should read:

> "We could never have continued our evangelical efforts had it not been for the financial help of Mrs. Poitier," Leavis said.
>
> Mrs. Poitier's generous support will be remembered by hundreds touched by the Open-Hand Ministry, said Leavis.

In general, just about every paragraph should have some sort of attribution.

✦ LONG QUOTES

Because newspapers typeset paragraphs in narrow columns, the traditional term-paper method for including a long quotation—indented one-half inch from regular text and single-spaced—does not make sense for the news writer. For a long quote (a quote longer than one sentence), add attribution at the end of the first sentence.

Following the tenet of accuracy, be certain that every word contained in quotation marks is exactly what the source said. Suppose the police chief said:

> The two cars appeared to have been drag-racing down Knight Street. At the light at the bottom of the hill, they were going too fast to stop and ran across the road into the front of Broadway Jewelers.

A reporter would place the attribution at the end of the first sentence, placing quotation marks around everything else, and thus write:

> "The two cars appeared to have been drag-racing down Knight Street," said Leroy Thomas, Amityville police chief. "At the light at the bottom of the hill, they were going too fast to stop and ran across the road into the front of Broadway Jewelers."

A comma goes before the attribution, a period follows it. Double quotes go around the quoted material, and all punctuation goes inside the quotation marks.

If the quotation is only one sentence, attribution goes at the end, as in:

> "The nature of the crime is unclear, but we'll keep Jenkins in jail until we understand what he was planning," said Chief Tomotla.

Often a quotation will run too long for one short newspaper paragraph. When the same person continues to speak in a second paragraph, the writer does not close the quotation after the first paragraph but, instead, reopens the quotation at the start of the second paragraph.

Suppose the police chief said:

> The two cars appeared to have been drag-racing down Knight Street. At the light at the bottom of the hill, they were going too fast to stop and ran across the road into the front of Broadway Jewelers. That building took a one-two hit. The front of the building was wiped out, and both cars were totaled.

A reporter would punctuate like this:

> "The two cars appeared to have been drag-racing down Knight Street," said Leroy Thomas, police chief. "At the light at the bottom of the hill, they were going too fast to stop and ran across the road into the front of Broadway Jewelers.
>
> "That building took a one-two hit. The front of the building was wiped out, and both cars were totaled," said Thomas.

There is a quotation mark at the start of the first paragraph and no quotation mark at the end of that paragraph. Then, to remind the reader that this is still a quotation, a quotation mark goes at the start of the second paragraph, and the quotation ends with a quotation mark. Notice that a second attribution goes in paragraph two because every paragraph should contain one (and only one) attribution.

One especially troublesome trap awaits beginning newspaper writers who interview a particularly knowledgeable or quotable source. Sometimes the writer lets the source talk on and on in the article. A source who talks on too long, though, ends up stealing the writer's voice. The story starts to sound as though the source had written it. The reporter ceases to be the writer, becoming a mere stenographer of someone else's words. To avoid this problem, a writer should never let a quotation run longer than two newspaper paragraphs. If the quotation contains more good information than will fit in two paragraphs, paraphrase the rest.

And, in general, a reporter should remember that conflict lies at the heart of the newspaper story. The best stories contain opposing viewpoints about an event, about an idea, or about people. The writer should not cede too much space to any one voice for too long. A writer with strong and essential quotes from two or more sources should try to alternate each person's appearance, using appropriate transitions. For example:

"The new tax ordinance puts an unfair burden on middle-class taxpayers," Steiner said after the council meeting. "We can't go on like this. Eighty percent of our taxes come from small businesses that make up only 38 percent of total firms in our town."

Councilman Wladek, however, disputed Steiner's assertions in a press conference after the meeting.

"Where Steiner gets his numbers I don't know," Wladek said. "I have the figures, and 80 percent of our revenues come from about 80 percent of our firms. That sounds fair, doesn't it?"

Steiner, who attended Wladek's press conference, argued that Wladek was merely grandstanding.

"It's a shame that the people of Salem have to put up with such foolishness," Steiner said.

Here, the final quotation goes in its own paragraph, since quotations should always appear separate from summary material.

✦ SAIDISM

English teachers rail about avoiding the use of *said*. They have even come up with a cute nickname for the repeated use of *said:* **saidism.** News writers should ignore their advice. Words like *suggested, shouted, raged, whispered,* and *implied* all insert the writer's opinion into an article. At best, fancy equivalents of *said* will merely irritate the reader. At worst, they insert pure opinion. Consider:

"I want to thank my supporters in advance for voting for me tomorrow," Selectman Smith blubbered.

"It's been a hard race, but we can still win," Smith squeaked, dabbing his eyes with a handkerchief.

Certainly, in this example, Smith comes across as weak and simpering, and nobody would bet any money on his chances of success. A change in the words used to attribute the quotations, however, completely changes the force of the paragraphs.

"I want to thank my supporters in advance for voting for me tomorrow," Selectman Smith crowed.

"It's been a hard race, but we can still win," Smith proclaimed confidently, dabbing his eyes with a handkerchief.

Not only does Smith sound far more confident; the eye-dabbing sounds like he's got something in his eye rather than like he's weeping. The writer should avoid editorializing, instead going with:

"I want to thank my supporters in advance for voting for me tomorrow," Selectman Smith said.

"It's been a hard race, but we can still win," Smith said, dabbing his eyes with a handkerchief.

Even with a thesaurus, a writer can run out of reasonable synonyms for *said* and end up with interviewees who gibbered and hooted before the end of a long story.

Similarly, writers should avoid the attribution *according to.* It takes more space than *said,* but says the same thing.

Some writers substitute the word *stated* for *said,* but they generally misuse the word. *Stated* implies that the source made a formal and well-thought-out statement. It only accurately describes actions at a speech or formal press conference.

A beginning reporter really should just use *said* for all attributions.

Writers sometimes insert their opinion by using single quotation marks, as in:

"The Arts Center can be thought of as a community 'benefit,'" Mrs. Waters said.

The use of single quotes around *benefit* implies that the event might not really be a benefit. It may or may not be, but the writer should offer evidence instead of opinion.

Think of attribution—as in a phrase like "said Smith"—as punctuation. Attribution appears constantly in a news story, just as does punctuation. Writers do not vary their periods and commas, and they do not need to vary their attributions.

✦ LEADING QUOTES

A writer who **leads a quote** precedes the quotation with attribution—often "according to . . . ," as in:

According to Smith, "The whole plan was cooked up over coffee."

Since the quotation mark at the start of the quotation tells the reader that someone besides the writer said the next set of words, a quotation needs no more introduction. Also, leading quotes, by emphasizing the voice of the writer—putting the reporter's words first—takes attention away from the source. A reporter should try for a sort of invisible presence in the story, necessary but unseen. In general, then, avoid constructions like:

According to Leavis, "My office will do everything in its power to help victims of the flooding."

Instead of leading a quote with attribution, put the attribution at the end.

✦ FIXING UP QUOTES

A reporter should not repair other people's language unless no other solution exists. Spoken English has a faster, breezier tone than written English, and all people make grammatical mistakes when they speak— but it is cruel to quote these mistakes in writing.

A person speaking during an interview has no chance to go back and edit the language to make sure that subjects and verbs agree in number, but a writer can clean up grammatical errors in a first draft. Since reporters translate spoken English from their sources into written English for articles, they owe it to their sources not to make them look stupid.

Kind reporters paraphrase when using interview material containing grammatical errors. Since the information represents the opinion of the source, the writer includes attribution. Since the passage does not contain the source's exact words, the writer does not include quotation marks.

Suppose the police chief mentioned earlier had said, "When George Stallings saw his jewelry store he was pretty tore up."

A kind reporter would write the following:

Jewelry store owner George Stallings was very upset, said the police chief.

It would be wrong to write:

"When George Stallings saw his jewelry store he was pretty upset," said the chief.

A writer who reported this sentence would be lying, plain and simple. Direct quotations should always report exactly what the interviewee said.

Quotes must always mean exactly what the source meant to say. Editing quotes or shuffling sentences in ways that change meanings can land a reporter in court.

✦ PARAPHRASING

In general, reporters do not get into trouble when they use direct quotations rather than paraphrasing. Usually, experienced writers report direct quotes carefully, word for word—but paraphrasing can cause trouble when the reporter assumes knowledge about the inner state of a source. An example from the early newspaper career of one of the authors might be instructive. A police chief told the reporter:

> I can't believe anybody could be as stupid as the mayor. He doesn't know as much about running a city as a pregnant sow knows about Neiman-Marcus lingerie.

An editor excised the quotation, and substituted:

> Chief Yarborough questioned the judgment of the mayor in the recent turmoil over the construction of the new jail building.

A reasonable assumption, but an assumption nevertheless. Had the story reported the chief's exact words, which were on tape, all would have been well. (See Chapter 9 for more information on using a tape recorder.) The chief, however, objected to the paraphrase. He accused the reporter of guessing his thoughts, and rightly so. When paraphrasing, then, never draw conclusions about the inner states of sources.

A second issue in paraphrasing has to do with comprehension and empathy. Reporters should make certain they understand what their sources mean before they start to paraphrase, and the best way to do that is to ask, on tape.

> CHIEF: I can't believe anybody could be as stupid as the mayor. He doesn't know as much about running a city as a pregnant sow knows about Neiman-Marcus lingerie.
> REPORTER: Could I say, then, that you're casting doubt upon the mayor's abilities?
> CHIEF: Hell, yes, you could say that.

When the article comes out in the newspaper the chief may regret saying this, but the wise reporter will have preserved a tape of the interview.

✦ TAPE RECORDERS

All too often, as in the above example, sources regret having said something after seeing their words in print. Angry people call the source to say, "How dare you tell the newspaper that?" And, although it is perhaps not the moral or brave thing to do, sources often lie. "I didn't say it. That damn reporter misquoted me," they will tell angry callers.

Such people sometimes convince themselves that they did not say things they really did say, and will go so far as to demand retractions. A reporter's best protection is to answer such demands with, "Would you like to hear your words on tape?" Further, in the event of a court case, nothing shuts down a source's attorney like an offer to replay the tape in court.

Beginning reporters sometimes worry that sources may not talk freely when they see a tape recorder. While this is a legitimate concern, a reporter might better ask, "Do I want to quote somebody in the newspaper saying something he would not say into a tape recorder?"

The tape recorder serves two useful functions. First, it captures what the source says for easy future reference. Second, it lets sources know that they are on the record—that they are speaking to a reporter who has every intention of quoting their exact words in print in the newspaper.

When reporters set tape recorders on the table in front of sources, with the little red flashing light that says the machine is running, sources get a very clear indication that their words will appear in the newspaper. A reporter should not get one of those spy-type micro-recorders, or try to use surreptitious microphones or the like, because the tape recorder does more than help a reporter get accurate quotes. It also helps a source understand the circumstances of an interview. It lets sources know, very emphatically, that they are speaking for publication.

✦ QUOTE-OUTS

Quote-outs are word- or phrase-long quotes, inserted into paraphrases. For example:

> Bartleman described American newspapers as "wimpy."

When used sparingly, quote-outs are a good tool for paraphrasing. When overused, they show lazy reporting.

A reporter should use quote-outs when the phrase or word has enough importance and interest to deserve such special treatment. In a good quote-out, the words themselves must have news value, as in:

> During his press conference, Menger called Thompson "a garden-variety crook.
> "The fact that she's fooled everybody in town tells us about the corporate mentality of this city," Menger said. "I'll see that woman in court, and then we'll see what everybody thinks."

Here, the phrase "garden-variety crook" states an opinion strongly. The author includes quotation marks in the paraphrase to emphasize that these exact words originated with the source.

✦ WHEN TO QUOTE

Quotation marks signal the reader that a new voice is speaking. A news story always contains at least two voices—the voice of the reporter and the voice of a source. Usually, stories have multiple sources, and hence more than two voices. Passages with no quotation marks represent, by definition, the voice of the reporter, who must speak in a dry, unemotional tone without expressing opinions. In contrast, readers expect lots of opinion from the news sources, the voices within quotation marks. A story lacks life when the tone of voice in a direct quote does not differ from that of the plain, reporter-generated text. If a quotation lacks compelling language, a reporter should just paraphrase it.

> "We could have driven through the blockade," Lieutenant Johnson told reporters, "but there was a significant chance that some officers might find themselves in a personal injury type of situation."

Better to write:

> Lieutenant Johnson told reporters that the police did not drive through the blockade because they wanted to avoid injury.

At best, dull quotes make dull stories. At worst, a dull quote creates a **double-decker**—a quotation that merely echoes what previous summary paragraphs have already said.

> Officer Richards said the police were afraid to enter the Overtown neighborhood.
> "We're scared of Overtown," Richards said. "That's why we won't go in there."

Better to just let the paraphrase in the first paragraph stand on its own.

Good quotes use lively language. Almost always, somebody says something interesting. A writer should pick quotes carefully, though. Use only the ones that put a distinct new voice into the story. As a writer, the reporter has the responsibility of selecting only interesting quotes for use in a story. As an interviewer, the reporter has the responsibility of encouraging sources to say interesting things.

> CHIEF: I really have to tell you that I don't think much of the jail occupancy cap. We'll be putting people out on the street that we shouldn't be releasing. This all goes back to some things I've said about the mayor.
> REPORTER: What things?
> CHIEF: Well, I'd better not say. I've just got some opinions, that's all.

REPORTER: What are your opinions about the mayor?
CHIEF: Well, you asked. I can't believe anybody could be as stupid as the mayor. He doesn't know as much about running a city as a pregnant sow knows about Neiman-Marcus lingerie.

If the chief knew plainly that he spoke for publication, then the reporter got some exciting quotes. The reporter did not force the chief to give his opinions. The reporter merely gave him the chance, and the chief took it.

◆ THE FOLLOW PARAGRAPH

Quotations have a special role in the structure of news stories. Since the lead has to be objective and factual, writers usually put a punchy quote into the second or third paragraph. This follow paragraph gives life and a sense of accuracy to the story. For example:

Four children and their mother are homeless tonight after an early-morning fire destroyed their house at 47 Delaware Ave.
"A log rolled out of the fireplace after we went to bed," Alma Smith, 47, said. "I shouldn't have kept all that kindling and newspaper so close."

This follow paragraph highlights the safety angle of the story as soon as possible by giving the story a human dimension. Ideally, the quotation should sum up the personal angle of the story in the same way the lead summarizes the facts. More commonly, though, the follow paragraph displays the most striking quote of the story.

The follow paragraph only works with a strong quote, though. Weak quotes with no human interest or conflict, or quotes that merely paraphrase the lead, turn into boring double-deckers, as in the following:

After trying for six months, BARCO unions and management have reached a stopgap agreement to continue manufacturing soap while they negotiate a final contract, said union officials Tuesday.
"We've tried for six months," union president Jack Charitos said. "This agreement will give us time to negotiate a permanent contract."

Another problem with the follow paragraph is predictability. Student government presidents, actors, appointed officials, athletes, and the new dogcatcher will all call a new job "a great challenge." Do not quote clichés, especially in a follow paragraph.

Mayor Burton (Tiny) Smart Monday named Helen Shapiro, 47, the first full-time tax collector of Salkehatchie County.

"It will be a great challenge," Shapiro said. "I thank the people of Salke-hatchie County for their confidence in me."

All new recruits say something like that. Equally weak and clichéd quotes are: "open lines of communication," "encourage cooperation," and "do the best job possible." Instead of using these lines, call the official back and ask, "Why will the job be a challenge? Can you give me an example of what you're talking about?" These questions might have yielded:

"We want to improve our collection rate," Shapiro said. "The county now has only an 89 percent success rate at tax collections while national averages say we should be collecting on 95 percent of the tax bills we send out."

That adds a little life to the story, particularly for the 11 percent of county property owners who are not paying their tax bills. The story might then read:

Mayor Burton (Tiny) Smart Monday named Helen Shapiro, 47, the first full-time tax collector of Salkehatchie County.
"We want to improve our collection rate," Shapiro said. "The county now has only an 89 percent success rate at tax collections while national averages say we should be collecting on 95 percent of the tax bills we send out."
Smart said he had no idea that the collection rate in Salkehatchie County was below that of comparable counties in the nation.

Not every story will have a quote that hops with vitality, miraculously summing up the whole event in a tidy package. Almost every story, though, will have some quotation that sparkles. Show it off well up in the story. If no quotation deserves display, then do not use a follow quote.

The follow paragraph can also reveal details about the subject of a story. As discussed in Chapter 3, few names should appear in leads.

Police today arrested a Louisville man in connection with the robbery of a Frankfurt video rental store.
John Nathan Jessup, 41, who gave his address as St. Matthews St., was leaving a fast food restaurant on Jessup Ave. when police arrested him.
"His car was loaded with the stolen tapes," Officer Sharon Dunsmore said. "He was armed, but he didn't offer any resistance."

The two follow paragraphs name the otherwise anonymous suspect and the police officer and play up the conflict angle of the story.

Quotations, when used properly, give important life to a well-written news story. Strong quotes make readers feel like eyewitnesses to the action, but quotations in news stories differ in several respects from quotations as they appear in standard written composition. The news formula formats quotations into short paragraphs, with an attribution in each paragraph. A reporter often paraphrases quotes, although paraphrasing requires considerable skill and judgment.

The difficulty with paraphrasing, however, should not discourage the news writer from using it liberally.

SUMMARY

- Newspaper paragraphs should run no more than five typed lines long.
- The newspaper term *attribution* refers to the part of the sentence that names the source of the words in quotation marks.
- Despite lessons learned in English composition, use *said* for all attributions.
- Don't repair other people's language. Instead, paraphrase an ungrammatical quote.
- Use a tape recorder, making sure that your source knows that he or she is being taped.
- For direct quotations pick lively passages with emotion, color, and interest.
- Put a punchy quote into the second or third paragraph. This follow paragraph gives life to the story by varying the voice.

IN-CLASS EXERCISES

1. Find a newspaper story that uses extensive quotes. What do the quotes add to the story? Would the story have worked as well without them?

2. Interview a classmate, using a tape recorder. Now write your classmate's quotes in the appropriate format for a news story.

3. Using the tape from Exercise 2, arrange the quotes topically by how interesting they are. What portions of the interview would you transcribe word for word, and what parts would you quote via summary?

4. Find a newspaper story using quote-outs. Were the quote-outs interesting and essential? Why or why not?

5. With the information you gathered in Exercise 2, write a news story using the news formula.

6. Attend a speech held on your campus, or nearby. Use a tape recorder. Now arrange the quotes topically according to how interesting they

are. What portions of the speech would you quote directly, and what portions would you paraphrase?

7. Using the information you gathered and processed in Exercise 6, write a news formula news story.

OUT-OF-CLASS EXERCISE

Attend a local event where a speech is given, or listen to a speech on C-SPAN. Tape the speech with a tape recorder. Arrange the quotes in order of topical interest, as described above, and write a news formula news story from them.

CHAPTER 6

Stylebooks,
Dictionaries, and
Other Tools

Stylebooks, dictionaries, computer spelling checkers, grammar checkers, and on-line services help journalists improve their writing. Stylebooks and dictionaries have been around for a long time, but newer tools, like on-line databases and spell checkers, make a writer's task even easier.

✦ STYLEBOOKS

A stylebook lists rules developed over the years to help writers make their copy fit the form that their newspapers want it to take. For example, the *Associated Press Stylebook and Libel Manual* contains an incredible wealth of useful information. Like the referee in a football game, the *AP Stylebook* generally makes the final decision about the rights and wrongs of usage and style.

Many newspapers, particularly the larger ones, have their own stylebooks that supplement or replace the *AP Stylebook*. Other news-gathering agencies, like United Press International, have their own stylebooks. In essence, a writer should think of the stylebook as the rule book for the game of news writing. The stylebook answers frequently asked questions about how to write.

Stylebooks answer a variety of questions. How should a number be printed—as 12 or twelve? Should an article refer to the head of the Catholic Church as the pope or as the pontiff? Is it *dogcatcher* or *dog catcher* or *dog-catcher?* A journalist must follow the stylebook's rulings on such questions.

The remainder of this chapter presents general stylistic rules and some clues as to how to most effectively use a stylebook.

✦ NICE-NELLYISMS

A writer who uses **nice-nellyisms** substitutes sweet euphemisms for blunter or more common words and phrases. Although nice-nellyisms can occasionally help an article, usually they get in the way of telling a story. A classic, and useful, nice-nellyism is *s---*. Obscene language offends some readers, so most newspapers use this fill-in-the-blank method of reporting such four-letter words. More often, though, nice-nellyisms stand in the way of important meanings. In general, unless the word appears regularly scrawled in public restrooms, a writer should use the word rather than the euphemism.

Sometimes, though, the news requires a reporter to print the word itself. It would make news, for instance, if a presidential candidate yelled a vulgar word at a journalist who had written an unkind story about the candidate. Part of properly informing the public would be to print the word the candidate used. Fortunately, the decision on how to put the word in print without offending lies with the editor, not with the reporter. In cases like this, a reporter should ask.

✦ ORGANIZATION NAMES

Groups have a right to the name they choose as long as the term does not mislead. Muslims dislike the term Muhammedan because it falsely implies that they worship the prophet Mohammad. Sometimes, though, additional information helps to make the terms that groups use more understandable. Many people do not know what the Church of Jesus Christ of Latter-Day Saints means, so most papers, and the church itself, will also use "Mormon." A group affiliated with the Ku Klux Klan once called itself Truth in God—a name that obscured the group's mission. One newspaper decided to go with:

> John (Big Daddy) Stewart, leader of a Klan-affiliated group called Truth in God, today said that his group was "declaring war on the media."

Note that the writer didn't say *calling itself.* The snide tone of that phrase would count as an editorial comment.

✦ MEDICAL TERMS

A similar problem comes up with terms used to describe people with AIDS. AIDS is a syndrome—a group of symptoms, like a fever and chills. The term "people with AIDS" accurately describes only those with immune deficiency symptoms. People infected with the AIDS virus do not necessarily have AIDS yet. The proper term for people who carry the virus is "HIV positive." A writer could add a parenthetical aside linking HIV and AIDS. "AIDS victim" implies a state of helplessness that many people with AIDS find offensive. Here again, a journalist would do better to use the phrases and words that the people involved in a group or situation have chosen. The writer can add a note of explanation to avoid confusion. Use sensitivity in labeling physical difficulties. Call people by the label they choose.

A reporter can be too sensitive, however. Calling criminals the legally underprivileged, as one newspaper did for a while, is just silly and confusing. Sometimes a journalist treads a fine line between calling people what they want to be called and writing a nice-nellyism. An editor will help define this line for a new journalist.

✦ EDITORIAL COMMENT

Some nice-nellyisms make unintended editorial comments. A word like, *underprivileged* implies that the people involved have somehow been systematically excluded from opportunity. Maybe they have, but the word choice implies that the writer has thought about the issue and believes this explanation. Terms like *poor* or *economically disadvantaged* deal more directly with the issue of not having enough money, and do not involve the writer in the ongoing debate about the nature of economic opportunity in the United States. Since the short and plain always works better, use *poor* in this situation.

✦ COMMONLY USED STYLE RULES

The editors of newspapers that are members of the Associated Press have addressed many of these style questions, and they suggest solutions in their stylebook. Much writing involves small decisions about word choice and spelling. If two people shared the award, does the reporter write two or 2? Is it Vietnam or Viet Nam? To give a consistent feel to the newspaper as a whole, editors have established a list of rules or conventions that govern these minor decisions.

Editors take the issue of style very seriously. They expect their reporters to know the newspaper's style rules and to follow them. Most American newspapers use the *Associated Press Stylebook* as their basic reference. Individual newspapers have their own stylebooks as well, to tell reporters how to handle unique local situations.

A reporter should flip through the stylebook to learn its organization. The following section lists the most commonly used style rules. A journalist could get to know the organization of the stylebook by looking up each of these rules in it.

Capitalization

Determine whether the newspaper you write for is upstyle or downstyle. Upstyle newspapers capitalize frequently. Downstyle newspapers use as few capitalizations as possible. In general, in the body of a story, capitalize only the first word of each sentence and proper nouns—the names of people, organizations, cities, and the like.

An upstyle headline might read:

Four Killed in Terrorist Blast

while the same headline, downstyle, would be:

Four killed in terrorist blast

Increasingly, newspapers have moved to downstyle.

Titles

Capitalize a person's title if it comes before the name. Lowercase the title if it comes after the name. Always put long titles after the name. For example:

Professor Ingrid Schwarz of Halliburton University gave the lecture.

A longer title would appear as:

Ingrid Schwarz, Richard Tallman professor of linguistics at Halliburton University, gave the lecture.

Mr.

Never use the title *Mr.* in a news story. Check the individual newspaper's policy on the use of *Miss, Mrs.* and *Ms.* Most newspapers do not use these courtesy titles. Important exceptions, though, are the *Wall Street Journal,* the *New York Times,* and the *Christian Science Monitor,* all of whose in-house style sheets demand the use of courtesy titles.

Time

Always refer to time as follows: 2 p.m. or 11 a.m. Don't write 2 pm or 2 o'clock or two this afternoon.

Dates

Generally abbreviate the names of months: Jan. 29, not January 29. Always spell out the following months: March, April, May, June, and July. Always spell out months standing alone without specific dates.

Spell out the names of the days of the week when used alone: Monday. Do not use days of the week in conjunction with the date. Do not say Mon., Jan. 31. Use either the day or the date.

Numbers

Spell out a number if it has one digit (the numbers one through nine). Use numerals for two-digit numbers (10 and above).

Names

The first time an article mentions a person, give the first and last name: Amadi Wilson, Franchesca Bertagnolli. After that, use just the last name (Wilson, Bertagnolli), as in:

> Winifred Wolcott, the director of the Center for Population Studies, said that the birth rate in Delmore and in Becchia County had decreased in the last 10 years. Wolcott's group, which tracks demographic information in the northern part of the state . . .

Organizations

On first reference give the organization's entire name: Department of Health and Human Services. On second reference use a generic term (the department) or an acronym (HHS) if the stylebook gives an acronym for this particular organization, as in:

> The Center for Population Studies tracks demographic information in the northern part of the state, and gets its funds from the state legislature. Founded in 1991, the CPS . . .

✦ USING THE STYLEBOOK

The stylebook contains an immense body of information—far too much information to memorize. Thus, reporters need strategies for looking things up in the book.

Newspapers usually recommend using a dotting system: After completing first drafts of stories, reporters print them out, then dot every word or phrase they need to look up. Some reporters prefer to check after a preliminary reading, but before printing out the story.

The one piece of advice that remains constant is to separate writing the first draft from checking word choice, grammar, or style. Writing is loose, creative work easily killed by interruption, especially a tour through the stylebook looking for arbitration of a particularly tricky question. Reporters should always wait to check style rules until after they have completed the creative part of their writing, producing the first draft.

✦ SPELLING CHECKERS

Computerized **spelling checkers** rely on a list of about 200,000 words. The computer takes each word in the word processing file and checks it against this list. If the word is in the computer's dictionary, then it stays; if the computer cannot find the word in its dictionary, the computer questions the writer. This means, of course, that almost every name in a piece of copy pops out in spell-checking. Schmit, Frannie, Letterman—the computer will question these, but it will miss the errors in a sentence like:

> Northington said he hat been instructed to tare the paper up by Williams the day before the Grand Jury investigation.

The computer's word list includes *hat* even though the writer certainly did not intend to use it here. *Tare* means the empty weight of a container, so the spelling checker passes on it. The spelling checker will stop twice in this paragraph—once on *Northington,* once on *Williams*—and will miss the two incorrect words *hat* and *tare.*

Journalists should think of spelling checkers as typo checkers. They will catch typographical errors like *hwich,* where the typist inadvertently transposed letters, but they will miss words used incorrectly. In general, then, use a spelling checker to catch typos; also check the article visually. Do not interrupt the creative process by worrying about spelling while writing a first draft. Instead, after writing, run the spell checker and then proofread the article thoroughly.

✦ GRAMMAR CHECKERS

The warnings given above for spelling checkers go double for **grammar checkers**. A grammar checker, usually a separate program from the word processor, goes through the sentences in a document and looks for violations of a list of rules. Since the program cannot understand the text, it does not identify the subject, the verb, and the objects in each sentence. Instead it looks for unlikely constructions—a singular verb and a plural noun, a comma directly preceding a *that,* a comma outside a quotation mark, and the like.

The problem with grammar checkers comes in sentences like:

> "That day, that evening, in fact, I saw Gunn driving on 14th St.," Elnor said during the cross-examination. "I don't see how he could have robbed a store in Lewiston if I saw him here that night."

Many grammar checkers would object to this short paragraph. In general, grammar checkers will object to so many acceptable items, and miss so many flawed constructions, that some find little point to using them at all.

Others find that a grammar checker forces them to isolate individual sentences and view them independently from overall context. Studying sentences in isolation can sometimes help a writer see an overall organizational problem in an article.

✦ COMPUTERIZED DATA SOURCES

More and more journalists are acquiring wide and ready access to computerized **databases**. The availability of such information via computer may well revolutionize the news business.

A new kind of news story has already arisen from these databases. A reporter searches news articles in a database to see how often a term appears. For instance, a reporter might look to see how often the term *spouse abuse* appeared in the year before the O. J. Simpson murder case and in the year after. Based on the results, the reporter would write an article about the nation's growing interest in the issue of spouse abuse.

Some newspapers are already putting their backfile of stories onto CD-ROM. This makes it easy to search for all the previous stories in that publication on a given topic. Other newspapers are placing their information onto on-line databases, which can be accessed by remote computers. Journalists may soon be able to log on to an information service and download onto their computer articles from other papers about a topic similar to the one they're working on. (Needless to say, the reporter who picks up another newspaper's exact wording risks losing a job because of plagiarism.)

Reporters can already download information from government and university sources about public opinion polls and about Census Bureau studies. The U.S. government has pledged to make most, if not all, of the immense amount of information it gathers available on-line.

Consider the difference between the following two versions of a story.

The Tidewater Regional Council released unemployment data for the region yesterday, indicating that the unemployment rate in the area has risen to 12.2 percent, up two percent from the same time last year.

A different picture emerges with the addition of some information gathered on-line.

The Tidewater Regional Council released unemployment data for the region yesterday, indicating that the unemployment rate in the area has risen to 12.2 percent, up two percent from the same time last year.

Historical data, however, indicate that 12 percent may be closer to the normal unemployment rate for the region. Unemployment in the region ranged from a high of 12.8 percent in 1978 to a low of 9.9 percent in 1992.

The story might play in a different manner with the use of Census Bureau data.

The Tidewater Regional Council released unemployment data for the region yesterday, indicating that the unemployment rate in the area has risen to 12.2 percent, up two percent from the same time last year.

Data from the Bureau of Labor Statistics, however, indicate that the Tidewater region is doing better than the nation as a whole. Unemployment this month for the nation sat at 13.3 percent, and for the state at 12.9 percent.

Data available from on-line sources can provide the perspective and background that stories frequently lack.

A reporter can find more than statistical data with a computer. The *Oxford English Dictionary,* the final arbiter of word origins and meanings, and the *Encyclopaedia Britannica* are now available on CD-ROM. A journalist writing a story about the reintroduction of the banded lynx into a nearby forest preserve can now, with a few keystrokes, look up an encyclopedia article about the history, life, and decline of the animal.

✦ THE INTERNET

The **Internet** started out as a system for interconnecting computers at universities, research institutes, and defense-related sites. Since the groups linked up over a period of time, no system of administration ever evolved for the net. Instead, net users began to collect into interest groups dealing with a wide range of subjects from politics to art to sports to dogs. Now the Internet links millions of sites and more than 10,000 interest groups. One group dealing solely with recreational fishing, for example, will at any given time have upward of 1,000 notes or comments. Other groups, such as the one addressed as sci.stat.research, circulate cutting-edge statistical studies before they ever appear at a conference or in a scientific journal. Another group, alt.barney.die.die.die, posts hate mail for the children's television character Barney the Dinosaur.

No one takes charge of most of these discussion groups and anyone can post anything. Sometimes this means that discussions degenerate into screaming arguments or name-calling, but a reporter who needs an answer to a question can post in the appropriate discussion group. For example:

POST: rec.arts.tv.comedy
FROM: Keisha Kelley <kelley@htn.com
MESSAGE: I'm writing a news story about Hal Walberg, who starred in "Bob and Aileen" back in the 60s. What other shows was he on?

To which the reply comes:

POST: rec.arts.tv.comedy
FROM: Mike Miller <miller@utsc.edu
MESSAGE: Hal Walberg was Captain Ed on "Captain Ed and the Princess," 1964–1966, and had guest roles on "Star Trek" (a Klingon commander) and on "Car 54, Where Are You?" (Officer Toody's sophisticated brother). Walberg was, I think, one of the

funniest bit players of the 1960s. People like him made the golden age of TV golden.

Mike Miller, Ass't Professor, UTSC School of Communication

After a phone call to get permission to use a direct quote, the story might then lead:

NostalgiaFest, an annual convention for fans of old television shows, will meet in Phillips Convention Center Jan. 19 and 20, said Leana Odell, organizer of the event.

Hal Walberg, who starred in the situation comedy *Bob and Aileen* from 1960 to 1962, will be the master of ceremonies for the event.

"Walberg was, I think, one of the funniest bit players of the 1960s," said Mike Miller, assistant professor of communication at the University of Texas at Santa Cecelia. "People like him made the golden age of TV golden."

Walberg also played the title role in *Captain Ed and the Princess,* 1964–1966, and had guest roles on *Star Trek* and *Car 54, Where Are You?*

Each discussion group usually has a few "netGods"—people with a great deal of knowledge about the subject discussed in the list and a willingness to dispense that information. Most netters include an address or a phone number, and, if necessary, a reporter can use the old-fashioned telephone for follow-up questions. Some groups even have what net slang terms FAQs, which are lists of answers to frequently asked questions. If a FAQ exists, check it first. Failing that, post a question.

There are three things to remember about the Internet. First, since most people read their electronic mail only once a day, there is usually a day's lag between posting a question and receiving a reply. Second, the anonymity of the Internet leads some people to levels of rudeness they would not dare display in person. Just ignore them. Finally, people with Internet access should never leave their terminals logged on and unattended. Occasionally, some practical joker will send a message to a group like rec.sport.baseball that reads something like:

Baseball is a sissy game, and anyone who likes it is stupid.

Of course, the message goes out under the name of the owner of the terminal, and then that person receives an avalanche of electronic hate mail.

✦ SOURCE BOOKS

Many institutions (universities, state governments, and research institutes) have as part of their mission informing the public not only about their activity but about their field of endeavor. Such institutions often provide **source books**—directories of people in that institution and subjects in which they have expertise and which they are willing to discuss. An entry might look like this:

> Bullman, Iva. Department of Sociology. Subjects: Infants, child-rearing practices. 414–3881.
> Burac, Thomas "Tom." Department of Anthropology. Author, "Understanding Subsistence Farming: The Example of Peru." Subjects: Peru, South America, Third-World Agriculture. 414–2992.

These entries would be cross-referenced by subject, as in:

> Peloponnesian War, Paul Cranford
> Peru, Tom Burac
> Peter, St., Millicent Radford

Most universities provide such a service. So do many advocacy groups, such as the National Organization for Women. Commercial sources also prepare such books, sometimes even ranking sources as radical, outspoken, and the like. In general, the reporter should try to find local sources, but using the Internet or source books will produce experts on almost any subject, no matter how obscure.

✦ THE NEWSPAPER'S LIBRARY

One of the most invaluable sources to a reporter is the newspaper's library. This contains the **backfile**—clippings of previous stories in the newspaper—and reference materials, usually encyclopedias, gazetteers, and other sources.

A writer should always check the backfile for information. Almost always, the newspaper will have covered some aspect of any topic before. Sometimes reporters from different divisions of the paper get asked to do essentially similar stories. Checking the backfile can prevent embarrassing wastes of effort, and the background provided by stories in the backfile will almost always make a news story better by providing context for the events of the day.

Many critics of American journalism have suggested that one of the primary problems with modern reporting is the lack of context. Articles often present the news as disconnected and singular events without history or future. Coverage dwells on the unusual without examining continuities.

Tools like the backfile, the Internet, on-line data sources and the like can help reporters in the effort to provide the context and history readers need to help them fully understand news stories. Placed in a larger historical and regional context, the news can make better sense.

Tools like a stylebook can help guarantee that stories look uniform and read easily. Seeing a number written as "10" in one place and as "ten" in another jars readers, making it more difficult for them to pay attention to the news itself. By following style rules, and by paying careful attention to spelling issues, the reporter can help the reader understand the news by removing distractions.

SUMMARY

- A stylebook lists rules that help writers make their copy fit the newspaper format.
- A writer should avoid nice-nellyisms—sweet euphemisms for blunter or more common words and phrases.
- Organizations have a right to see the name they have chosen used in a news story as long as the term does not mislead.
- Wait to check for spelling and style until after completing a first draft.
- After running a computer spell checker, always read copy over again to look for errors.
- Not everything a grammar checker flags is truly an error.
- Computerized data sources can produce a great deal of information.
- The backfile—the library of articles the newspaper has already published—provides lots of background about local people and events.

IN-CLASS EXERCISES

1. Use a copy of the *AP Stylebook* to proofread an article from your campus newspaper. How many errors did you find? Would these errors have been obvious to you without the *Stylebook?*

2. Run something you have written through a grammar-checking program. How many suggestions did it make? How many of those were sensible?

3. Use a computerized database to research information on a topic like regional unemployment levels. Was the process difficult? Did you find information that would be of use in writing a story?

4. Use the Internet to pose a question to a discussion group concerning a topic of interest to you. Did the information you gained help your understanding of the topic? Why or why not?

5. Find out whether your local campus has a source book listing faculty experts available to do media interviews. Find a source on a topic of

interest to you. Find a national source book, and use it to locate an expert on the same topic. Why did you select these sources?

6. Examine a list of the discussion groups available on the Internet. Are there any that would be of particular use to a reporter? Are there any that are of particular interest to you?

7. Using a local campus source book, locate an expert on the local economy. What are that person's credentials? Do you believe that person would make a good source for a news story? Why or why not?

OUT-OF-CLASS EXERCISE

Attend an event where a speech is given, and use the speech as the basis of a story. Then use the Internet and a source book to locate a source who disagrees with the person who gave the speech, and incorporate an interview with that source into the news story.

CHAPTER 7

Editing

Books on writing present a daunting amount of advice. How can a writer create while trying to keep all these rules in mind? It is important not to let the rules create writer's block.

No one can, or should, think about all this composition advice while writing. Instead, you should wait to think about the rules until you begin editing. To write anything—a news story, fiction, or poetry—first just write. Get words down on paper in some form without worrying about sentence structure, paragraphs, and vocabulary. Just write. A writer with a completed draft has already accomplished the hard work. Enough editing will easily turn any draft, no matter how poor it may be, into a much better piece of writing.

Research has shown that most people hit writing problems when they try to edit too early. Writers have a shy creative voice, and it fades away when criticized. The best, and perhaps the only, way to write productively is to write first, and then edit later. A writer with a first draft in hand can retire the shy creative voice, and attack that draft with a new, aggressive, and critical voice.

When you edit, begin by first going through each sentence, checking sentence structure, word choice, spelling and the like. Then edit for overall sense, tone, and structure. Finally, edit to be sure that the article complies with the news formula.

✦ EIGHT EASY WAYS TO POLISH COPY

The "Recommended Reading" section of this book names some of the many excellent books of advice on improving writing style. Rather than duplicating those works, this section lists eight mechanical copyediting devices a writer can use quickly to improve a piece of work.

A writer should not worry about these suggestions when composing a beginning draft. These are devices for improving a completed draft. The computer can help here—use the search function on a word processor to make these editing changes quickly.

1. Use Spelling Checkers

When editing, always run the word processor's spelling checker first. In addition to finding misspellings, the spell checker will also pick up typographical errors. Quickly weeding these problems out of a piece of writing makes it easier to find and fix other difficulties.

Always do a visual check for spelling as well. Remember that the spelling checker on a word processing program only points out words missing from the dictionary. It does not indicate words that do not fit the context. If a writer meant *the* but typed *thee,* the spell checker will miss this mistake. *Thee,* after all, will show up in the spell checker's dictionary. Always run the spell checker again as the last step in editing. This will pick up any spelling or typing errors inserted during editing.

Do not rely on the spelling checker, but also do not hesitate to use it.

2. Eliminate *Is*

Verbs push sentences forward. Strong verbs push harder than weak ones. *Is,* the weakest verb of all, adds no information to a sentence. To eliminate *is,* use the search and replace function on the word processor. Have the computer search for (space)is(space), and delete each occurrence. Just tell the computer to leave a blank space for each *is.*

Then, read through the piece. Some sentences, the ones that contained *is,* will lack verbs. Select the strongest word in each of these sentences and convert this strong word to a verb. Then reword the sentence using that verb. Usually, a writer tosses out a lot of excess verbiage along with *is,* and this makes the piece read better.

For example, take this sentence:

The plan is to purchase combination bed-desk units to furnish rooms in the new dormitory.

With *is* deleted, the sentence reads:

The plan to purchase combination bed-desk units to furnish rooms in the new dormitory.

With *is* deleted, potential verbs like *plan, purchase* and *furnish* become apparent. A stronger sentence could say:

The housing office plans to purchase combination bed-desk units to furnish rooms in the new dormitory.

Or:

The housing office plans to furnish rooms in the new dormitory with combination bed-desk units.

A second example:

There is an increased likelihood that state universities that lose enrollment will also lose state funding, said Williams.

With *is* deleted, the sentence looks like this:

There an increased likelihood that state universities that lose enrollment will also lose state funding, said Williams.

Since *increased* could make a good verb, the improved sentence could read:

The likelihood has increased that state universities that lose enrollment will also lose state funding, said Williams.

3. Eliminate the Passive Voice

Reporters should tell the public who has taken the actions that are affecting their lives. The passive voice evades that responsibility by not naming the doer. Consider this lead:

The property tax rate was doubled today.

Readers who want to complain to somebody will want to know who doubled the tax rate. Bureaucrats love the passive voice because it allows them to evade responsibility for their actions. The newspaper should tell readers who made the decision. A better lead:

The county council voted today 3-2 to double the property tax rate.

The passive voice avoids naming the person responsible for the action in a sentence. The passive voice always uses two or more verbs: a form of the verb *to be* plus a past participle or past-tense word. To find the passive voice, search copy for the following:

- be
- is
- are
- was
- were
- been
- -ed

To eliminate the passive voice, ask this fill-in-the-blank question: Who _____? Fill in the blank with the past-tense verb, and then use the answer to this question as the subject of the new, rewritten sentence. In the example above, ask, "Who doubled the tax rate?" The answer is the county council. Rewrite the sentence to make the county council the subject.

Newspaper stories try to establish who did what, with what effect on whom. Passive-voice constructions, such as the notorious phrase "mistakes were made" (said of a recent scandal), let people off the hook.

4. Check for Accuracy

Go through the copy looking at the following:

- Are all proper nouns spelled correctly?
- Are all times and dates and locations consistent?
- Do all numbers add up correctly?

Look at all uses of the words *not* and *no*, and try to rewrite the sentence to eliminate them. Because accidental omissions of these words can create humiliating errors, avoid using them. Experienced court reporters have learned to write:

A jury today found Alice Wolcott innocent of the charge of murder.

The pro avoids saying "not guilty" in such stories because the accidental elimination of the word *not* can create a horrible error.

Examine carefully any material within quotation marks. Make sure the quotation does not contain any typographical errors. A typo in a direct quote can create an appalling misquote.

5. Ease Transitions

The news formula can create awkward transitions, because the writer brings up topics based on importance to the reader instead of logical order. If a writer can find no other transition, a trick that often works is to pick a word from the last sentence on the old topic and repeat this word in the first sentence of the new topic. The following two sentences lack transition:

> "I know I'll probably lose the election because of that vote, but I couldn't feel good about the county's future unless we doubled those taxes," said Spinks.
> Workers plan to cut down the 200-year-old oak tree on Fayette Dr.

Notice in the following example how the repetition of the words "county's future" aids the transition:

> "I know I'll probably lose the election because of that vote, but I couldn't feel good about the county's future unless we doubled those taxes," said Spinks.
> The 200-year-old oak tree on Fayette Dr. will be missing from the county's future. The county department of public works says the tree is dying at its core and could fall at any time.

6. Create Parallel Structure

Check the copy for series of three or more items connected by commas and *and*. Make sure each item in the series uses the same grammatical structure—that is, make sure to string together all nouns, all verbs, or all prepositional phrases. For example:

> The city council discussed raising taxes, potholes on State St., and will hold their annual retreat Jan. 10 to 11 at the Houston Inn.

The sentence could read much more smoothly by making items in the series parallel. The following revision makes each item in the series a noun followed by a prepositional phrase:

> The city council discussed taxes on property, potholes on State St., and the annual retreat Jan. 10 to 11 at the Houston Inn.

The following revision makes each item in the series a gerund:

> The city council discussed raising property taxes, fixing State St. potholes, and holding the annual retreat Jan. 10 to 11 at the Houston Inn.

Creating parallel structure quickly adds fluidity to a beginner's writing.

7. Eliminate Sexism

Avoid using the pronoun *he* as a generic term. Do this by recasting the sentence in the plural whenever possible. This allows the use of the gender-neutral pronoun *they*. This book, for instance, tries to use *reporters–they* rather than *reporter–he*.

8. Search and Destroy

Use the search function on the word processor to find each of the following items and eliminate them from the copy.

You   A news story should never address readers directly. This comes too close to editorializing, to commanding the reader to do something. The newspaper just presents the facts and leaves the reader the freedom to decide what action to take. A warning, though: Do not alter direct quotes to eliminate *you*. Sources can and should express their wishes in print.

We   A reporter who uses *we* automatically inserts opinion in the article. Of course, *we* works fine in a direct quote.

I   A reporter who uses *I* automatically inserts opinion in the article. *I* works fine in a direct quote.

Our   A reporter who uses *our* automatically inserts opinion in the article. Naturally, *our* works fine in a direct quote.

", and *".*   Since punctuation always goes inside quotation marks, let the search function find typing accidents in copy where a comma or a period ended up outside punctuation marks.

Search for the following items and consider deleting them from the copy. Deleting any of these items will create copy with more punch.

That   Since good news formula sentences are very short, the sense of a sentence will usually survive with *that* deleted.

Which   Most people use this word incorrectly. In many cases they should have used the word *that*. (See the detailed discussion in Chapter 13.)

, and   Check to see if a comma followed by *and* is used as a conjunction between two clauses, as it generally is. Making each of the clauses into separate sentences can add punch to a piece of writing.

;   Only the rare writer uses the semicolon correctly. Look for every semicolon in copy and consider deleting it. The same goes for colons, dashes, and other infrequently used punctuation.

✦ CHECKING FOR NEWS FORMULA STRUCTURE

In the final pass through a story, the writer should examine the article to see if it meets the requirements of the news formula.

Does the Lead Contain All the Required Elements?

A lead should contain identification (who and/or what the story is about), location (where the story happened), a time angle (when the story happened), and, if at all possible, a conflict angle (how whatever happened was opposed). The lack of any of these elements is a violation of the contract with the reader because it defers important information until later in the story.

Does the Story Clearly Identify the Main Characters or Organizations in the Lead or Soon Thereafter?

Usually, proper names do not appear in a lead sentence, but they need to come up soon thereafter. To do this, insert the appropriate information in the next paragraph after the lead.

> Police arrested two men last night in North Waynesboro after a high-speed chase through four counties.
>
> Wally Tipton, 19, of Waynesboro, and Wilfred Gouge, 18, of North Waynesboro, face charges of reckless endangerment and driving while intoxicated.

Is the Brightest Quote in the Second or Third Paragraph?

When editors use the word *bright* in connection with quotes, what they usually mean is the quote that most plainly plays up the conflict angle of the story. This quote should appear as high up in the story as possible, usually falling immediately after the lead.

> Wally Tipton, 19, of Waynesboro, and Wilfred Gouge, 18, of North Waynesboro, face charges of reckless endangerment and driving while intoxicated.
> "They were going at least 120, right through the middle of the Kenwood development," Police Chief Ralph Shattuck said. "We're just lucky that nobody got killed, and that we didn't have to shoot them."

Does Any Backfill Appear After the Follow Paragraph?

If additional information or stage-setting appears, it should fall right after the bright quote, as in:

> "They were going at least 120, right through the middle of the Kenwood development," Police Chief Ralph Shattuck said. "We're just lucky that nobody got killed, and that we didn't have to shoot them."
> Several high-speed chases, one resulting in the deaths of two officers, have taken place in North Waynesboro in the last year, according to police records. The county board of aldermen is considering enacting a new policy forbidding such chases.

Is the Summary–Quote Material That Falls After the Backfill Organized in Action–Reaction Pairs?

The body of the story, the part that falls after the specialized lead, follow, and backfill paragraphs, consists of brief summary paragraphs, followed by quotations. Since these paragraphs should make the conflict angle of the story clear, they should usually fall in action–reaction units.

In these units, one source or a set of sources makes a contention, followed by a rebuttal or response from another source. Each contention or rebuttal consists of several paragraphs. These begin with an introductory summary followed by quotations, as in:

> Several high-speed chases, one resulting in the deaths of two officers, have taken place in North Waynesboro in the last year, according to police records.

The county board of aldermen is considering enacting a new policy forbidding such chases.

North Waynesboro residents label these high-speed chases dangerous and futile, but the police chief contends he needs the ability to do chases for proper enforcement of the law.

"These kids may get a little rowdy, but they don't mean any harm," said Linda Rochelle, president of an organization called Protect Our Safe Streets, Everyone (POSSE).

"The real harm comes when these cops decide to act like cowboys. If they want to drive fast, they can go to Daytona. But we don't want them driving like Richard Petty through our neighborhoods."

"High-speed chases, while undesirable, are an essential part of our total commitment to safe streets and neighborhoods," said Ralph Shattuck, police chief. "We don't want to sit in parking lots and watch violators of the law drive by without fear."

Are the Paragraphs Short?

Beginning news writers often write long paragraphs. Paragraphs in newspaper stories do not have the same structural purpose they do in every other sort of writing. The news formula calls for short paragraphs because stories appear in print set in long, narrow columns. Long, narrow paragraphs can look gray and forbidding. Paragraphs should run only two or at most three sentences long, and often are only one sentence long.

Are the Summary–Quote Sections Arranged From Most Interesting to Least Interesting?

Because reporters usually turn in a much longer story than appears in the newspaper, the most interesting quotes, generally the ones with the strongest conflict angle, should go up higher in the story than dull quotes.

> . . . "We don't want to sit in parking lots and watch violators of the law drive by without fear."
>
> The county board of aldermen has voted several times on this issue, deadlocking four to four on each vote.
>
> "Everyone's opinion on this issue is set," said Parham Welles, an alderman who opposes a ban on high-speed chases. "This issue won't be resolved for a long time."

Note here that the quotes that have the strongest conflict angle (the accusation that the police enjoy conducting high-speed chases and endangering lives) appear before those dealing with a deadlocked board of aldermen. The aldermen are fighting less powerfully than the POSSE group and the police, so that quote appears later.

Is There a Concluding Paragraph, or Anything That Looks Like One?

News formula stories should never have a concluding paragraph. Often, the information the writer would like to put in the concluding paragraph describes the future plans of the people in the story, but these future plans should go up higher in the story. It would, for example, be incorrect for the story to end with:

> "We'll fight this thing through the courts," Rochelle said. "They haven't heard the last of POSSE."

Both these final sentences have too much power to run the risk of getting edited away.

✦ EDITING: AN EXAMPLE

Here's an example of how to edit a story. The first version is:

> In connection with a series of robberies in the Brightwater district, Robert T. Mallons, of 119 White Horse Drive, and his half-brother, William L. Tyree, of the same address, were arrested yesterday on charges of breaking and entering, according to police records. The men were charged with 14 counts of breaking and entering, three counts of possession of stolen goods, and one charge of felonious entry.
>
> Hayward Jennings said, "The police have no proof that my clients knew the equipment was stolen," their attorney said. "There's a reasonable explanation for what was going on at 119 White Horse Drive, and we'll present that explanation when the time is right,"
>
> "Their basement looked like a stereo store. You could go to their front door, ask for a specific piece of stereo equipment, and they'd just go downstairs and get it for you. The prices were right, too, since everything was stolen," said Officer Reynolds Thomas.
>
> Thirty-eight break-ins have been reported in the Brightwater neighborhood in the last year; most of these have involved the theft of sterio equipment, televisions and radios, and cameras and other photographic equipment.

Thomas believes the two robbers can be connected to almost all the thefts, and promises that others connected to the robberies will be apprehended quick.

First, look at the lead paragraph. Who, what, where, and when appear in the lead, but the lead does not read easily because it provides far too much information. For instance, the names of the characters involved appear in the first paragraph. Also, the lead paragraph begins with a prepositional phrase, and the paragraph, at 66 words, is too long. Edited, it would be

> Police charged two men yesterday with breaking and entering in connection with a series of robberies in the Brightwater district.
>
> Robert T. Mallons and his half-brother, William L. Tyree, both of 119 White Horse Dr., face 14 counts of breaking and entering, three counts of possession of stolen goods, and one charge of felonious entry.

Next the writer examines the quotations.

> Hayward Jennings said, "The police have no proof that my clients knew the equipment was stolen," their attorney said. "There's a reasonable explanation for what was going on at 119 White Horse Drive, and we'll present that explanation when the time is right,"
>
> "Their basement looked like a stereo store. You could go to their front door, ask for a specific piece of stereo equipment, and they'd just go downstairs and get it for you. The prices were right, too, since everything was stolen," said Officer Reynolds Thomas.

The brightest of the quotations here is the stereo store quote from the police officer, because it provides a strong visual image. Further, the stereo store quotation is long enough that the attribution could fall after the first sentence rather than at the end of the quotation.

The Jennings quotation needs some help as well. The attribution leads into the quotation, and needs to move. The last sentence of the quotation ends with a comma rather than a period.

In editing, then, the writer could reverse the order of the quotations and provide a transitional paragraph between them to set up the change in voice. Including the modifications suggested above, the example would read:

> "Their basement looked like a stereo store," said Officer Reynolds Thomas. "You could go to their front door, ask for a specific piece of stereo equipment, and they'd just go downstairs and get it for you.
>
> "The prices were right, too, since everything was stolen," Thomas said.

An attorney for the defendants contends that the police have overreacted to rumors about the sale of stolen high-fidelity audio equipment.

"The police have no proof that my clients knew the equipment was stolen," attorney Hayward Jennings said. "There's a reasonable explanation for what was going on at 119 White Horse Drive, and we'll present that explanation when the time is right."

Now for the final paragraph.

Thirty-eight break-ins have been reported in the Brightwater neighborhood in the last year; most of these have involved the theft of sterio equipment, televisions and radios, and cameras and other photographic equipment. Thomas believes the two robbers can be connected to almost all the thefts, and promises that others connected to the robberies will be apprehended quick.

The most serious problem in the last paragraph is the phrase "the two robbers." Since no court has convicted them, it is not accurate to call them robbers, and hence this sentence libels the two men. "Sterio" is a misspelling, and that sentence uses a semicolon to form a run-on sentence. The series listing stolen goods reads awkwardly because it lacks parallel structure. Both sentences use the passive voice, and the last word of the paragraph, *quick,* modifies *apprehended* and so needs to be an adverb. Finally, the paragraph is too long, and the final phrase beginning with "and promises" functions as a concluding sentence here. After editing, the last paragraph would read:

Residents have reported 38 break-ins in the Brightwater neighborhood in the last year. Most of these have involved the theft of stereo, video, or photographic equipment.

Police can connect the two defendants to almost all the thefts, said Thomas.

Putting the whole story together, and moving up the final sentence, a final version would read:

Police charged two men yesterday with breaking and entering in connection with a series of robberies in the Brightwater district.

Robert T. Mallons and his half-brother, William L. Tyree, both of 119 White Horse Drive, face 14 counts of breaking and entering, three counts of possession of stolen goods, and one charge of felonious entry.

"Their basement looked like a stereo store," said Officer Reynolds Thomas. "You could go to their front door, ask for a specific piece of stereo equipment, and they'd just go downstairs and get it for you.

"The prices were right, too, since everything was stolen," Thomas said.

Police expect to make further arrests soon, said Thomas.

An attorney for the defendants contends that the police have overreacted to rumors about the sale of stolen high-fidelity audio equipment.

"The police have no proof that my clients knew the equipment was stolen," attorney Hayward Jennings said. "There's a reasonable explanation for what was going on at 119 White Horse Drive, and we'll present that explanation when the time is right."

Residents have reported 38 break-ins in the Brightwater neighborhood in the last year. Most of these have involved the theft of stereo, video, or photographic equipment.

Police can connect the two defendants to almost all the thefts, said Thomas.

SUMMARY

These steps will quickly polish copy.

1. Always run the spell checker as the first and last steps in editing.
2. Eliminate *is* from copy whenever possible.
3. Eliminate the passive voice.
4. Examine all nouns for accuracy and all numbers to make sure they add up.
5. Ease transitions by repeating words when the subject changes.
6. Create parallel structure.
7. Delete sexism by using plural nouns and pronouns when possible.
8. Eliminate *we, you, I,* and *our* from copy. Consider eliminating each use of *that, which,* the semicolon, and the word *and* as a conjunction between clauses.
9. Check the sequencing in the story to make sure the most important information comes up first.

IN-CLASS EXERCISES

1. Take a news story you wrote in a previous session, and edit it using the rules presented here. Did you find that your copy changed very much?

2. Examine five stories from your local newspaper. Are the main characters identified early on in the story? If there are characters who are identified later, how do they differ from the characters identified earlier?

3. Examine five stories from your newspaper for sexist language. Did you find any, and, if so, how would you eliminate it?

4. Examine a news story from a local or campus newspaper for use of the passive voice. Did you find instances of it? Were some of those uses appropriate? In what instances do you think it would be appropriate to use the passive voice?

5. Rewrite a news story you wrote earlier in class, eliminating each use of *that, which,* the semicolon, and the word *and* as a conjunction between clauses. Did you find it difficult? In what instances did it improve your copy, and in what instances did it not?

6. Locate a news story that you believe uses sexist language, and rewrite it to eliminate the sexist language.

7. Find a story that identifies a main information source only late in the story, and rewrite it to identify this source earlier. Which version do you like better, and why?

OUT-OF-CLASS EXERCISE

Attend a meeting of a government body, and use that as the basis of a story. Then edit the story using the guidelines presented here. Now, compare the edited and unedited versions of your story. Then make a list of the writing errors you tend to make.

PART TWO

Gathering
the News

CHAPTER 8

Interviewing

A good journalist must have strong interviewing skills, because all the information in news stories comes from only two sources: written documents and interviews. Knowing this, some beginning journalists find interviewing intimidating. They see themselves as humble college graduates about to take on experienced experts, and they worry about whether or not they'll succeed.

In reality, experienced reporters enjoy interviewing. An interview gives the reporter a chance to take a break from the office and all the deadline pressures lurking there. Most sources really enjoy talking with reporters because it gives them a chance to talk about their area of expertise, a subject they usually love. Many people say that interviews with journalists help them see new things, or think about their fields in new ways.

Interviews go successfully if the source relaxes and if the reporter keeps the final article clearly in mind.

✦ PREPARING FOR AN INTERVIEW

Reporters do most of their interviews over the telephone, because this saves a huge amount of time. The reporter does not have to drive all the way to the subject's office and back. During the interview itself, two people talking on the telephone can get through the social niceties much more quickly and therefore the interview does not take as long. A journalist sitting at a computer to do an interview can type notes directly into a computer file. This makes writing up the story a much faster process because reporters never have to retype word-processed notes. Instead, they use their computers to move quotes from the notes file to the file that contains the draft of the article.

For example, reporter Joyce Takahashi needs to write a roundup of highway patrol calls for the last 24 hours. She has covered the cops for six months and knows them. Besides, she already has two other stories she needs to finish by deadline. Instead of driving out to highway patrol headquarters, she may well telephone and ask for her good buddy, Officer Fred Gomez, and say, "Hey, Fred. You got anything good from last night?" Gomez will reel off the accident reports.

Many stories, though, need the personal touch. Often in a face-to-face meeting a person will give more detailed information on a subject. A reporter should get to know anyone who could become a continuing source of information. A face-to-face interview can help establish long-term rapport. In addition, many people prefer to talk in person because the telephone intimidates them.

Takahashi has just added local schools to her beat. She needs to write her first article describing a proposed county school budget. She got a copy of the budget at last night's school board meeting, and the document weighs five pounds. She needs a guide to help her make sense of the mountain of data. Before arranging an interview, a reporter does some thinking about the information she wants. Here, the reporter knows what she wants—help. Unfortunately, Takahashi knows that calling the main number for the school administration and screaming "Help!" won't work.

Instead, she tries to find out who she should interview. She asks her editor and her fellow reporters for names. "Which of the school's administrators has the patience to explain the budget to a novice? Is there someone who likes dealing with the press?" she asks.

Some interview subjects think a reporter should spend lots of time researching a story before seeking an interview—but in reality, reporters don't have lots of time. A reporter should find out as much as possible ahead of time, but basically reporters do research by interviewing people. The reporter's ignorance makes the interview necessary—that is, she needs to do the interview as part of the research necessary to write a thorough story. Reporter Takahashi needs an expert on school budgeting who is willing to work with her ignorance of accounting.

The editor suggests School Superintendent Shirley Wesley. "She's a good guy and, besides, you need to get to know her," he says. Now Takahashi at least knows who to call.

She also needs to prepare a list of questions to ask. For the budget story, she needs to get the editor to show her the basics of reading a budget and preparing questions.

✦ SETTING UP AN INTERVIEW

Takahashi calls Superintendent Wesley for an appointment. She describes her story assignment. Takahashi warns the superintendent that the interview will take about an hour. While making the appointment she tries to make sure her source schedules enough time. Since she wants the superintendent to start thinking about the information she wants to appear in the newspaper, making the appointment ahead of time gives the source a chance to prepare for the interview.

The setting for the interview matters. A reporter and a source can talk in the newspaper office (the reporter's territory), at the subject's home or office (the subject's territory), or in a park or restaurant (neutral territory). In most interviews, a reporter wants a calm source.

Setting the interview in the subject's territory, the place where the person will feel the most relaxed and in control, will help create a relaxed interview. A newsroom interview may save time. But keep in mind that sources may give more information in surroundings they find familiar.

Avoid doing interviews in restaurants. Documents and notebooks tend to get lost among the cups and saucers. Besides, just as a reporter thinks she has developed enough rapport to ask a tough question, she may be interrupted.

Takahashi wants to avoid a restaurant interview because she knows what will happen. She will be saying to the superintendent, "Dr. Wesley, it looks like the Yucca High Wildcat football coaching budget has doubled from last year." Just then, the waiter will come up: "Hi, I'm Heathcliff, and I'm your waitperson for today!" This kills everybody's train of thought.

Reporter Takahashi will schedule her meeting for the school district offices. Superintendent Wesley can help her more if she has her files handy.

Takahashi also wants to make the interview a twosome. Too often an added person tries to take over an interview. Takahashi knows what will happen if, for example, School Business Manager Robert Smith sits in. He may keep interrupting the superintendent to tell the reporter something like, "This is far too complex. Hardly anyone understands the difficulties here. You shouldn't bother to write a story about this." Takahashi cannot respond simultaneously to a cordial superintendent and a hostile business manager.

✦ UNWILLING INTERVIEWEES

The newspaper has a new editor who has decided to begin covering school board budgets in depth for the first time. What if the superintendent tells Takahashi she will be out of town and designates the business manager as the source of information on the budget? Takahashi calls him for an appointment and he says, "This is far too complex. Hardly anyone understands the difficulties here. You shouldn't bother to write a story about this."

A reporter can try two routes to convincing an unwilling source to grant an interview. The reporter can threaten to quote him in the story saying, "No comment." Takahashi would say: "Well, OK. Here's how the story will read: 'Business Manager Bob Smith refused to discuss the budget. "This is far too complex. Hardly anyone understands the difficulties here. You shouldn't bother to write a story about this," he said.' "

A more humane approach usually gets more cooperation. The reporter says, "We're doing the story anyway, and this is what it's going to say. Don't you want to include your side?"

In the county budget example, Takahashi would say, "Mr. Smith, I know I'm asking a lot of you to take time with me to go over the budget, but my editor insists that we write the story and the superintendent told me you would be happy to help me."

Usually one of these approaches will convince a person to grant an interview, but remember that no one is required to talk to the press. Everyone has the right to say, "No comment." Government officials who refuse to discuss their work can end up out of work, but in the end they have the right to make this choice.

If the person opts for "No comment," then a reporter finds other sources and includes the "No comment" if it seems necessary to the story.

✦ AT THE INTERVIEW, MAKE SMALL TALK FIRST

Smith, the business manager, has relented and will go over the numbers with Takahashi. At the interview, she tries to put Smith at ease. She does not walk in the door shooting questions about the Wildcat football budget. At first, she does not ask any questions.

Instead, she tries to establish common ground, to put Smith at ease by first making small talk. She goes through the social niceties. Takahashi shakes hands with Smith and thanks him for agreeing to help her out with the story. She begins the conversation by discussing little things—sports, the weather, the traffic, or the pictures on the office wall.

The reporter tries to establish herself as a decent and professional human being.

Eventually even someone hostile like Smith will relax and say he wants to start answering questions. "Well, let's get to it," he might say.

After a sign from her source, Takahashi starts the interview. She signals that she wants to start the formal business of the interview by taking out a notebook and asking, "How do you spell your name?" A reporter should always start an interview with this question. This holds true even for someone with a name as obvious as Bob Smith. Takahashi would ask, "That's R-O-B-E-R-T S-M-I-T-H, right?"

This question has several effects. First, it serves as a conversational bridge from small talk to work. Second, it establishes the reporter as trustworthy and interested in accuracy. Third, it puts the reporter in charge of the interview. It says that the reporter will ask the questions and decide in what direction the interview will flow.

✦ DURING THE INTERVIEW

At this point, Takahashi does not remove her list of prepared questions from her purse. Instead, she asks what comes to mind. Then she follows up with whatever flows naturally from the previous question and answer. She avoids peppering Smith with questions. Instead, she converses with him. A reporter should try to leave the expert free to explain the topic instead of letting a preconceived list of questions limit the conversation.

Takahashi will save her prepared list for the end of the interview. She'll refer to the list only when she draws a blank and cannot come up with anything else to ask.

During the interview, new questions will come to her if she keeps in mind the story she plans to write. With a story idea in her head to guide the conversation, she asks questions to get quotations to support her approach. Then she follows up the person's answers with more questions on the same topic.

For the school budget story, Takahashi's central question is: "Why has the school budget gone up over last year?"

Smith answers, "Well, we're paying the teachers more."

Then the reporter follows up: "Each teacher got a big raise?"

"No," the business manager answers. "They just got cost of living, but we filled four new positions."

Then Takahashi follows up: "How big was the cost-of-living raise?" and "What were the four new positions?"

During the interview, Takahashi tries to keep her source on track. If the person really relaxes, he may wander off the topic. Smith may say,

"One of the new teachers went to Arizona State. That's my alma mater, you know. I had the best teacher there. That guy really made accounting interesting."

Takahashi smiles to acknowledge the statement, but she brings Smith back on topic by asking, "What will the four be teaching?"

✦ USEFUL QUESTIONS

There are three questions in particular that can keep an interview going and get good, quotable information:

1. "Why?" Out of shyness or hostility, a source will sometimes give one-word answers to questions. The person will answer all questions with "Yes" or "No" or "Sometimes" or "Maybe." "Why?" works so well in interviews because the source cannot give a one-word answer. A person has to answer this question with sentences.

   Takahashi asks Smith, "Do you think the school board will approve this budget?"

   He says, "Nope." And then sits back quietly.

   "Why?" she asks.

   "I don't think they'll want to raise taxes much," he says.

   "Why?" she asks.

   Occasionally someone will toy with a reporter and give the only possible one-word answer to the question, "Why?" "Because," the person will answer. When this happens, the reporter should look the person dead in the eye and say, "Because why?" Usually, this will make a person return to giving complete answers.

2. "Can you tell me a story about it?" The new budget includes $4,000 to install video surveillance cameras on school buses. Takahashi might ask the business manager, "Can you tell me a story about that? Can you describe one of the incidents that caused you to decide to buy the cameras?"

   Usually this question will bring forth an interesting anecdote that will help illustrate a point in the newspaper article. Because most people love to tell stories, they seem to enjoy answering this question.

3. "Best?" "Worst?" The reporter tells the source, "I'm going to ask you two questions. Can you tell me what's the best thing about this? What's the worst?" About the surveillance cameras, Takahashi might tell Smith, "I'm going to ask you two questions. What's the best thing these cameras could make happen? And what's the worst outcome of buying these video cameras?"

   People usually have to stop and think before they answer the Best? Worst? question, but they usually give very telling responses.

✦ ASK DUMB QUESTIONS

Never worry about asking a dumb question. If a reporter does not understand something a person says, she should stop him and ask for an explanation or a definition.

Occasionally a source will be rude.

Smith might mention "the capital budget."

"What's that?" Takahashi might ask.

"You don't even know that? How am I supposed to work with someone like you?" Smith might respond.

The best answer to rudeness is, "Look, I'm sorry, but I don't understand, and I do want to get it right in my article."

A part of the art of journalism is figuring out how to write an accurate story about a topic a reporter knew little about at the start of the research. While school budgeting may involve complex and difficult concepts, the public still needs to know how its schools spend tax dollars.

Takahashi tries to keep in mind that she is asking questions because she needs information about the school budget. She can find the answers only by asking questions, even if some of them seem dumb to Smith. If she does not ask dumb questions, then she risks including in her article something she does not understand. If she puts in something she does not understand, she will probably use it inaccurately. A reporter can either ask dumb questions or write a dumb article.

✦ OFF THE RECORD

During an interview, a source will sometimes ask, "Can we go off the record?" Sometimes an interviewer will volunteer, "Do you want to go off the record?" If a reporter learns something **off the record,** it means that she has promised not to publish the information. Reporters, then, should avoid promising to keep information off the record. An example of why this is a good rule to follow occurs in the Smith interview:

Takahashi asks, "Do you think the school board will approve this budget?"

"Nope," Smith answers.

"Why?" Takahashi responds.

"Look, can we go off the record?" Smith asks.

His boss, the superintendent, has submitted an unpopular budget to the school board, who are also his bosses. Smith worries that if the newspaper quotes him describing a fight among his superiors, he could lose his job. He wants to share the information, but he certainly doesn't want to see himself quoted as the source of the information.

Some journalists argue against ever going off the record. If a source asks to go off the record, they advise saying, "I don't go off the record. If you don't want it in the newspaper, don't say it." That response may mean the journalist misses some good news.

Rarely should a reporter agree to go off the record. The agreement means that the reporter will not use the information. Instead, negotiate. Offer, "If I find it out from someone else, I'll print the information, but I won't report I got it from you." Most people will agree to this bargain.

◆ INACCURATE INFORMATION

Very rarely will a person tell a complete lie during an interview, but routinely a person will give misinformation. Lying means deliberately attempting to mislead. This happens, but rarely. Often, though, a source will unintentionally mislead a reporter. Reporters interview experts, but even experts don't know everything, and even they can make mistakes.

Takahashi wants to ask Smith about a new budget item—$2,000 for special events. Smith explains that the money will fund holiday celebrations.

"I think they're planning a big program for Martin Luther King Day," he says.

"When will that be?" Takahashi asks.

"Sometime in January," he answers.

"When?" she presses.

"Oh, Jan. 15," he says.

Takahashi goes back to the office and writes:

The school board will spend $2,000 on a Martin Luther King Day celebration Jan. 15.

That one sentence will cause her real trouble. The school superintendent will make an angry call to the editor.

"What do you mean saying we're going to spend $2,000 on Martin Luther King Day? I only wish. That special occasions money will barely cover crepe paper for Thanksgiving, Christmas, King Day and all the other holidays. And, you fools, you didn't even get the right date for the King holiday," the superintendent tells the editor.

When the angry editor arrives at Takahashi's desk, the reporter has no defense. She can try arguing that that's what Smith told her, but it won't work because it isn't true. Smith did not tell Takahashi this.

In the interview itself Smith hinted about the inaccuracy of his answers. First, he said, "I think they are planning . . ." These words say that Smith has no direct part in the planning. He's saying that he thinks this will happen, but he could be wrong.

During the interview, Smith tried to evade the question about the date for Martin Luther King Day. First, he answered, "Sometime in January." The word *sometime* shows a hesitancy. Then, when Takahashi pressed him, Smith said, "Oh, Jan. 15." By using the word *oh,* Smith was saying he was guessing.

Smith did not lie to Takahashi. He did not even deliberately mislead her. He gave all sorts of clues that he was not sure about his information. A truly kind and wonderful source would answer Takahashi's questions with "I don't know" or "I'm not sure." Many people, though, hate to admit they don't know something. Instead they subtly signal that they may be saying something inaccurate.

The good reporter must stay alert during an interview for tentative statements that may contain inaccuracies.

✦ DON'T TALK—LISTEN

Interviewing, then, involves careful analysis and listening. Reporters should try to talk very little.

A really enjoyable interview can frustrate a reporter. The reporter and the source hit it off. They like the same music, the same restaurants. They are politically simpatico. The reporter thinks she has made a new friend. She leaves the interview thinking, "This is a great person, and it's going to be a wonderful story."

Back at the office, though, when the reporter starts to write, she cannot come up with any words. Oops—she discovers that her notebook contains only two pages of very sketchy information. What happened?

The reporter talked too much. Instead of doing an interview, the reporter engaged in a conversation, a give-and-take in which both people talked the same amount and traded information and ideas. In an interview, a reporter should ask questions, listen carefully, and take lots of notes. A reporter should say very little.

✦ WHEN TO STOP

An interview can end when the reporter has enough information to write a story. Two things tell a reporter she has enough.

First, the reporter can see clearly in her mind the story she will write. As she talks with the source, she starts to write a lead in her mind.

Second, she has enough notes. Most reporters need about four hand-written sheets of notepaper to write a four-page double-spaced story. Six pages of notes work better. The more information a reporter has, the more she has to choose from to craft a good piece.

✦ CLOSING QUESTIONS

Once a reporter knows she has enough to write the story, she has three more things to take care of:

1. Always save the tough questions for last. At the end of the interview Takahashi can at last ask Business Manager Smith why the budget for the Wildcat football coaches has doubled.

   Reporters hold the tough questions until last for two reasons. First, by then the reporter and the source have usually established some sense of trust and rapport, and the source, therefore, will be more likely to give an honest and detailed answer. Second, sometimes a really tough question can get this response: "That is it. No more questions. This interview is over." Just in case this should happen, a careful reporter gets enough notes to write a story before shoving in the tough questions.

   A tough question will more likely get an answer if the reporter asks it in a humane and professional manner. The reporter should maintain the stance of an unbiased news gatherer whose job, unfortunately, includes the asking of tough questions. For instance, reporter Takahashi could pose this question to Smith: "I see the Wildcat coaching budget will double this year. How are you going to explain that to the Moms for More Math group who want the school system to buy computers and other teaching tools to improve math instruction?"

   Phrase the tough question in this way: "Some people will be unhappy with this. A good newspaper has to report their unhappiness. How would you respond to their criticisms?" This approach establishes the tough question as neutral and professional.

2. After the tough questions, the reporter, at last, can get out her prepared list of questions. Takahashi might say, "Let me look over my questions and see if there is anything else I meant to ask you." Up to this point the natural flow of conversation has guided the interview, but Takahashi wants to make sure she asked everything she intended.

3. Before leaving, a reporter has one final question to ask. This question can often bear more fruit than any other in an interview. While closing up the notebook, the reporter turns to the source and says, "Is there anything else I should have asked you?" The answer will often surprise the reporter and will usually produce some newsworthy information the reporter knew nothing about.

   Knowing that a reporter was coming for a chat, the news source will have thought in advance about what to say. For instance, Business Manager Smith might have answered: "Well, this has nothing to do with the school budget, but we're all really excited here. We just learned that Morris Yu, a kindergarten teacher at Ida B. Wells-Barnett Elementary, has been named one of America's 100 most outstanding teachers. Mo's going to get to eat dinner at the White House with the president of the United States."

◆ COPY CHECKING

At some point during an interview a source will sometimes make an offer that at first seems helpful and generous. The person will volunteer to read over a draft of the article to check it for accuracy. Business Manager Smith might say, "Look, I know you haven't had a course in accounting, and I don't expect you to understand the crazy bookkeeping system the state makes us use. I'd be happy to go over your article for you to make sure you have everything right."

NEVER, NEVER let a source read an article before publication. Even the most well-meaning of people cannot resist rewriting the piece. If a source reads a draft of an article, an argument with the reporter may result. At best, the fight will concern the source's wish to have more technical or bureaucratic language in the piece. At worst, the source will begin to regret statements and demand to rewrite the quotations.

Interestingly enough, people rarely complain about an article once it has been published. They fear the consequences of every word in an unpublished draft. After an article has appeared, they see that their friends and coworkers confine their comments to, "Hey, I saw your name in the paper." Usually sources like any accurate, balanced piece of writing.

A reporter who receives an offer to read over a story should say, "Thank you so much. That's really generous. I'll call you back with questions if I hit something I don't understand when I'm writing up the story."

SUMMARY

- Interview someone who likes dealing with the press.
- Make up a list of questions ahead of time.
- Make an appointment to talk in the source's office.
- During the interview, move from small talk to substantive questions.
- Make the interview a conversation rather than just reading from a list of prepared questions.
- Ask: "Why?" "Tell me a story." "What's the best and worst part of the topic?"

- Ask dumb questions if you need to.
- Avoid going off the record.
- Listen carefully for tentative statements that could be inaccurate.
- Don't talk much. Listen instead.
- Stop the interview when you have enough notes to write a story.
- Ask tough questions last.
- Don't let the source read the article before it appears in print.

IN-CLASS EXERCISES

1. Select a news story from the local newspaper. Make a list of questions you would ask of the sources in the story if you were going to do a follow-up on it. What do you think the lead of your follow-up story will be? What questions will help you construct it?

2. In a story from your local newspaper, deduce and list the questions the reporters must have asked each source to get the information in the story. Are those the questions you would have asked? Why?

3. Find a story in which two sources are giving contradictory information. Can you tell which one is lying? What approach would you use in a follow-up story to find out which of the people was telling the truth?

4. Locate in your local newspaper an article you think one of the sources might have wanted to read over and edit before it was printed. What changes might the source have demanded? Would the changes have substantially altered the story? What conclusion can you draw from this concerning whether or not it's a good policy to let sources review stories?

5. Locate a story that you found confusing. Draw up a list of questions you would have asked to clarify the questions you have.

6. Imagine yourself interviewing a famous person. Who is the person, and what questions would you ask? What follow-up questions would you have for each primary question?

OUT-OF-CLASS EXERCISE

Interview a campus or local official. Write your questions down beforehand, and write the source's responses in a question-and-answer format. Would the information you got have been sufficient to generate a story? What changes would you make in the interview if you could do it over again?

CHAPTER 9

Covering Speeches

Many if not most reporters dislike doing speech stories. During an interview, a reporter has the freedom to interrupt to get explanations and clarifications, but during a speech a reporter must sit quietly, taking copious notes and praying for their accuracy. Just as most people prefer a conversation to a lecture, so most reporters prefer interviews to speeches.

This chapter follows a beginning reporter, Shalanda Johnson, as she covers a speech by Bernard King, an expert on lead in water pipes, who has visited town to give a speech.

A reporter assigned to cover a speech might want to try to avoid the task by interviewing the speaker instead. In Johnson's case, the expert will address a local consumer rights group, but the reporter will try to arrange a personal interview, because in a person-to-person interview she can interrupt King when he says something she does not understand.

"We've found high concentrations of lead in much of the nation's household water supply," King may say.

"I don't understand," Johnson can interrupt. "People have known for years that lead is dangerous. Lead pipes have been banned forever."

"The problem is not with the pipes themselves," King responds. "The problem is with the solder used to join the pipes together."

During a speech, reporter Johnson does not have this freedom to interrupt to get clarification. Also, during a speech, Johnson cannot interrupt to ask speaker King to slow down, to speak more distinctly, or to make any other modification to his presentation style.

In an interview, the water expert may get very enthusiastic about his subject and start quickly throwing out a stream of really good information. The data can come too quickly for the reporter to get it all down. In an interview, she can hold up her hand and say, "Wait. Wait. This is really good information. Stop for a minute while I catch up with you." Obviously, a reporter cannot do this during a formal speech. Also, during a speech or formal talk, sources do not project the personality they do in person. During a speech, the speaker tries to keep to a schedule, worries about how the audience is receiving the speech, and tries to remember to speak distinctly. Under such circumstances, most people have trouble achieving any sort of genuine enthusiasm.

Reporters avoid speech story assignments, then, because they have to work to get good notes, and because they can control almost nothing about the situation. Someone giving a speech to 100 people cannot stop to help one reporter who does not understand the vocabulary or who cannot write quickly enough to get down every word.

◆ ADVANCE COPIES

Unfortunately for reporter Johnson, the water expert does not have time for a private interview with her. She will have to attend his speech. Johnson may now try to ditch the assignment—but the editor does not buy her excuses. "I know the school board controversy is taking a lot of your time, but I want this guy covered," the editor tells her.

The reporter can only pray that King has a good publicist or some knowledge of public relations.

Public relations people, who know that many reporters hate to write speech stories, have a simple way to entice reporters into covering a speech story. To get coverage of a client's speech, a publicist will try to make the task easier for reporters by handing out **advance copies**—written transcripts of the speech—before the client stands up to talk.

Johnson prays she can get her hands on an advance script of the speech. With the text of the speech in her hands, she can figure out a lead even before the speaker begins to talk.

Television commentators can begin analyzing and quoting from a presidential address within five minutes of the end of the speech not because they have brilliant memories and instantaneous analytical abilities. They can do the analysis so quickly because they have already read the speech before the president even began talking.

With an advance in hand, covering a speech by an expert on the content of lead in household water becomes a simple task for Johnson, and she again likes her assignment. One major danger still haunts Johnson's speech story, though. This danger could get her fired.

Suppose the water expert's publicist mails a copy of the speech to Johnson. She has the speech transcript in her hands at the office as she sits in front of her computer. She decides to just go ahead and write up the story and duck attending the speech itself. She rationalizes that she will just hear King read to her what she already has in her hand.

So Johnson writes up a story about the speech on water quality given at 7 p.m. Friday to the Activist Consumers of America meeting at the Civic Center. And she gets fired.

She gets fired because the lead-in-water expert did not give the speech. When he drove up to the Civic Center, he parked his car. When he stepped out, he set his foot down on a patch of black ice. He slid. He fell and broke his leg. At 7 p.m. Friday when he should have been telling the Activist Consumers of America about water quality, he was sitting in a hospital emergency room waiting for a doctor to look at his leg.

Johnson had published a false story and every member of the consumer group had called the editor to point this out. So no more job for Johnson.

Even with an advance copy, a reporter still has to attend the speech. The script almost never accurately transcribes what the speaker says. Those reporters covering a presidential speech sit with their transcripts in hand and read along while the president talks. They look for sections of the speech he leaves out, and they look for ad-lib remarks he may add to the talk. Only after the speaker has finished do they complete their stories.

✦ NOTE TAKING

What if Johnson cannot get an advance copy of the water speech? Then she is stuck. She has to attend the speech, take good notes, and write up a story.

Ironically, although journalists find it hard to write a speech story with no advance copy, assignments like this usually go to beginners. Most of the people who give speeches in the small towns where beginning reporters get their first jobs lack sophisticated public relations skills. They hand out no advance copies. Even at papers in larger towns, the more experienced reporters pick the big-name assignments—the people with public relations operations. Besides, the old hands tell the beginners that writing speech stories provides good training in accurate note taking.

Although reporters can more easily craft news stories from written material, they can also take down good notes more easily than many beginners think. Reporter Johnson may have just begun her first job as a reporter, but she brings special qualifications to her work.

After all, as a recent college graduate, she does have some expertise in note taking—she has spent 16 years of her life in school taking notes. Especially in history and humanities classes, she knows how to get down everything the professor says. All new reporters need to develop a system for taking notes, and most just refine or adapt the system that worked for them in college.

Since almost no one can take down everything the speaker says, most note takers develop a personal system of shorthand. Most importantly, every reporter develops a way to mark direct quotations. Reporter Johnson uses this system:

Just before writing down a direct quote, she draws two quick lines across the page. Then she draws a big, exaggerated quotation mark. She writes down the speaker's exact words. Then she draws a big end quotation mark and two more long horizontal lines.

She continues taking sketchy, paraphrased notes until the speaker says something else she wants in the story exactly as he said it.

She uses the note-taking trick of starting long words, but not finishing them. Usually when she writes the story she can reconstruct these words. For instance, the speaker says, "I can't speculate about the damage this lead is doing to the nation's health."

Johnson might write, "I can't specu about dam this lead doing to nat's health."

The context of the sentence and the words she got down accurately will help her reconstruct the whole sentence correctly.

✦ DON'T LEARN SHORTHAND

Reporters have trouble taking notes on a speech because they cannot write down, even in the fastest, most illegible cursive scrawl, everything a speaker says. Some beginners, looking at this challenge, take a course in shorthand, since with shorthand they can get down every word. A very small group of reporters do swear by their shorthand, but most advise against it.

If reporter Johnson takes notes on the speech in shorthand, she will have to laboriously type a transcribed version of her notes before she starts writing her story, and the writing will take much more time than it should. Even if reporter Johnson writes her story directly from her shorthand notes, she will still have a harder time than the reporter who took notes without shorthand. During the speech she has concentrated on the wrong thing. Instead of working on getting the speech down word for word, she should have worked on seeing the main points in the speech. Eventually she will have to decide what to include in her article. If she goes back to the newspaper with her shorthand transcription, she will have to read over the entire speech in order to highlight the main points she wants to feature in her story.

A reporter can approach note taking at a speech in two ways. Beginners sometimes see their goal as getting down on paper, as accurately as possible, everything the speaker has said. This is the wrong goal. More seasoned reporters see their notes as the very first and very rough draft of the news story that will run in the newspaper. The final article in the newspaper cannot include every word in the speech—the story would occupy far too much space. In addition, it will include other information besides what the speaker said. In this instance, for example, the article needs to mention the sponsor of the speech.

Sometime between the end of the speech and the publication of an article, the reporter has to do some boiling down of material. To write a good article on the speech, the reporter has to throw out most of the words of the speaker.

This throwing-out process begins during note taking. A reporter, aware of this, makes a set of notes on a speech into the rough draft for the article to come. Since reporter Johnson knows she cannot get down every word of the speaker, she ignores sentences she knows she will leave out of her article.

"I want to thank the Activist Consumers of America for inviting me to your city to talk this evening," says the water quality expert. King must make this courteous comment. It helps him establish rapport with his audience, but Johnson knows she will leave the sentence out of her final story. Surely the speaker will say something more newsworthy than that. So this quotation does not make it into her notes.

✦ TAPE RECORDERS

For the same reason that some reporters learn shorthand, many reporters use tape recorders to cover speeches.

The news business contains both advocates and haters of tape recorders. The contrasting attitudes are illustrated by what happened at two different newspapers that came under new ownership.

At one of the papers, the new editor arrived and announced, "Anyone who does not use a tape recorder isn't a professional, and I only want pros working with me." At the second paper, the new editor arrived and walked from desk to desk in the newsroom. "Give me your tape recorder," he demanded of each reporter. "I'm confiscating all these things. They destroy good writing."

The tape recorder has a major advantage. Reporter Johnson knows that the machine will give her an absolutely accurate record of the speech without also giving her writer's cramp. With a tape recording of a speech, she knows she will have no misquotes. She knows she can get the speaker's phrasing down absolutely accurately.

The tape recorder becomes an essential news-gathering tool for dealing with a source who may accuse a reporter of inaccuracy. Once every year or two, every reporter encounters this problem. A source will regret something he said to a reporter. But instead of owning up to the regretted remark, the source will lie.

"That lousy reporter, Shalanda Johnson. I never said that. She misquoted me," he will scream.

Sometimes, his friends or his boss will pressure him. "You ought to get that damned newspaper to print a correction," they will advise him.

He will roar into the newsroom, shouting, "You misquoted me. I demand a retraction."

Johnson loves to answer, "Really! You think so? Let me get out the tape and let's check and see."

"Oh, ah, you've got it on tape," he will say. Then he will slink back out the office door.

When a particular source has a reputation for denying the things he says, a tape recorder becomes an essential tool for talking with him.

Using a tape recorder does, however, have major disadvantages. It is a machine, and therefore handicapped. In the middle of the speech the tape may run out. While the owner fumbles to turn it over, important words may tumble from the speaker's mouth. Worse yet, the battery can choose to die in mid-speech, or the microphone may lack the power to pick up what the speaker has to say.

To use a tape recorder to cover a speech, then:

- Be sure the tape will run the length of the speech.
- Be sure to have a fresh battery.
- Be sure to put the tape recorder within microphone range of the speaker.

Using the tape recorder to cover a speech has another disadvantage. Even if reporter Johnson goes to the water quality speech and sets up her recorder just right, at some point, she has to decide which quotes to include and which to exclude. She will then have to search through the tape to find the quotations she wants.

If she just tapes the speech, she may find herself doing her note taking back at the office while she listens to the tape recording. In essence, the reporter ends up listening to the hour-long speech twice.

To eliminate this problem, she uses a tape recorder with a counter that she sets to zero at the start of the speech. Then she also takes notes. When the speaker gives a quotation that reporter Johnson really wants to use, she writes down the number that appears on the tape recorder. Then she has no problem finding that wonderful quotation.

A tape recorder, then, gets really accurate quotations, but it can give only minor help in writing up a speech story. Think of it as a technique of self-defense rather than as a writing aid.

✦ LISTEN ACTIVELY

To cover a speech efficiently, a reporter must take copious and accurate notes while the speaker talks. This means listening in a very different way from the rest of the audience.

To take good notes, reporter Johnson begins writing her article in her head while she listens to the speaker.

"Lead in the pipes of elementary school water fountains may be hurting our children," King says.

"That's important. I need that," Johnson thinks, and she gets that quotation down accurately.

While she writes about the school fountains, though, the water expert keeps talking. Now he gives a list of numbers and scientific measurements. Since Johnson cannot write down everything the expert says, she has to let these numbers go by while she gets the water fountain quotation into her notebook. She will have to catch King after the speech to get those numbers down accurately, or she will have to leave the numbers out of her story if her tape does not come out.

During the first 15 minutes of the speech Johnson tries to take down everything the speaker says. She will lead her speech story with the most important thing the speaker had to say, but when she first sits down to listen to the speech she does not know when King will make this most important statement.

She starts out taking lots of notes so she can get something for a story. The speaker may make his most important statement at the beginning of the lecture. She does not know. After she has enough in her notes to know she can write something, then she relaxes the vigilance of her note taking. For the rest of the speech, she continues to listen carefully, but at this point she knows she has a story. Now she just looks for additions to an already existing story.

✦ SIT AT THE FRONT OF THE ROOM

Besides taking good notes, a reporter should do several other things when covering a speech.

Reporter Johnson always sits at the front of the room, preferably in the front row. If she uses a tape recorder, sitting at the front will let her get the mike of her recorder close to the speaker. Even when she comes to a speech without a tape recorder, sitting at the front allows her to hear really clearly.

She sits at the front of the room mainly so that she can quickly get to the speaker after the talk. At the end of a speech, a reporter always finds a few things that need clarification. During the speech, the water quality expert may have spewed forth a lot of statistics. In her notes Johnson only got, "?? parts per million of ??" Yet those numbers would add a sense of veracity to her story.

After the speech she needs to get those numbers. If she has sat at the back of the room, she will have to push and shove her way against the flow of a crowd streaming toward the exit. By the time she has worked her way to the front of the room, the speaker may have ducked out a side exit.

Also, a reporter covering a speech story should remember that the speech itself may not make the only news at the event. What about the audience? Is the hall packed? Is the crowd bored or enthusiastic?

At rare speeches, something else may happen that has even more news value than the content of the speech itself. Johnson has already covered a speech by a congressional candidate at which one prominent citizen stood up and began screaming at another just as the speaker was beginning to talk. The two citizens almost came to blows about a matter that had nothing to do with the political candidate. The candidate became a sideshow and a very small part of the resulting news story.

If something more important than the content of the speech itself happens, the reporter should cover it.

✦ CLEANING UP QUOTATIONS

What does a reporter do about a source who speaks ungrammatical English? The newspaper should set a standard of good English, and should quote people accurately. Yet speakers routinely make grammatical errors. For instance, almost every extemporaneous speaker fails to have nouns and pronouns agree in number.

"Now, I don't want to worry anyone. If a student takes one sip out of that water fountain, they won't get sick," the speaker may say.

A grammarian would say that the speaker should have used a singular pronoun—*he* or *she*—to agree in number with the singular *student*. Instead King used the plural pronoun *they*. The speaker knows the rule and would never commit this error in his writing—writers find it much easier to keep track of rules like this because they have the opportunity to edit their work. Speakers lack this luxury.

Reporters work as translators as they change spoken English into written English. So should reporter Johnson clean up the speaker's grammatical error? Should Johnson write the following quotation for her article?

"If a student takes one sip out of that water fountain, he won't get sick."

After all, the story addresses water quality, not the speaker's grammatical abilities—but the act of cleaning up quotations does create white lies. The newspaper has claimed King used words that he did not use.

Many speakers object strongly to this cleanup service. For example, the ethos of athletics seems to include the misuse of adjectives as adverbs.

"We played real good last night. I'm proud of the girls," the women's volleyball coach may say.

A grammatically correct version of this sentence would read, "We played really well last night." But should a reporter fix the coach's English? Some coaches and athletes complain vigorously when the press alters the very nature of their language and syntax.

Reporter Johnson solves this problem by finessing it. When a quotation contains a grammatical error, she doesn't use the quotation word for word. Instead, she paraphrases it. She changes the wording, attributes the ideas to the speaker, but doesn't use quotation marks.

For instance, Johnson would write:

One sip of water from a fountain will not hurt a child, the water quality expert said.

The coach said she was really proud of her team's play last night.

✦ SPEECH STORY LEADS

Always remember the news formula when writing up a speech story. Do not lead with the title of the speech. Instead, lead with the most important or newsworthy thing the speaker said.

The lead for a speech story, then, should start with a paraphrase of the speaker's most newsworthy idea. This is the *what* of the five Ws. The first sentence in the speech story also should include *who* and *when*. For example:

> America's children risk getting lead poisoning from elementary school drinking fountains, a water quality expert said Wednesday.

Because describing an idea takes up a good bit of room in a sentence, putting all the five Ws into a speech story lead makes for a long and clunky sentence. For example:

> America's children risk getting lead poisoning from elementary school drinking fountains, water quality expert Bernard King said in a speech Wednesday at 7 p.m. in the Caldera Room at the Civic Center to the Activist Consumers of America.

Because the speaker's central idea should dominate a lead, this first sentence should leave out details about speakers themselves. Save a description of the details of his qualifications and of the sponsors of his appearance for the second paragraph.

In the first paragraph, a reporter does not even have to identify the speaker by name. Most people have never heard of Bernard King anyway. In the lead, Johnson just identifies the speaker in a few words to explain his qualifications to address the subject. She saves the rest for later.

Into the lead, though, must go the *when* element of the five Ws. The news formula's timeliness requirement demands this *when*, but a reporter can make a bow to timeliness very, very briefly. Johnson just gives the day of the week the speech occurred.

In the lead, a reporter does not need to go into the details of the exact time, 7 p.m., or the exact location, the Caldera Room at the Civic Center. The readers have already gotten this information in the advance story announcing the talk. Readers need to know where to show up, and at what time, if they want to hear the speech. After the speech, though, readers do not need the exact *when* and a precise *where*.

The lead for a speech story, then, starts out with a fairly lengthy paraphrase of the speaker's central idea. Next comes a brief and often generic identification of the speaker. Instead of giving the speaker's name, a good lead often just uses nouns to describe the speaker's expertise.

The speech story lead sentence ends with two words, the verb *said* and one word (the day of the week) to tell *when*.

✦ THE CONTEXT PARAGRAPH

This leaves the second paragraph of the speech story with much work to do. It must sketch the details alluded to in the first paragraph. It also has to outline the rest of the five Ws, *where* and *why*.

For this second paragraph, a reporter shelves the central idea that will make up the theme of the entire article. Instead, this second paragraph gives the context of the speech. It tells *where* and *why* the event occurred.

Johnson starts the second paragraph of the speech story with the speaker's name and a more detailed description of him:

> Bernard King, a professor of chemistry at Wilsonia University . . .

After identifying the speaker, she uses the verb *spoke* and prepositional phrases to explain where and why he gave his talk.

> Bernard King, a professor of chemistry at Wilsonia University, spoke to the Activist Consumers of America at their annual membership dinner in the Caldera Room at the Civic Center.

The next two paragraphs of a speech story should offer direct quotations from the speaker. These quotations should tie back into the central idea reported in the lead.

> "Lead in the pipes of elementary school water fountains may be hurting our children," said King.
> "Now, I don't want to worry anyone," King continued. One sip of water from a fountain will not harm a child, he said.

After this opening, reporter Johnson will compose the rest of her story using the system outlined in Chapter 4. She will structure topical sections beginning with a quotation or paraphrase of a main idea and follow with more information on that idea.

✦ POOR SPEECH STORY LEADS

Beginning reporters often make one classic mistake in writing leads for speech stories. Instead of talking about the speaker's ideas in the lead, beginners often start their stories by merely announcing that the speech took place.

If reporter Johnson took this approach her story would begin:

> Water quality expert Bernard King Wednesday spoke to the Activist Consumers of America about lead in household water.

This lead fails because it adds no new information. The advance story in the paper announcing King's speech gave this information. That lead probably said:

> Water quality expert Bernard King will speak to a meeting of the Activist Consumers of America about lead in household water Wednesday at 7 p.m. in the Caldera Room at the Civic Center.

The lead to a story describing the speech itself must go beyond this information. It must report what King has to say about lead in water fountains.

Also, a reporter should not necessarily lead with the first topic the speaker brings up.

"I have invented a new process that allows me to find trace amounts of lead in water," the speaker may say.

While this interests King a lot, most readers could not care less about this technicality. The lead content of water matters to them much more. Chronological order never makes a good structure for any news story, including a speech story. Avoid including information in the story in the order in which the speaker brought it up. Instead, bring up information based on its newsworthiness.

For the same reason, Johnson will not necessarily lead with the thing the speaker considers most important. The foundation of King's success may rest on the new chemical process he has invented. His invention may even earn him promotion to full professor, or make him rich, or land him on the "Oprah Winfrey Show"—but in this case the important issue—the thing readers want to know—is whether the local water supply is safe.

SUMMARY

- Try to get an advance copy of the speech.
- Do not take a course in shorthand.
- Use a tape recorder to get accurate quotations, but take notes, too.
- Make the notes the rough draft of the news story to come.
- Sit at the front of the room.
- Paraphrase statements where the speaker used faulty grammar.
- Do not lead with the title of the speech.
- Lead with the speaker's most newsworthy idea.

• Put Where, Why, and details about the speaker in the second paragraph.

IN-CLASS EXERCISES

1. Turn the following speech transcript into a news story.
TEXT, SPEECH
Charles M. Lewis
Cartoonist, "Percy Potato"
Before the Albemarle Sound Civic Club, today

Thank you for your kind invitation. I realize it may seem odd to
have a cartoonist appear before a group that is involved in civic affairs
and betterment, but I hope before you leave I can convince you we're
really in the same business.

You see, I began drawing Percy Potato for the Wausatch College
"Beacon," back in 1961. When I graduated from college, I was an editorial cartoonist for several midwestern papers before Smith and Smith
Syndicate picked up Percy for national distribution. For the years that
Percy appeared in only a handful of newspapers, I worked in total (or
at least near-total) obscurity. In 1968, though, Percy became enor-
mously popular, both here and overseas, and today appears in some
2,200 daily newspapers across the world. And that's how I became a
social activist.

You may think that 2,200 newspapers printing your cartoon would
make you rich, and you'd be right. At least, I was a lot richer than I
was before. But I also found that I had a forum, and an audience. The
popularity of Percy meant that I was very unlikely to be dropped from
a newspaper, and the readership of the comic meant that I had an
audience. I found that I had things I needed to say, and I decided in
1970 to start saying them.

Percy came out against racism in 1971 in a three-month series of
strips. You may recall the outrage, the charges that I was out of my
place. But, I think, time has proven otherwise. Percy has dealt with
homophobia, with drug abuse, and with aging. I won't say Percy has
made the world a better place, but I will say I did what I could.

And that's the major point of my speech tonight. Someday, you may
find that you have an opportunity to do some good through whatever
it is that you're doing. And then I would encourage you to go boldly,
to ignore the criticism of the timid and the small-minded, and make a
difference. That's the path to a happy and a meaningful life.

I spend all day drawing vegetables. You wouldn't think that that
would make a difference in the world, but it has. Remember that when
you think that what you do doesn't make any difference.

2. Every weekend, the president of the United States gives a speech on the radio. Listen to that speech, take notes, and write a news story from it.

3. In your local paper, find the story that covers the president's Saturday radio address, and compare it with the story you wrote. Which do you think is better? What makes it better?

4. Interview someone in your class, taking notes and using a tape recorder. Then write up the interview in the inverted pyramid format. Then ask the person you interviewed to read the story, checking any quotes that he or she questions against the tape recorder. Whose memory was better—yours or your interviewee's? Why do you think that was so?

5. Examine a news story about a speech in your local newspaper. Locate the lead, the context paragraph, and the summary–quotation units, labeling them as such on the story.

6. Watch a videotape of a famous speech: Martin Luther King's "I Have a Dream" or Franklin Delano Roosevelt's "Day of Infamy." Write a news story based on this speech.

OUT-OF-CLASS EXERCISE

Attend a speech, taking notes and using a tape recorder. Write a news story based on the speech, checking all pertinent quotes against your tape recorder.

CHAPTER 10

Narrative Leads

The news formula forms the basis for American newspaper writing because it gives reporters a quick and efficient way to analyze information. Using the structure that the formula offers, an experienced reporter writing on deadline can produce a lead immediately after an event occurs, and this structure also helps browsing readers who like to scan the information in the entire newspaper quickly and then select a few articles to read completely.

The news formula does have a serious flaw, however. A study by the American Society of Newspaper Editors found that it does not make for particularly easy reading. Often, the formula discourages readers from finishing an article.

◆ WEAKNESSES OF THE FORMULA

Poorly written straight news leads can overburden a reader with complex facts and obscure vocabulary. The necessity to cram the meat of a story into a lead often overburdens that first sentence with ideas. In addition, even well-written news formula stories can challenge readers, because the structure makes the writer bring up new topics in the order of their importance or newsworthiness. This makes for difficult transitions.

Essay writers bring up topics in a logical order. Each new topic grows out of the previous subject. But news formula writers, because they try to squeeze all the essential information into the top of an article, have a tendency to hop around disconnectedly from topic to topic.

Also, the news formula defines the end of an article as boring—so boring that when an editor lops off that section, the overall article will lose none of its real meaning, interest, or importance. Since the writer must end the piece with the least important information, the end of the piece is assumed to be uninteresting to the reader.

A reading of the articles published any day in an American newspaper will reveal these inherent flaws in the news formula approach to writing.

◆ THE STORYTELLING APPROACH

In frustration with these inherent drawbacks of the news formula, many newspaper editors encourage their staffs to write articles using the narrative structure. This way of organizing information in a news story draws on the structure many authors of fiction use to tell their stories.

The term **narrative structure** generally means the telling of a story in chronological order from the first event to the concluding event. For example, Charlotte Brontë's famous novel *Jane Eyre* opens with a pivotal incident in the heroine's childhood and moves with her through life in an orphanage and then on to work as a governess.

Brontë waits until Chapter 12 to begin the real story of Jane Eyre's adventures at Thornfield Hall. Only at this point does the hero, her employer Edward Rochester, enter the story. The author spends the first 11 chapters explaining Eyre's childhood as a way of establishing the heroine's identity. Because readers by then know Eyre as a well-rounded person, they can understand the things she does once she goes to work at Thornfield Hall.

Newspaper writing cannot take the space for such leisurely storytelling. On the other hand, a news formula lead for the love story of Jane Eyre and her employer would rob the story of all its charm and interest. A writer using the news formula might write an opening sentence to tell Jane Eyre's story in this way:

> A young governess who grew up a poverty-stricken orphan has found happiness as the wife of her employer Edward F. Rochester, who lost his eyesight when his mansion burned to the ground in a fire started by his deranged wife.

Obviously that lead is no fun. Dull and lifeless, it reduces Eyre's story to the clichés of a romance novel. The pleasure of reading the story of Jane

Eyre and Edward Rochester comes in the early establishment of the heroine's courage and then the slow unfolding of the many mysteries that surround Thornfield Hall. Revealing the backbone of the plot in the first sentence would destroy the novel. Many argue that using all five Ws in the lead can just as easily destroy a news story.

So newspapers have found a compromise—a storytelling approach to writing the news. Many newspapers try to print some articles each day that use this storytelling structure. Roy Peter Clark of the Poynter Institute calls this approach the narrative structure; the authors of the Missouri Group news writing text call it the *Wall Street Journal* **lead**.

The narrative structure is as much a formula as the news formula. It has three key sections. At the beginning of an article, the reporter writes a little three-to-six-paragraph chronological narrative that relates a story about a particular person involved in the news event. Then, the reporter writes a **nut paragraph** or **nut graph**, sometimes also called a **so what graph**—a paragraph that summarizes the basic newsworthiness of the story. The reporter then completes the article with the basic facts of the story often arranged in an inverted pyramid.

◆ THE FIVE Ws

To write a news article with a narrative structure, a reporter still has to find the answers to the five Ws: Who? What? When? Where? and Why? With the narrative structure, though, the reporter does not give the answers to the five Ws in the first paragraph. Instead, the narrative formula calls for the reporter to insert the five Ws in the article after an introductory story about a specific person.

For example, the five Ws for the novel *Jane Eyre* might be:

- Who? Jane Eyre, an orphan who works as governess at Thornfield Hall
- What? Marries her employer, Edward Rochester
- When? After a disastrous fire started by his deranged wife has left Mr. Rochester blind and Mrs. Rochester dead
- Where? At Thornfield Hall
- Why? Because Eyre has fallen in love with Rochester

With the five Ws listed, the writer looks for a key event or person who illustrates the main point of the story. This person provides a source of human interest in the story. Then the writer takes several paragraphs to describe this key event. For example, a news writer using the narrative lead might begin Eyre's story this way:

Shortly after she arrived, Jane Eyre, the new governess at Thornfield Hall, began noticing odd events.

Her employer was at times gruff and at other times charming.

Her pupil was French but lived in an English household.

Mysterious wails emanated from the attic of the venerable mansion.

The housekeeper, although friendly to Eyre, refused to answer any of the governess' questions about the mysteries at Thornfield Hall.

But Eyre liked the job, and she had had no other job offers when she left school.

First, the narrative writer hooks the reader into Eyre's personal story, picking out a few specific and telling details to open the story. This opening section usually runs five or six paragraphs, but occasionally a narrative lead can work with two or three tightly written paragraphs.

Only after introducing the topic by telling a story does the writer draw on the five Ws to tell the reader why the story matters. This nut paragraph offers the tight kernel of meat that summarizes the story. It sketches the context in which the reader should understand the opening.

Here is a nut graph for Eyre's story:

Only after falling in love with her employer, Edward Rochester, did Eyre discover that he kept his deranged wife locked in the attic of the family mansion. After Mrs. Rochester died in a fire that she had set and after her husband was blinded trying to save her life, Eyre and Rochester found happiness.

After this nut graph the newspaper writer of Jane Eyre's tale would then complete the article by recounting the rest of the plot.

The narrative lead can give a reporter an excellent way to open an article. The structure works especially well to open an article that might otherwise be very dry and boring. Much of the news comes from bland lists of statistics produced by government agencies. A narrative lead provides a vehicle for bringing life to these statistics.

✦ THE NARRATIVE LEAD

The lead for the narrative structure sets out a series of intriguing facts on a very human level. The writer tries to establish a human, emotional connection with the reader, and to convince the reader to empathize with the real people involved in the news story. The narrative lead rests on the idea that a person who gets interested in one person's story will keep reading the article to find out why that person became involved in the events reported.

The narrative lead has three major characteristics:

1. It focuses on specific people caught in a large news story.
2. It uses chronological order to tell these people's story.
3. It relates a story in very specific and human language, using words that people use every day.

The *Wall Street Journal* has employed this approach very effectively to explain the human impact of the business statistics that the paper specializes in reporting. To make the newspaper more readable, the *Journal's* editors avoid the five Ws lead in featured pieces. For example, an article reporting on a rise in home mortgage interest rates could start with a traditional five Ws lead like this:

> Five major lenders yesterday announced their intention to raise home mortgage interest rates by half a percentage point.

Some readers with enough background will immediately understand the implications of this sentence. They will see that this action by the major banks will price some people out of the housing market. Many other readers, though, may miss this major ramification.

The five Ws dictate that a writer must state the lead in a dry way. This means that many readers will miss the full implications of the story, while even those who understand its meaning may not think about its human implications. The five Ws report information efficiently, but the news formula can force a writer to boil a story down to the point where the news loses its essential humanity.

To deal with this problem, the writer of a narrative lead finds a particular family and concentrates on telling its story in very human terms.

Here is a narrative lead for a story on rising home mortgage rates:

> When Jim and Mary Ellen Winston married in 1985, they knew they wanted to buy a house, but they found they could not afford one. She's a secretary, he's a janitor. Their combined income is $31,249.
>
> In the late 1980s they had searched and searched for a home they could afford, but finally they gave up and continued to rent.
>
> But this year when interest rates hit historic lows, the Winstons tried again for a home, and last month they and their two children moved into a neat bungalow on Marshall St. in Albany, Ga.
>
> Today, the Winstons are celebrating. Five major lenders yesterday announced their intention to raise home mortgage interest rates by half a percentage point.
>
> "We can just squeeze out our payments at 7 3/4 percent interest," commented Mrs. Winston. "This raise to 8 1/4 percent would have meant we couldn't buy this house."

The narrative lead uses a human story to explain to the reader the full implications of what may at first appear to be very dry facts. The Winstons' search brings to life the real meaning of that half a percentage point rise in home mortgage interest rates.

✦ LOCAL GOVERNMENT NEWS

Although the *Wall Street Journal* pioneered the narrative approach, this method of structuring an article can really help any reporter explain the kind of dry news generated by local governments. For example, a local reporter covering the City Council could use the narrative structure to excellent effect. Many measures presented for action by local government appear on the agenda in dull, bureaucratic language.

For example, say the City Council has refused to build sidewalks along a major feeder street. The five Ws lead might say:

> The City Council today rejected a proposal to build sidewalks along both sides of San Antonio Rd., saying that the budget could not handle the $200,000 expense.

The narrative lead might say:

> Two months ago eight-year-old Maria Oviedo left home so excited about the field trip her class was taking that she forgot her math homework.
>
> She told her friends waiting for the school bus that she had to run back home to get her homework. That's the last time her classmates saw Maria.
>
> She missed the bus and tried to walk the mile and a half to school along busy San Antonio Rd.—a road that has sidewalks on only one side of the street for most of its length. When she tried to cross the street, a car traveling at normal speed struck and killed her.
>
> Her mother, Linda Oviedo, has retraced her daughter's walk and says the eight-year-old had to cross the busy thoroughfare three times to find sidewalks where she could walk.
>
> "If we had sidewalks on both sides of San Antonio Rd., my daughter might not have died," said Oviedo.
>
> The City Council today rejected a proposal to build sidewalks along both sides of San Antonio Rd., saying that the budget could not handle the $200,000 expense.

By telling the story of a little girl who died in a traffic accident, the reporter hooks the reader much more compellingly into the article. The tragedy of a child's death attracts a reader's attention. The reader immediately wants to know why San Antonio Rd. lacks sidewalks on both sides of the street. By focusing on real people caught in a news event, the narrative lead shows a reader why this particular story matters.

The writer lets the reader focus first on Jim and Mary Ellen Winston as they struggle to buy a house, or on Linda Oviedo as she grieves over the loss of her daughter. The reader sees how the impersonal actions of bureaucratic entities like major banks and city governments can have an impact on the lives of ordinary people.

✦ CHRONOLOGICAL ORDER

The narrative lead tells one story about one person or family in the order in which the story occurred. Chronological order becomes an important marker for a narrative lead. This emphasis on the chronological ordering of events represents a major break from the traditional news formula, which requires a writer to ignore chronological order and bring up the information in a news story in the order of its importance or news value.

In traditional journalism, chronological order is a mark of amateurish writing, but the writer of a narrative lead uses chronological order because readers understand this familiar storytelling technique. People are used to reading fiction that starts with the first event in the plot and relates the story chronologically to the last event.

Because readers already know this technique, the telling of a story in chronological order allows them to focus emotionally on the plight of the particular person whose story the writer is narrating. Readers can feel some human empathy for the person involved in the story. Because they can identify with and understand an individual and that person's situation, they can use their imaginations to supply additional information that the writer has left out. The very ordinariness of the people a writer features in a narrative lead helps readers to visualize these people's lives.

The reader can see the Winstons going to realtor after realtor; can imagine the Winstons carefully setting aside a certain sum each month to go toward the down payment on their first home; can feel the family's joy when they finally get to buy a house. The reader also can think about how that joy gave the Winstons the energy to endure the disruption of moving their possessions to a new home. The reader can share the Winstons' relief when they see how close they came to missing out on home ownership.

In the same way, the reader can share in Maria Oviedo's excitement over her field trip; can admire her because she went back home to get her homework; and can feel the horrible pain of her mother and her classmates after her death. The reader can sense her mother's frustration and anger that Maria died in an accident that an obvious city service like adding sidewalks could have prevented.

Instead of hitting a reader with abstract ideas like mortgage interest rates and city capital improvement budgets, the chronological narrative simply tells a very human story in the order in which the story happened. The readers see real people in the story living out their lives in the way everyone else does. The story features people who are not politicians or money managers working in the realm of power politics and national commerce. These people are not rich and powerful. They're just normal.

✦ THE NUT GRAPH

The narrative lead draws its solidity from the nut graph, also sometimes called a so what graph, as mentioned earlier. The reporter concludes the telling of the story about real people by writing a paragraph tying these real people to a larger issue in the news.

Here is the nut graph from the narrative lead about the rise in home mortgage interest rates:

> Today, the Winstons are celebrating. Five major lenders yesterday announced their intention to raise home mortgage interest rates by half a percentage point. "We can just squeeze out our payments at 7 3/4 percent interest," commented Mrs. Winston. "This raise to 8 1/4 percent would have meant we couldn't buy this house."

Notice that a traditional five Ws lead sentence for this story suddenly appears along with quotes from Mrs. Winston. Instead of starting with the five Ws, the writer has concluded the narrative lead with the five Ws.

Here is the nut graph from the narrative lead for the story about Maria Oviedo's death:

> The City Council today rejected a proposal to build sidewalks along both sides of San Antonio Rd., saying that the budget could not handle the $200,000 expense.

Here again, the nut graph that ends the narrative lead is identical to the first sentence that a reporter would write for a traditional news formula story that led with the five Ws.

The nut graph is absolutely essential to a narrative lead because the writer has to show readers why they should care about the stories of specific people like the Winstons or the Oviedos. The sheer force of reading a story about one person in the order in which the events happened will keep most people working through several paragraphs.

Eventually, though, the busy reader will begin asking, "So what? It's nice that the Winstons bought a house and I'm sorry little Maria is dead, but what does this have to do with me? Why should I care? Why should I keep reading this article? What is it going to tell me?"

The nut graph answers these questions. In one little meaty paragraph, the narrative writer explains the news of the story. The nut graph explains that the individual actors in the narrative share their dilemma with many other people. Other families like the Winstons may miss the chance to buy homes because interest rates have gone up. Other children like Maria may die in traffic accidents because the City Council has decided that it cannot afford to build sidewalks.

The nut graph, then, serves a crucial purpose in a narrative lead story. It provides a transition from the small world of specific people to the larger world of social policy. Huge bureaucracies may deal in dry statistics and incomprehensible jargon, but many of their actions have a major impact on readers. The stories of people like the Winstons or Maria serve the purpose of telling readers why they really must pay attention to these larger abstract issues.

✦ THE REST OF THE NARRATIVE ARTICLE

The rest of a narrative article works much like the body of a traditional straight news story. The writer can bring up new topics and discuss them in the order of their importance or news value. From the nut graph to the end, a story with a narrative lead will often read exactly like an inverted pyramid story. After hooking readers with a human story, many *Wall Street Journal* articles switch to a reporting of dry statistical data. When an article lapses into a recitation of detailed facts and figures, it can drive away the reader who first started the article for its human story.

The article on city sidewalks could begin to read like an annual auditing report, recounting expenditures for other competing city departments. The article on the Winstons might lapse into high-finance-speak, discussing the minutiae of monetary policy in technical terms. However, the best narrative articles preserve the human interest element from the lead throughout the story. The writer keeps using human stories to illustrate the important points that surround the issue.

The article on city sidewalks could describe another city program that also needs an increase in the budget, and could tell the story of a particular person who needs that service. A writer could continue the article in storytelling mode, using chronological order and a lot of direct quotations to preserve a human feel.

For example, the article on sidewalks might tell the story of the Pine Valley Jets. The Little League team has to drive 45 minutes across town and compete with other Little League teams for a chance to use the city's only lighted ball field. They could use the field next to the site of an old elementary school near their home, but it has a problem: The Jets hate the nearby ball field because it lacks toilets.

After the nut graph, the article on sidewalks for San Antonio Rd. could continue:

> Across town, Pedro Fuentes, also eight years old, dreams of playing major league ball. He's the star first baseman for the Pine Valley Little League Jets, but when he plays in the city recreation league, a personal problem interferes with his concentration.
>
> The Jets want to use the ball field of abandoned Pine Valley School as their home field, but the Pine Valley site lacks toilets. "What are you supposed to do when your kid has to go?" asks his mother, Maria Fuentes.
>
> The Jets can drive 45 minutes across town and play on the Cisneros Recreational Park field, but because Pine Valley is a new league, they must wait until 10 p.m. to get their chance at bat. "We get home way after bedtime, and that's just not good for my kid. He's a mess the next day," says Fuentes.
>
> Upgrading the Pine Valley field and building toilets would cost about $200,000—the same as the cost of building sidewalks on San Antonio Rd.

The body of a good narrative story continues in this manner. The writer brings up each new topic by telling the story of a person involved in that topic and including a telling quote spoken in a simple human voice. For example, next the sidewalk story could describe the finances of a typical city homeowner. The writer could explain that this person's taxes would have to go up to pay for both upgrading the ball field and putting in the sidewalks.

✦ PROBLEMS WITH THE NARRATIVE STRUCTURE

The major advantage of the narrative structure is that it allows a writer to humanize what could otherwise be a very dry story. Instead of discussing monetary policy or city budgets, the narrative writer describes a specific person who is affected by the policy and tells how that person's life may change. The article uses direct quotations to let these specific people speak, and the writer explains with specific and human examples how the new policy will impact their lives.

A narrative creates a much more accessible and readable structure because it does not force people to master abstract ideas like budgeting and finance, and instead emphasizes the ordinary things in life. The narrative structure, though, does have several major drawbacks.

First, the narrative approach eats incredible amounts of space. The telling of little human stories takes several paragraphs. The five Ws use one paragraph to report what the narrative structure takes three to six paragraphs to cover. If the article length stays the same, that means the writer can use the narrative structure to discuss only a few topics. The lack of space may mean that the narrative approach leaves out many of the basic elements in a story. All journalism oversimplifies, but the narrative structure forces writers to simplify even more than the news formula does.

In reality, a city spends its budget on hundreds of services. Instead of discussing the new ball field, the reporter could just as easily have described the need for new police cars, for repainting all the firehouses, for new furniture for the mayor's office, or for city employees to get raises. Confining an article to the need for sidewalks and the need for toilets at a ball field ignores the complexities of the city's budget.

The narrative structure has a second flaw. Its focus on storytelling can create editorial comment and bias. For instance, a writer who chose to contrast the need for new furniture for the mayor's office with the need for sidewalks would be slanting the story heavily in favor of sidewalks. On the other hand, a writer could contrast the need for sidewalks with a tale of a police officer driving a patrol car with bad brakes in hot pursuit of a criminal. This would make the need for sidewalks seem less urgent.

When writing narrative stories a reporter should pick human stories of equal weight. For example, in the article about sidewalks used as an example here, the writer balanced the tragic death of one eight-year-old against the inconvenience of many eight-year-olds.

◆ USE NARRATIVE LEADS JUDICIOUSLY

Not all readers like narrative leads, and not all stories lend themselves to these leads. A Poynter Institute study found that well-educated, loyal newspaper readers, particularly women, prefer the news formula, probably because they have developed the habit of relying on the formula to help them scan through the newspaper. The news formula tells them the meat of an article immediately. These readers see a narrative lead as just a waste of space before the article finally gets to the nut graph and explains the news.

In the Poynter study, other categories of newspaper readers—less-seasoned readers, younger people who had not attended college, and particularly men—preferred the narrative approach. The storytelling technique allowed them to move into a story. They got an idea of the issues involved before having to master the large number of difficult ideas that the news formula throws at a reader at the start of a story.

Both types of people kept reading farther down into a narrative story than they did in a straight news article. The Poynter study found that readers were much more likely to read the continuation onto another page if an article used the narrative structure instead of the news formula.

This works for the writer of that specific narrative article but not necessarily for the welfare of the newspaper. If people read one story in depth, that may mean they do not read another story at all. By definition, the narrative approach, by encouraging deep reading, also discourages scanning. For this reason, not every article in a newspaper should use the narrative approach. Readers who expect to scan much of the newspaper, reading in depth only those articles that pique their interest, need the news formula.

Newspaper reporters should definitely use the narrative structure, but not in all the articles they write. Instead, a reporter should reserve the narrative approach for a few articles, particularly those on topics that the news formula renders dry and lifeless.

✦ CLICHÉS

The narrative structure does create one final problem for some writers. Because narratives force a writer to simplify material and relate it in basic human terms, the writer can easily lapse into a string of clichés, and readers grow tired of clichés very, very quickly.

Here is the Winstons' story told in clichés:

When Jim and Mary Ellen Winston married in 1985, they knew they wanted the American Dream, a home of their own, but things have been tough for the Winstons. She's a secretary, he's a janitor. Their combined income is $31,249.

In the late 1980s they had searched high and low for a house within their means, but finally decided it was a lost cause and continued to rent.

But in 1993 when interest rates hit historic lows, the Winstons began their search anew, and last month they and their two children moved into the proverbial ivy-covered cottage. Theirs is on Marshall St. in Albany, Ga.

Today, the Winstons are breathing a sigh of relief. Five major lenders yesterday announced their intention to raise home mortgage interest rates by half a percentage point. "We can just squeeze out our payments at 7 3/4 percent interest," commented Mrs. Winston. "This raise to 8 1/4 percent would have meant we couldn't buy this house."

Here is Maria Oviedo's story told in clichés:

When little Maria Oviedo left her mother's roomy turn-of-the-century home two months ago, all she could think about was the big trip that her class was going to take to farmer Sam Brown's.

When she woke up to the fact that she had forgotten her math homework, she told her friends waiting for the yellow school bus that she would be back in a minute. That's the last time anyone saw little Maria alive.

When she discovered the school bus had left without her, Maria began the trek to school down crowded San Antonio Rd.—a road that has sidewalks on only one side for most of its length. A car traveling at normal speed struck and killed her.

Her mother, Linda Oviedo, has retraced her daughter's last steps and says the eight-year-old must have had to cross the busy thoroughfare three times to find sidewalks where she could walk.

"If we had sidewalks on both sides of San Antonio Rd., my daughter might not have died," said Oviedo.

The City Council today rejected a proposal to build sidewalks along both sides of San Antonio Rd., saying that the $200,000 expense was more than the budget could handle.

Notice that the clichés rob the narrative lead of its emotional impact. Since a writer uses the narrative structure to reach readers on an emotional level, the use of clichés destroys the effectiveness of the approach. A writer who can only render a narrative lead in clichés should abandon the technique and revert to the straight news formula.

SUMMARY

- The news formula can produce boring stories full of technical jargon and difficult transitions.
- Telling one person's story, relating the events in the order in which they occurred, can make the information in an article more accessible.
- The narrative structure has three parts: an introductory story about one person, a nut graph, and the rest of the story.
- A writer still has to identify the five Ws for an article using the narrative structure.

- A narrative lead focuses on specific people caught in a larger news story and relates the events in their story using ordinary, commonplace vocabulary.
- Narrative leads can help a reporter bring local government news alive.
- Chronological order makes a narrative easier to read because it takes a reader step by step through the events as they happened to a specific person.
- The nut graph, which comes up about four to seven paragraphs into the story, explains the news elements of the five Ws that appear in the lead of a news formula story.
- The rest of an article with a narrative lead can revert to the news formula, or it can continue to relate mini-stories that illustrate the topic.
- A narrative approach can create a bias in a news story, depending on whose story the writer chooses for the main focus.
- Many readers dislike the narrative structure because it inhibits scanning.
- The narrative lead can inspire a writer to use clichés, which destroy the impact of the story.

IN-CLASS EXERCISES

1. In your local newspaper, find a narrative lead story. In it, locate the five Ws. Where are they placed? How do the locations of those items differ from those in a news formula story?

2. Using something that has happened to you recently as the opening, write the first page of a narrative lead story. Be sure to use your anecdote to lead into a nut graph, and then to move into summary–quote pairs.

3. For many important stories, newspapers will have both a narrative lead story and a news formula story. Locate such a pair of stories, and write a comparison of the two. Which is more interesting? Which is more informative? Why? Do you have a preference? If so, why do you prefer this story?

4. Locate a narrative lead story in a national newspaper. In it, isolate (a) specific people caught in a large news story; (b) the story of these people told using chronological order; and (c) the specific and human language used to tell the story.

5. Locate a narrative lead story in a national newspaper. Transform it into a news formula story.

6. Locate a news formula story in your campus newspaper. Using phone interviews if necessary, transform it into a narrative lead story.

7. Find five stories in your local newspaper that you think would work well as narrative lead stories. Who would you interview for each, and why? What questions would you ask of them, and why?

OUT-OF-CLASS EXERCISE

Locate someone whose experiences you feel are somehow indicative of a larger story, and write a narrative lead story using his or her experiences as the anecdote, following the format given in this chapter.

CHAPTER 11

Words

A small roadside eatery posts a sign: "Shirt and Shoes Must be Worn to be Served." What does that sign say? Read literally, it says that if a shirt or some shoes wish to order a meal, they have to be old and worn. The restaurant will not serve food to new shoes or a new shirt, but only to old shoes and shirts.

A person with the courage to ask the proprietor—a rough-looking man with cauliflower ears—why he won't feed lunch to a pair of new shoes would probably receive the answer, "Hey, cut the wisecracks. You know what I mean."

In one sense, he would be right. He means that no barefoot or shirtless people will get food. That reading makes so much more sense than the alternate reading that his customers figure out what he means.

For most newspaper articles, settling for the nearly right word rather than seeking the right word will not make much difference. But whenever writers settle for the nearly right word, they take a chance on losing their readers. Instead, reporters should try to write so clearly and simply that readers just cannot misunderstand them. Why not pick the right word, even if it takes a little more effort?

Writing starts with word choice, and picking the right words matters far more than most beginners, and even some pros, think. Words stock a writer's tool chest, and their misuse can lead to all sorts of trouble. At best, choosing the wrong word can make the editor groan and readers write insulting letters. At worst, wrongly chosen words can libel the innocent.

Words establish the tone of a news story, and therefore, by themselves, create the possibility of inadvertent editorializing. Choosing the wrong words can also drive readers away. They will not tolerate obscure words and phrases. Since they skim newspapers quickly, readers will not take the time to look up words in a dictionary.

✦ $50 WORDS

The use of fancy language, another trap for news writers, stems from American higher education. High school and college English teachers have united to indoctrinate American students in a writing voice that works well for graduate-level scholarly reports. Beginning news writers naturally adopt the voice that made their high school teachers happy and earned them high marks in college.

But an elaborate vocabulary will not help a bad story, and it will hurt a good one. A fancy word will irritate even readers who understand it, because the word slowed them down; those who do not understand the word will move on to another story, confused.

For example:

Chilton, whose residence burned down, said he would seek a new domicile elsewhere.

Residence? Domicile? A house is what burned (not *burned down,* which makes as little sense as its companion phrase *burned up*). And the phrase *seek a new domicile elsewhere* tells the reader nothing; he's not going to buy a house tonight. Is he going to live with relatives, or stay in a hotel, or what? Better:

Chilton, whose house burned, is looking for a place to rent.

Another example:

Attorney General Boyles said the matter would be adjudicated as soon as possible.

The matter is vague, and *adjudicated* is a fancy word for *tried.* Better:

Attorney General Boyles said the Levine case would go to trial as soon as possible.

Here's another example:

A substantial number of the underprivileged fail to employ social services because they are ill-informed about their existence, said State Senator Harlan Pruitt today.

Replace *a substantial number* with *many, underprivileged* with *poor,* and *ill-informed* with *do not know,* and you get a much more direct version:

Many poor people do not know about help offered by the government, State Senator Harlan Pruitt said today.

Writers often face a choice between a multisyllable word with Latin origins and a shorter word with Anglo-Saxon origins. *Domicile* or *residence* versus *home* is an example. A good rule of thumb: Always prefer the Anglo-Saxon to the Latin, the short over the long, and the simple over the complex.

In the days when newspapers calculated paychecks by the length of a writer's work, perhaps it made sense to use the longest and most complex words available. On college term papers in some courses, a similar logic may hold true. But for newspaper writers today, the best word is the shortest and simplest one. Don't use a $50 word when a 25-cent one would work just as well.

◆ WORD CHOICE

Beginning news writers usually need to work on mastering the subtleties of word choice. Consider, for example, the sentence:

Jamison's specializes in native azaleas grown under the most delicate soil conditions, according to Mary Levi, production director.

Delicate soil conditions? Can soil conditions be delicate? What the writer meant was that the precise soil conditions needed for the azaleas exist in only a few places. A better sentence would read:

Jamison's specializes in native azaleas grown in acidic soil, said Mary Levi, production director.

The word *delicate* conveys the meaning—sort of. Readers understand from *delicate* that the conditions are hard to maintain, or something like that, and from that can infer that the plants themselves are delicate. But why put the reader through such mental gymnastics, when another word would work better?

A similar example:

Constantin called Lehigh Valley one of the world's perfect places to live.

In general, words like *perfect* or *greatest* imply singularity. There can't be two greatest places in the world to live. A better usage would be:

Constantin called the Lehigh Valley a marvelous place to live.

Sometimes, the difference between the right word and the nearly right word is minor. Consider:

Thompson called living conditions in the migrant camps deplorable, with most of the housing heated by kerosene wick stoves. One family, according to Thompson, nearly smothered when a stove malfunctioned.

Smothering implies being unable to breathe because something covers one's mouth and nose. The correct word here is *suffocated,* which implies that the air was unbreathable.

Thompson called living conditions in the migrant camps deplorable, with most of the housing heated by kerosene wick stoves. One family, according to Thompson, nearly suffocated when a stove malfunctioned.

Reporters should make every effort to use precisely the right word. As in the above cases, readers can often figure out what the reporter meant, but a writer should make things clear enough that readers can spend their time pondering the events of the day rather than a reporter's meaning.

✦ *ALLEGEDLY* AND *ALLEGED*

Two words that often give reporters trouble are *allegedly* and *alleged.* These words appear often in stories dealing with people charged with some crime but not yet convicted. For example:

Hammond allegedly misappropriated $180,000 from Constance Jewelers over a 10-year period.

A reporter would do better to name the person making the allegation:

The district attorney has charged Hammond with misappropriating $180,000 from Constance Jewelers over a 10-year period.

Sometimes reporters find themselves using *alleged* in contexts where it works poorly, or not at all. Consider this use of *alleged*:

Hammond, an alleged extortionist, will hire Julian McBride as his lawyer, according to a friend.

The use of *alleged* almost always sounds odd. Consider:

McBride said evidence putting his client at the scene of the alleged crime was circumstantial.

Did the crime happen, or not? Reporters, anxious to avoid convicting people in print, sometimes sprinkle *alleged* throughout their stories. But if the crime really happened, then *alleged* makes no sense.

Avoid using *allegedly* and *alleged*. On rare occasions each word may help a sentence, but almost always a reporter would do better to seek an alternative construction.

✦ *HE, SHE,* OR *THEY?*

Although some newspapers have not yet adopted a policy on the matter, gender bias has become unacceptable in any form of writing. Consider:

According to management consultants, when the boss cordially invites a worker to his Christmas party, he'd better go.

Are all bosses men? Are all workers men? Of course not, and so this use of *his* excludes many people. Similarly:

The attorney general warned that the cabdriver has a legal responsibility for the safety of his passengers.

Are all cabdrivers men? No.

Many writers have struggled with the problem of the gender-specific pronoun *he*. Some of the solutions they have devised do eliminate the gender problem. When they substitute alternative forms like *one, he or she,* or *s/he* that eliminate gender bias, however, they sometimes create awkward sentences.

For example:

According to management consultants, when the boss cordially invites a worker to his or her Christmas party, he or she had better go.

And:

The attorney general warned that the cabdriver has a legal responsibility for the safety of his or her passengers.

Writers can take a much easier and more graceful route to eliminate this bias. Fortunately for the news writer, plural pronouns in English are gender-neutral. Often a writer can efficiently eradicate gender bias from a sentence by recasting it in plural rather than singular terms.

According to management consultants, when bosses cordially invite their workers to Christmas parties, the workers should go.

The attorney general warned that cabdrivers have a legal responsibility for the safety of their passengers.

Besides the pronoun *he,* other words can also imply unintended gender bias. Again, here, the writer needs a combination of sensitivity about bias and sensibility about the readability of language.

Calling the individual who chairs a corporation's board of directors a *chairman* eliminates the possibility that a woman could head a board of directors. *Chairperson* is correct usage, but awkward. Lately, there has been a search for gender-neutral but still mellifluous terms. Just substituting the word *person* for *man* often creates an awkward construction. A writer could call the person who leads a board of directors the *chair, head,* or *president of the board.* Similarly, a *fireman* can as easily be a *firefighter,* and a *policeman* can be an *officer.*

One unsuccessful attempt at gender neutralization has come in America's restaurants, which tried calling the person who brings the food to the table a *waitperson* or *server* and the people who work a particular shift the *wait staff.* The point about words that indicate gender is not to eliminate them from the news, but instead to include people of both genders in newspaper articles.

For example, the person who brings food to the table must be either a male or a female, therefore a writer can use the gender-specific term *waiter* or *waitress* to describe that person. The people who staff a particular shift are both male and female. Therefore, a writer would refer to them as *waiters and waitresses.*

Fortunately, the editors of the Associated Press have given a lot of thought to the issue of gender-freighted language. In the *Associated Press Stylebook,* beginning news writers can usually find suggestions of graceful substitutions for most gender-biased words.

✦ THE DANGERS OF ADVERBS

Adverbs modify verbs. They describe how the action occurred. Since they tell how something happened, adverbs often require a judgment by the writer. While some forms of writing demand these judgments, in news writing adverbs can often force the writer's opinion into an article. A reporter should tell what happened, and not judge how it happened.

Here are some examples:

> In an all-night session, the state legislature unexpectedly passed a stopgap spending bill.

The *unexpectedly* changes the whole thrust of the story, and, in doing so, offers an opinion. This wording says the writer did not think the legislature could pass the bill.

> Amazingly, Wilson said he had not noticed his wife's disappearance until the next day.

With that *amazingly,* the reporter implies that Wilson is lying, and worse, that Wilson may have had something to do with his wife's disappearance.

> "My home really isn't all that nice," Lieutenant Treves said frankly.

Here, *frankly* is an editorial comment suggesting that Treves is telling the truth, though it may somehow harm his cause. Perhaps Treves seems honest, but a reporter should not provide character assessments for readers.

> The Senate confirmed only 52 percent of Ronald Reagan's Supreme Court nominees.

Only 52 percent? Is 52 percent some historical low? If it is, and that fact is germane to the story, present the fact, rather than the editorial comment *only.*

Fireman Nelms then ran quickly from the building, carrying the last pup cradled in his arms.

Ran *quickly*? Can one run slowly? Perhaps. But nobody would run slowly from a burning building. Instead, use a more visually specific and descriptive verb. For example:

Cradling the last pup in his arms, fireman Nelms charged out of the building.

Here's one more example of an adverb messing up a sentence.

Boss Tweed quickly came to hold or control most of New York City's political power.

How long did Tweed take to gain that control? Is that less time than others have taken? Better to stick to the facts, and if Tweed did it in a year, just say so. Let the reader assess the speed of the takeover.

A news writer cannot use an adverb without inserting opinion into a story, because adverbs demand that the writer make an assessment about how an action happened. The safest approach to adverbs in news writing is to avoid using them.

✦ *ALOT* AND *HOPEFULLY*

Sometimes reporters use words that aren't really words, as in:

McNemara said he had learned alot in the Elderhostel classes.

There's no such word as *alot,* as the computer's spelling checker will point out. The spelling checker, however, will suggest *allot,* which means *to allocate,* and that would be no better.

Another word that gives reporters trouble is *hopefully,* as in:

Jarvis said that the new technologies would hopefully give "five to ten years" of life to those with myocardial failure.

Hopefully is an adverb, and the problem with its use in the above sentence becomes clear with the substitution of another adverb.

Jarvis said that the new technologies would gladly give "five to ten years" of life to those with myocardial failure.

Hopefully is an adverb, but many writers use it as an adjective. Avoid using *hopefully* in news copy.

✦ SCIENCE TALK

Often, reporters find themselves having to quote technical discussions verbatim, as in:

> "We feel that the new fifth-generation cyclosporins have been overused, contributing to the development of resistant strains of staphylococci," said Baignet.

Few readers would know what a *cyclosporin* is, or a *staphylococcus*. A reporter could try glossing the quote:

> "We feel that the new fifth-generation cyclosporins have been overused, contributing to the development of resistant strains of staphylococci [the bacteria that cause a variety of common infections]," Baignet said.

Glossing *staphylococci* only makes the quote tougher to read. In this case, paraphrasing usually works better:

> Baignet said that overuse of new, powerful antibiotics had led to the development of strains of common bacteria that are far more resistant to antibiotics.

The following direct quotation contains too many technical terms, but it also includes strong opinions that should be quoted.

> "We feel that the new fifth-generation cyclosporins have been overused in a stupid and unethical manner, contributing to the development of resistant strains of staphylococci [the bacteria that cause a variety of common infections]," Baignet said.

In such a case, orphan quotes can include the important (and, in this case, inflammatory) words, while paraphrasing covers the technical material.

> Baignet said that overuse of new, powerful antibiotics had led to the development of strains of common bacteria that are far more resistant to antibiotics. Baignet described this overuse as "stupid" and "unethical."

Tech talk also pops up in sports stories, where reporters who wouldn't dream of using a phrase like *fifth-generation cyclosporins* without glossing are perfectly happy to talk about *spikes, netters,* and *back-court* as if everyone knew what they meant. The same is true in political stories, which sometimes run like this:

> Halliburton suggested that the governor pocket veto the gambling bill, said Nunez.

When an article must use a technical term, the writer should pause to define it. A better paragraph would be:

> Halliburton suggested that the governor block the gambling bill with a pocket veto, said Nunez. To use this indirect veto the governor would keep the legislation on her desk unsigned, until the current legislative session ends.

Some reporters like to use technical talk, thinking it makes them sound knowledgeable, but these words really only make their copy hard to read.

✦ WORDS AND TONE

Since newspaper writing takes a formal tone in general, a writer should avoid contractions, slang, and colloquialisms, unless in direct quotation.

Often, the use of colloquialism leads to confusion about whether a phrase is a direct quote or not, as in:

> Fortuna said he would not allocate another cent for the Center for Classics, arguing that the Center had spent plenty of money and had nothing to show for it.

Did Fortuna actually say that the Center had spent "plenty of money"? Or did the reporter choose that phrase? A writer should save controversial language for direct quotation:

> "I will not allocate another cent for the Center for Classics," Fortuna said. "The Center has spent plenty of money and has nothing to show for it."

What if Fortuna actually said, "We feel we've been generous to the Center, and thus we are reluctant to offer more money to them"? Then the first paraphrase exaggerates the speaker's views. Here, using colloquial speech caused a problem for the reporter. The colloquialisms "not another cent" and "plenty of money" made the sentence sound as if the actual words came from the speaker, Fortuna.

In general, then, attempt to use standard, formal English in news stories. Colorful dialogue and clever phrases should come from the mouths of sources, and the writer should label them plainly as direct quotations.

✦ DESCRIPTION

Often, reporters must describe people or places.

> Lafonda drove an old sedan, belying her current status as America's fifth richest person.

What is a *sedan?* How does it differ from a *coupe?* Some readers will miss the meaning in this sentence. What if the writer continues:

> Lafonda's husband, an attractive man with a flat-top haircut, looked no more wealthy than she.

What, precisely, is a *flat-top haircut?* In general, reporters should use phrases or words only when they know the precise meaning.

Descriptions can also insert the writer's opinion into a story.

> The Stewarts' house, a dilapidated old barn with a few threadbare curtains hung over open windows, housed a family of five.

Such condescension reveals the writer's contempt for the Stewarts. Similarly:

> Koenig laughed heartily as he hitched up his ample pants around his even more ample waist.

Here, the writer displays a disdain for overweight people and also perpetuates a false stereotype—that of jolly fat people. No sensible reporter would dream of perpetuating similar stereotypes about ethnic groups.

Another example of condescending description:

> Kolko, an attractive 30-year-old, dresses smartly in the latest styles; her charming manner and fashionable dress would never indicate to the casual observer that this woman possesses a keen business mind.

The writer evidently thinks that women can be either attractive or clever, but not both.

Because descriptions of scenes, people, and events give a reporter much creative freedom, they leave a reporter free to display bias. Reporters should write descriptions very carefully, and then double-check them for stereotypes and condescension.

✦ FOREIGN WORDS

Occasionally, foreign words creep into news stories, as in:

"We've been looking for la dolce vita in retirement," Heinemann said. "And we've found it here in Cape Cod."

Instead, paraphrase:

The Heinemanns were looking for the sweet life in retirement. "And we've found it here in Cape Cod," said Heinemann.

Avoid using almost any foreign phrase, with a few obvious exceptions like *vice versa*.

SUMMARY

- Don't use a 50-dollar word when a 25-cent one would work just as well. Complicated words impress no one, and irritate many readers.
- Choose the word which conveys the precise meaning you have in mind.
- Do not use *alleged, allegedly, hopefully,* or *alot.*
- To avoid the implication that only males inhabit the earth, cast sentences in the plural, which lets a writer use the gender-neutral pronoun *they* instead of the gender-specific *he.*
- Avoid adverbs, because they can slip unintended opinion into a news story.
- Avoid technical vocabulary and foreign words. When you must use them, provide translations.
- Adopt a sober tone and save colorful language for direct quotation.
- Keep bias out of descriptions.

IN-CLASS EXERCISES

1. Pick out a story in a local or national newspaper about a technical subject. Do you find any jargon or large words in it that you don't know? Are there any words that you don't think the average reader of that newspaper would know? Rewrite the story, replacing the technical jargon with plain English words.

2. In the sports page of your local newspaper, find a story that uses sports slang that not all readers would understand. Rewrite the story so that the sports terms are plainly explained.

3. Find a newspaper story in which adverbs are used outside of quoted material. Do the adverbs make the story seem less objective? Would removing the adverbs make the story less interesting? Explain whether you think the story would be better with or without adverbs, and why.

4. What part of the newspaper—news, sports, business news, family news—is the most likely to use jargon and slang? Examine your local newspaper, and justify your choice.

5. Interview one of your classmates, and write the interview using only summary, avoiding quotes. Then show the interview story to your classmate. Did your classmate think your paraphrase was accurate? What does this tell you about paraphrasing?

6. Find a story from your local newspaper that uses numerous, colorful quotes. Rewrite the story, using a sober tone to paraphrase all the quoted material. Do you think the new story reads as well as the original? Why or why not?

7. Find a television news story in which adverbs are used outside of quoted material. Do you believe that the adverbs make this story seem less objective? Do television news stories seem to use adverbs more often than do newspaper stories? Why do you think they do?

OUT-OF-CLASS EXERCISE

Find someone who is an expert on a technical subject, and interview that person about his or her current work. Write a story on your interview, being sure to avoid technical language.

Bureaucratese, ▬

Clichés, and ▬

Fluffy Phrases

When a writer picks out words, accuracy—finding the word with just the right meaning—must dominate the selection. Art in writing comes at the level of phrasemaking. Writers demonstrate their artistic ability when they hook words together into phrases. Apt phrases entertain the reader, while stale expressions make an article prosaic and imitative.

This book emphasizes that beginning news writing involves much more craft than art. In this chapter we discuss bureaucratese and fluffy writing, the two main phrasing defects that can create a bad piece of writing. A novice reporter should learn to identify and eliminate bureaucratese and fluffy writing, but that reporter should not worry about trying to substitute brilliant and artistic phraseology for the bureaucratese and the fluff. Forced brilliance makes for stilted and pretentious writing. Art grows in a writer's voice over time because entertaining writing grows out of the author's interest in and enthusiasm for a subject. Writers can strongly improve a piece by cutting bureaucratese and fluff, but they should not strain for art. Keeping a piece of writing plain and simple works best as a way to begin to learn news writing.

✦ BUREAUCRATESE

In bureaucratese—the peculiar almost-English that government officials use to conduct business—*revenue enhancement* replaces *more taxes,* *incidental malfeasance* replaces *petty theft,* and *at that point in time* replaces *then*. Bureaucrats toss commas like rice at a wedding and plant semicolons in every other paragraph. Their sentences grow to interminable lengths, and paragraphs stretch from page to page.

Imagine a paragraph like:

> Wilson suggested that new avenues of funding availability would be sought, but that the considered opinion of the council was that several budget lines for personnel would have to be consolidated.

That sounds innocuous enough. Written in plain English, though, it becomes ominous:

> Wilson said the council would try to find more money, but that the city would probably have to fire several employees.

Sometimes, officials use bureaucratese to hide the facts, as in:

> The continued utilization of improper waste management procedures and policies by the county could result in higher than acceptable levels of methacarbamate in local potable supplies, and possible sanctions by federal officials.

A plain English version might read:

> Continued dumping of toxic chemicals by the county could poison nearby wells, resulting in fines by the federal government.

Often, official sources who have to create a press release about a negative event will write in complicated and obtuse language to obscure the facts. The reporter who does not take the time to find out the definition of *methacarbamate* or to get a specific list of "sanctions" inadvertently helps officials conceal their actions.

Journalists, too, have their own peculiar language. Think for a moment about the phrase *brutal murder,* then try to imagine its opposite—a gentle murder. In journalese, rampaging rivers cut huge swaths through unprotected villages. The worst forms of American journalese label all leaders of unfriendly countries as *despots* or *strongmen*. Writers call guerrilla forces operating in countries supported by the United States *thugs* or *hooligans,* while insurgent forces the United States aids receive the title *freedom fighters*. Reporters who use nice cant for forces the United States supports, and ugly terms for forces the United States opposes, would do well to remember that sides change, and yesterday's freedom fighter could become tomorrow's thug.

The reporter who wrote the following excerpt was in full cliché mode:

> The Second Horseman of the Apocalypse, Pestilence, stalked the Earth in grim triumph yesterday when an outbreak of food poisoning struck 230 people at the Phil Johnson Evangelical Center.

More information and less cliché appear in the following revision:

> An outbreak of food poisoning characterized by nausea and fever struck 230 people at the Phil Johnson Evangelical Center yesterday.

✦ FLUFFY PHRASES

Most writers reach clarity when they edit their first drafts. Go through the first draft and eliminate every phrase that can go. Exchange fancy words for simple ones. The article may grow shorter, but the writer can lengthen it by adding more facts. For example:

> At that point in time, Marcos was also dealing with an internal power struggle.

The fluffy *at that point in time* takes five words to say *then*. The *internal power struggle* doesn't give many facts about what was going on. Better:

> Marcos was then dealing with an attempted coup d'etat led by members of his own cabinet.

This shorter improvement provides more information. Another example:

> The governor said that his cabinet was seeking additional modes of revenue enhancement.

Revenue enhancement means taxes, of course; politicians must think the public has a harder time reading their lips if they use fluffy phrases. The use of the fancy word *modes* makes this whole messy sentence almost incomprehensible. How about:

> The governor said his cabinet was seeking new ways to raise money.

The fluffy phrase *essentially* adds nothing to the sense of a sentence.

> Essentially, the state's program will require about $4 million a year in public funding.

Will it or won't it? Also, *in public funding* is redundant; that kind of money does not come from bake sales. Better:

> The state's program will require about $4 million a year.

Another example:

> Witnesses said Thomas, armed to the teeth, shouted wildly at his father before he began to fire.

Armed to the teeth? Were his teeth really armed? A factual description of his weapons would have worked much better. And *shouted wildly?* Knowing what he shouted, or that he shouted incoherently, makes more sense than *wildly.* Better:

> Witnesses said Thomas, armed with an automatic rifle and a hunting knife, shouted obscenities at his father before he began to fire.

✦ SCIENCE TALK

Many reporters use scientific jargon wholesale in a story. Often they fear trying to translate technical language. In the previous chapter we discussed scientific words; this section examines the ways in which complex phrases need not only simplification, but also explanation in terms readers can understand. Consider:

> Walston said the polymerized low-temperature bearings would have important applications in cryogenics and hyperbaric applications.

Reporters who write sentences like this either have not taken the time to find out what *cryogenics* and *hyperbaric applications* are, or do not trust their knowledge. Much easier to read is:

> Walston said the new process would make bearings that could work in high-pressure and low-temperature applications.

Better yet, a writer could explain those applications, as in:

> Walston said the new process would make bearings that could work in high-pressure and low-temperature applications such as space suits, deep-sea diving equipment, and decompression chambers.

That first sentence would make most readers turn to a new story. Those who kept reading would follow the second sentence with little interest. The third sentence, however, gives readers something to grab on to. Everybody can define a space suit or deep-sea diving equipment, and this "new process" that will help make those things becomes more interesting because the reader can visualize some of the products.

When scientists talk about scientific matters, jargon seems to be inevitable. A reporter must not only translate that jargon into words and phrases that every reader can understand, but also provide clues that help the reader understand the implications of the news story.

In this context, writers reporting on the size, cost, speed, or power of something often compare it with a familiar item, as in:

The new LandStar, while it is approximately the same size as a family sedan and costs about the same to operate, can travel at similar speeds on both land and water.

When reporters deal with scientific stories, they should take every opportunity to ground the new information in a way that makes it easy for readers to follow the story.

✦ CLICHÉS

The smoked turkey was done to a turn.

Many clichés really do not make much sense. Done to a turn? This phrase originally applied to meat cooked on a spit and meant that it had received the right number of turns over the fire. A clichéd phrase may once have had a meaning related to a specific visual image, but by repetition it has come to sound acceptable without meaning anything. "Done to a turn" means "cooked perfectly." If the visual image no longer makes sense, a writer would do better to abandon it.

Writers use bureaucratese and other forms of cliché because these words come up repeatedly. Clichés sound good because of their familiarity and because the first 20 people who used them sounded witty. People use them all the time, but clichés do not communicate anything except the writer's attempt to imitate someone else's wit. "Done to a turn" used to have a precise meaning, but a cliché like this adds little new information to the sentence.

Unfortunately, writers often use clichés in their first drafts. Because forcing oneself to come up with a new and witty way of saying something almost never works, a cliché tends to pop out instead.

✦ HOW TO AVOID CLICHÉS

The best way to edit for clichés is to try to keep from writing them in the first place. Anyone thinking of writing for a newspaper—that is to say, anyone who would be reading this book—already knows that he or she can write competently. Most journalism beginners have already written some articles or essays that they like. If these pieces had any merit at all, they probably were free of clichés. Subconsciously, then, most writers already know how to write cliché-free copy. To avoid clichés a writer needs to learn how, with a given assignment, to tap into that already existing ability to write without resorting to clichés.

A writer can turn on a no-cliché voice by learning to generate enthusiasm and self-confidence when approaching a new assignment. A writer who finds an assignment boring, or who worries about explaining the facts accurately, will produce clichés and bureaucratese.

Consider, for example, the weekly meeting of the city council. A beginning reporter sees all those unfamiliar bureaucratic terms, like *ad valorem tax rate* and *coliform bacteria,* and panics. A writer who worries about misrepresenting these technical concepts might try to be safe by reproducing the bureaucratic terms in the article. For example:

> The Medford City Council agreed last night to hire a consultant to investigate the appearance of coliform bacteria in the city water supply.

That creates an article so weighty that only people who attended the meeting will try to read it.

There is, however, another solution. A reporter who feels insecure about how to word a story should ask for help. Anyone starting on a new beat, be it the city council or the Pentagon, needs to find a few friendly sources to provide laymen's definitions of the bureaucratic terms. City council meetings always have regulars in the audience. Some retirees attend just for the theater of it all. Civic associations regularly send a member to monitor the politicians' activities. These people truly enjoy helping a new reporter. Even at the Pentagon, bored colonels delight in dazzling new reporters with in-depth explanations of the use of military power. If insecurity has produced the cliché, the reporter needs to ask more questions, get an education on the topic.

In the case discussed above, after a little explaining, the reporter has a stronger (and more alarming) lead:

> The Medford City Council agreed last night to hire a consultant to investigate the appearance of bacteria from raw sewage in the city water supply.

Clichés can also be committed by seasoned reporters who have covered the city council for many years. They have seen Sammy Snider of the West Gate Neighborhood Association complain about backed-up storm drains once a month for two years. "Here's Sammy again," they moan. "I'll bet I can tell you word for word what he has to say before he says it." Bored reporters quickly write up boring stories littered with clichés. When they do not care about the assignment, they fall back on clichés because they can get through the story faster that way.

An alive, enthusiastic reporter, on the other hand, can find something fresh and new in these events. While Snider laments, that reporter gets more information on a new move the council is planning. Or that reporter takes detailed notes on the bored agony on council members' faces and writes a piece about the tedium of public service. Or that reporter interviews Snider, takes a look at the West Gate storm drains, and writes a piece on the ineptitude of the city public works department. After all, Snider has been complaining for two years and the storm drains are still backing up.

An interested reporter looking for these fresh approaches to city council meetings will not parrot stale phrases made up by others. Instead, an enthusiastic reporter automatically generates fresh copy that describes the unique character of the particular situation.

✦ HOW TO CATCH CLICHÉS

All writers do, on occasion, produce clichés. While a writer has to work much harder to identify a cliché in a completed article than to keep from writing it in the first place, once a cliché has popped up in a piece, the writer faces the task of labeling a part of his or her personal creation as imitative. This takes great psychic strength, but here are some suggestions.

First, many writing texts contain lists of clichés. Reading over a list of clichés can attune a writer's ear.

Second, many people unconsciously build a cliché warning system into their copy. Some writers find themselves typing along, occasionally putting phrases in quotation marks. These phrases in quotes do not report what a source said. They just appear as the writer goes along. Usually, this stray punctuation marks a cliché. Other writers, while struggling along through a piece, will suddenly find a phrase springing forth fully formed. These phrases are probably clichés.

A writer can eliminate clichés easily just by taking them out. Since clichés by definition have no meaning, a reporter does not have to reword to fix a cliché. With the cliché gone, the sentence will be shorter, blunter, and more effective.

✦ WRITING CLICHÉ-FREE AND BUREAUCRATESE-FREE COPY

A beginning reporter, faced with turning a bureaucratese-laden press release into a news story, can follow a two-step process. First, the reporter writes a news story that uses whatever phrasing the original press release or story used. Then the reporter goes back through the article, translating the bureaucratic or scientific jargon into plain English.

An example might be the following press release from Michael Grimes, public relations officer for Aztec County Schools:

> Do our children come first, or last? That's the question the Aztec County School System asks of Aztec County.
>
> County residents currently pay the lowest taxes in the state, at only six cents a.p.t. This low tax rate shows in our schools, where Little Johnny can't get near a computer, and Little Suzy finds long waits for even the simplest gym equipment.
>
> The County seems reluctant to raise money, though. After the passage of Initiative Six in 1990, no new funding enhancements have been proposed by the County. Teacher salaries have stagnated, while class enrollments have increased.
>
> "We're going to have to do something if we don't want Aztec to become the poorest school system in the state," says Superintendent Wanda Lionheart. "Are the people of Aztec willing to pick up the gauntlet?"
>
> Ad valorem taxes are a fair and equitable way of raising money. So are property taxes. Can't our school system come first?

With the opinions deleted, and a new lead constructed, the story reads:

> The Aztec County School System has begun a public relations campaign aimed at encouraging county voters to approve a property tax increase.
>
> County residents currently pay the lowest taxes in the state, at only six cents a.p.t. This low tax rate shows in the quality of the schools. "Little Johnny can't get near a computer, and Little Suzy finds long waits for even the simplest gym equipment," said Michael Grimes, public relations officer for the schools.
>
> After the passage of Initiative Six in 1990, the county has proposed no new funding enhancements. Teacher salaries have stagnated, while class enrollments have increased, said Grimes.
>
> "We're going to have to do something if we don't want Aztec to become the poorest school system in the state," says Superintendent Wanda Lionheart. "Are the people of Aztec willing to pick up the gauntlet?"
>
> "Ad valorem taxes are a fair and equitable way of raising money. So are property taxes. Can't our school system come first?" asked Grimes.

The final version adds some additional data, eliminates the clichés and bureaucratese, and explains some of the unfamiliar phrases.

> The Aztec County School System has begun a public relations campaign aimed at encouraging county voters to approve a property tax increase.
>
> "We're going to have to do something if we don't want Aztec to become the poorest school system in the state," says Superintendent Wanda Lionheart.
>
> County residents currently pay the lowest taxes in the state, with the average home in Aztec paying $620 in real estate taxes, compared to the state average of $880.
>
> This low tax rate means that students do not have enough computers or recreational equipment, says Michael Grimes, public relations officer for the school system.
>
> Since the passage of Initiative Six in 1990, a tax-relief measure that required voter approval for any tax increases, the county has proposed no new taxes.
>
> Teachers have had no raises since Initiative Six, while class enrollments have increased, said Grimes.

SUMMARY

- Translate bureaucratic language like *revenue enhancement* into plain terms like *taxes.*
- Simplify scientific phrases.
- Sometimes it's hard to come up with a new and intriguing way of saying something. So out pops a cliché.
- Avoid writing clichés and bureaucratese by learning the meaning of technical terms used by sources.
- Avoid writing clichés and bureaucratese by finding an intriguing story angle. An enthusiastic writer does not see a topic in clichéd terms.
- Since clichés have no meaning, taking them out of copy only makes it work better.

IN-CLASS EXERCISES

1. Find a newspaper story that uses overly bureaucratic language or journalese. Rewrite the story so that it is in everyday, comprehensible English.

2. Find a story in your local newspaper containing clichés, and rewrite it in standard English.

3. Rewrite a news story from your local newspaper using as few words as possible. What did you eliminate, and why?

158 / GATHERING THE NEWS

4. Exchange the story you wrote in Exercise 3 for a classmate's rewrite, and repeat the exercise, adding words to improve the sound of the article. What did you add, and why?

5. Rewrite a news story from your local newspaper, eliminating all the fluffy phrases and obscure words and sentences. What did you change, and why?

6. Locate a story on the television news that contains clichés. Why might television news be more inclined to rely on clichés than newspapers? Is this necessarily a bad thing?

7. Rewrite a news story using no simple sentences. How does this story sound to you?

OUT-OF-CLASS EXERCISE

Write a story about unemployment rates in your area. To do such a story, you'll need to (a) interview someone at the local unemployment bureau; (b) use local data on unemployment; (c) use state data; (d) use national data. Be sure that your story doesn't contain any clichés or jargon.

CHAPTER 13

Sentences

The news formula is very specific about sentence structure. Newspaper editors want their reporters to write news copy that uses a simple and straightforward syntax. The information in this chapter all grows out of one underlying assumption—the assumption that editors prefer that their reporters opt for simple declarative sentences in creating news formula articles.

The writer orders such sentences by putting the subject first. Next comes the verb, and next comes the object.

Subject → Verb → Object.

Most of the sentences in this book take that form. Because the repetition of that form page after page gets tedious, however, a good writer occasionally throws in a sentence with a different structure. Like oregano in a salad, a complex sentence adds flavor.

The simple declarative sentence sets the standard for newspaper syntax because newspaper readers do not give sentences, or stories, a second chance. Research has shown that readers prefer simple sentences, sentences that a sixth-grader could readily understand. For whatever reasons, intricate and convoluted wording drives readers to other articles. Consequently, news formula stories should use, on the whole, simple sentences.

✦ PUNCTUATION

High school English teachers often encourage the use of fancy punctuation, like colons, semicolons, and dashes. They do not want their students' writing to stagnate at the level of the simple declarative sentence. They also, of course, want to teach students the correct use of these punctuation marks.

For a news formula writer the appearance of these punctuation marks is a warning sign. A colon or other fancy punctuation in a sentence may mean the sentence is too complex for use in a newspaper. Some writers overuse semicolons, putting them where periods would work better, as in:

> Steinman said that Johansen brought immense strength to the team; her fielding alone easily made her the most valuable player on the Rocket Squad.

That sentence reads better as:

> Steinman said that Johansen brought immense strength to the team. Her fielding alone easily made her the most valuable player on the Rocket Squad, he said.

Many writers misuse dashes to cram sentences into other sentences, as in:

> Only when Halliburton—who had landed on D-Day in Normandy—revealed his identity did the situation become clear.

The only reason to use a dash is to cram a sentence or a sentence fragment into a sentence in some location where it doesn't fit grammatically. Thus, writers of news formula stories almost never employ dashes.

In general, fancy punctuation doesn't belong in news stories. Even when used properly, it tends to irritate readers. When used improperly, fancy punctuation mystifies them. Since only the rare writer uses fancy punctuation marks properly, the beginning writer should avoid them.

Colons

In newspaper writing the colon is used only to introduce a list:

> Meyer claimed to have sold the following to Herve: diamonds, stocks and bonds, and French perfumes.

That same sentence, though, reads better as:

> Meyer claimed he sold Herve diamonds, stocks and bonds, and French perfumes.

Semicolons

Newspaper writing makes only one good use of the semicolon—to list a complex series. Consider the difficulty of reading the following paragraph:

> The Hainesville Elementary School PTA Tuesday elected the following officers: Mary Sue Allison, president, Virginia Dalquist, vice president, Dan Iovacchini, secretary, Sue Horowitz, treasurer, and Warner Sanchez, parliamentarian.

The author of this list set up a convention—name first and then title—but halfway through the list a reader forgets the convention. Is Iovacchini vice president or secretary? Semicolons do help in this situation.

> The Hainesville Elementary School PTA Tuesday elected the following officers: Mary Sue Allison, president; Virginia Dalquist, vice president; Dan Iovacchini, secretary; Sue Horowitz, treasurer; and Warner Sanchez, parliamentarian.

When commas are necessary to separate items within the sections of a list, the writer uses a semicolon to separate each section from the next one.

Newspapers, however, are moving away from the use of lists within the body of newspaper stories. Under the influence of *USA Today,* newspapers have begun to put lists of names, events, or dates in separate, boxed items. Readers interested in these specifics can check the boxed items and find the information they want. That way, the reader who wants to know what happened but has little interest in the specifics does not have to wade through the detailed list.

Even newspapers that do not use separate boxes use lists more often now. For example:

> The Hainesville Elementary School PTA Tuesday elected the following officers:
>
> - Mary Sue Allison, president
> - Virginia Dalquist, vice president
> - Dan Iovacchini, secretary

- Sue Horowitz, treasurer
- Warner Sanchez, parliamentarian

Newspapers call the dots in front of the listed names **bullets.** They enable readers to run through a complex list without having to struggle with the grammar of the sentence. They especially help in more complicated lists, as in:

School lunches for the next three days are:

- Monday: pizza, fruit salad, and peas
- Tuesday: macaroni and beef, turnips, and chocolate cake
- Wednesday: beef soup, green salad, and angel-food cake

Such a list works much better than the grammatically correct but difficult nonbulleted alternative:

School lunches for the next three days are: Monday, pizza, fruit salad, and peas; Tuesday, macaroni and beef, turnips, and chocolate cake; and Wednesday, beef soup, green salad, and angel-food cake.

Most newspapers have writing rules for the use of bullets, so the beginning reporter should check with an editor about when and how to use them at that particular paper.

Dashes

A dash in copy usually indicates a writer who has gotten about halfway through a sentence and then feels the need to cram another thought in.

Irving could not have been present at the shooting—as Loomis claimed—because at that time the Dallas Police Department had her in custody.

The suspended phrase "as Loomis claimed" spoils the flow, making the sentence harder to read and harder to understand. Also, the "as Loomis claimed" subtly injects the reporter's opinion into the article since it implies the reporter's evaluation of the accuracy of the claim. A better way:

Although Loomis claimed that Irving was present at the shooting, at that time the Dallas Police Department had her in custody, said Phelps.

The sentence reads better, and, with the attribution, is more accurate.

Writers most often use dashes when they are trying to get additional information into a sentence, as in:

A novice spends four weeks in training—at a cost of $1,500—to complete Killer Kriminski's wrestling school.

But, in general, the writer can easily punctuate such sentences to eliminate the dash.

A novice needs four weeks of training, and $1,500, to complete Killer Kriminski's wrestling school.

Usually the surgery just involves substituting commas or parentheses for the dashes.

Exclamation Points

Occasionally, a paragraph like the following will appear in a newspaper:

Despite having a student body only half as large as Central, Whitsett High has produced over twice as many college-bound students!

Never use exclamation points in a newspaper. They always make an editorial comment. An exclamation point at the end of a direct quote means that the reporter is saying that the source exclaimed, just as surely as if the reporter wrote, "he exclaimed." That represents opinion, the reporter's judgment alone, precisely what readers do not want. Even a piece written for the opinion or editorial page should not contain an exclamation point. In deliberately opinionated writing, the words a writer chooses can exclaim with much more power than a piece of punctuation can.

In the case presented above, the information in the paragraph effectively makes the point about the quality of the two schools. In the following example, the information does not stand alone.

Judge Orem could hear 14 traffic cases in one day!

Most readers do not know whether 14 traffic cases is a few or many, and the exclamation point does not help them to decide. A better version is:

Judge Orem could hear 14 traffic cases in one day, almost twice as many as any other judge in the department.

In most cases, when an exclamation point appears, the writer should replace it with information and allow readers to decide for themselves whether the information surprises them.

Question Marks

The question mark very seldom appears in news formula stories because the news story aims to answer questions. Question marks most often appear when sources ask questions within quotations, as in:

> "What would you yourself have done in a similar situation?" Trevor asked Lieutenant Phipps.

Note here that the sentence itself is declarative, ending with a period. The quotation ends with a question mark, which, like all punctuation used in a quote, appears within the quotation marks.

A situation that gives some writers trouble is the case where sources ask questions that aren't really questions, as when someone says something like, "Shall we go?" The speaker is really politely saying, "Let's go." Despite the implied meaning here, the sentence grammatically is a question, and needs a question mark, as in:

> "Shall we go?" Thompson asked the jury. "Shall we go in our mind's eye to the evening of the murder? Shall we look into the mind of a murderer?"

Single and Double Quotation Marks

The only use for single quotation marks is when a source's direct quote contains the exact words of someone else.

> "We now know what Gandhi meant when he spoke of 'soul force,' " Gemelin said.

There's no other use for the single quote, although writers improperly use them for partial quotes, as in:

> Westly described Trenton as 'a garden spot,' according to Travis.

News stories should use double quotes for all quoted material, even brief quotes or only a single word.

Commas

Commas seem to give most writers of English more trouble than any other item of punctuation. A writer can avoid semicolons, colons, and other fancy punctuation, but commas must appear in some sentences. Commas are hard to use because they have so many different purposes. Grammatical commas must appear in certain grammatical structures. Enumerative commas separate items in lists or series. Nonrestrictive commas set apart modifying clauses in sentences. Since news writers must vary sentence structures to avoid the "See Jane run" sound of grade-school writing, they need to learn the rules about commas.

The key to commas is understanding the four types of sentences discussed below, and understanding independent and dependent clauses. All sentences contain independent clauses, a combination of noun and verb that can stand alone as a complete sentence—for instance, *The boy ran.* Some sentences also contain dependent clauses, which as incomplete thoughts cannot stand alone; for instance, *although he went downstairs.* Dependent clauses can function within a sentence as nouns, adjectives, or adverbs. Independent clauses are sentences.

Comma Rules

Commas are used in five basic situations:

1. in compound sentences
2. in inverted sentences
3. for words, phrases, or clauses in a series
4. for nonrestrictive modifiers or clauses
5. for lists of two or more adjectives

Of these, only the last is not discussed later in this chapter. Adjectives that are coordinate can be joined either by *and* or by commas. Adjectives that are not coordinate sound odd used with *and.* An example might be:

Tall, handsome Bob Smith moved with ease in the political circles of Detroit.

With *and* added between the adjectives, the sentence still sounds fine:

Tall and handsome Bob Smith moved with ease in the political circles of Detroit.

But here is a different example:

> Smith wore a green tweed coat.

Substituting *and* between these adjectives sounds odd:

> Smith wore a green and tweed coat.

Thus no comma is necessary.

Apposition

A construction that often gives reporters trouble is apposition. Apposition is the use of a clause to give additional information about the subject of a sentence, as in:

> William Harshaw, president of the Film Society, said he would do "everything humanly possible" to bring Pornelle's film to Sedona.

Here, the clause *president of the Film Society* provides additional information about the subject. It does not, however, restrict the meaning of the subject in the way a restrictive clause does. Since it does not restrict, a writer sets it apart with commas. Most writers correctly insert the first comma for apposition, but many incorrectly leave off the second one.

✦ SENTENCE TYPES

The key to understanding punctuation is understanding sentence types. There are four types of sentences in English: simple sentences, compound sentences, complex sentences, and compound-complex sentences.

Simple Sentences

Simple sentences consist of just one independent clause.

> Officer Tom Bigbee arrested Johnson.

Sentences like this need no grammatical commas. Commas may appear in a simple sentence in lists or in an inverted sentence, in which a group of words appears before the subject:

> To squelch rumors, Bigbee held a press conference.

The comma indicates an inverted sentence structure. In this case a prepositional phrase precedes the subject. An uninverted version of that sentence would read:

Bigbee held a press conference to squelch rumors.

Compound Sentences

In compound sentences, a comma and a coordinating conjunction or conjunctive adverb join two or more independent clauses. Coordinating conjunctions include *and, but, or, nor, for,* and *yet.* Conjunctive adverbs include *although, therefore,* and *because.*

Bill had supper, and Mary went home.

Removing the comma and the *and* would create two sentences.

Bill had supper. Mary went home.

Complex Sentences

Complex sentences have one independent clause and one or more dependent clauses. When the dependent clause is restrictive, it contains information that is essential to the meaning of the sentence. An example:

The golfers who stayed away from the trees survived the lightning.

In this example, the "who stayed away" clause indicates a specific group of golfers. Those golfers who stayed away from the trees survived. Those who hid under the trees did not.

Adding commas around the "who stayed away" clause changes the meaning of the sentence:

The golfers, who stayed away from the trees, survived the lightning.

In this sentence, all of the golfers survived. The "who stayed away" clause adds more information. Without this clause the fundamental meaning of the sentence would stay the same. Therefore, the clause is dependent. Commas are used to set apart nonrestrictive clauses in complex sentences; restrictive clauses in complex sentences need no grammatical punctuation.

Compound-Complex Sentences

A compound-complex sentence is a compound sentence with at least one dependent clause added.

> The golfers who stayed away from the trees survived, but falling limbs killed the others.

This sentence consists of two independent clauses, the first of which includes a dependent clause.

✦ SENTENCE LENGTH

While the news formula encourages simple sentences, that does not mean the sentences should all be the same length. Series of sentences of the same type and similar length develop an annoying singsong rhythm.

> Nesmith said he was robbed. His assailants were three men. They fled down Park Street after the attack.

This sounds like a second-grade reading textbook, because both second-grade readers and this example use the same sentence structure over and over. By varying sentence structures, a writer's style can grow up.

> Nesmith claimed three men robbed him. After the attack, his assailants fled down Park Street, he said.

Research on readability and sentence length suggests an average sentence length of 20 words, but writers should remember the important word *average* contained in this recommendation. A few sentences should run 40 words long. Some can stop at five or ten words.

As in bricklaying, a writer should try to arrange sentences so that annoying patterns do not emerge. The "See Jane run" sound of the paragraph presented above can annoy a reader, but so can:

> Harris found the lost money in Riverside Park. Because he had no idea where it had come from, he took it to the police station. The police were baffled. Since they could not identify the owner of the money, they called in the State Bureau of Investigation.

Here, simple sentences alternate with inverted compound sentences, creating a peculiar, repetitive tone that becomes annoying.

✦ SENTENCE STRUCTURE PATTERNS

A problem of rhythm can occur in sentences. For example, the "See Jane run" problem often crops up in news stories written by beginners.

> Thieves hit the studios of a local artist last Thursday. The thieves walked away with several paintings. The most valuable of these was a woodland scene with a price tag of over $10,000. Jane Campelier, the artist, was unavailable for comment.

Here all the sentences have an identical structure. The phrases appear in identical sections of each sentence. Beginners, afraid of making punctuation errors, will often rely too much on simple sentences—subject, verb, object; subject, verb, object; subject, verb, object. A little editing to make some of the sentences complex or compound solves the problem.

> Thieves hit the studios of a local artist last Thursday, taking several paintings, including a woodland scene with a price tag of over $10,000.

A more complex phrasing problem occurs in:

> In a few instances, Hetrick's disease can develop into a full-blown paralysis. Most of these cases improve spontaneously. In some cases, improvement does not occur quickly. Some of these cases never improve at all.
> Radson's research indicates the saline-injection treatments may work. Some doctors use them regularly. But when Hetrick's disease strikes, other doctors refuse to give any treatment at all. They cite the 1990 CDC report urging further study before any treatment is attempted.

Here, the sentences alternate in form, with one sentence inverted, the next not. The effect is quite unpleasant, although diagnosing it isn't an easy task. Again, a simple rewrite—changing some sentence forms—can eliminate the problem.

> In a few instances, Hetrick's disease can develop into a full-blown paralysis. Most of these cases improve spontaneously. In some cases, improvement does not occur quickly, and in these cases there is seldom any improvement at all.
> If Radson's research is correct, the saline-injection treatments are the most likely to work. Some doctors use them regularly. But many doctors refuse to give any treatment at all, citing the 1990 CDC report urging further study before doctors attempt any treatment of the disease whatsoever.

Often, phrasing is the source of the problem when a story sounds wrong.

A writer should distribute sentence types randomly in a story. Simple sentences should predominate for ease of reading, but complex and compound sentences do break up the monotony. A beginning writer might want to try writing a news story using a predetermined list of sentence structures—say, compound, simple, simple with inversion, complex, simple—and repeat this pattern throughout the story. This sounds like a painful grammar exercise, but many people find it easy. Once writers feel assured of their ability to write using whatever sentence types they like, then they achieve control of phrasing.

✦ *THAT* AND *WHICH*

The words *that* and *which* probably cause more trouble for newspaper writers than any other pair of words. Many writers mistakenly use them interchangeably. The simplest way to remember their use is to put the clause introduced with *that* or *which* in parentheses, and see if the sentence means the same thing. If it does, use *which;* if not, use *that.*

If the clause does not alter the meaning of the sentence, and just presents additional information, use *which,* but if the clause is essential to the meaning of the sentence, use *that.* Eventually a writer automatically comes to use these two words correctly, but a beginning news writer should check each *that* and *which.*

The critical distinction between the use of *that* and *which* is the idea of the restrictive clause. *That* introduces a restrictive clause, one that restricts the size or number of the subject. *Which* introduces a nonrestrictive clause, a clause that presents additional information but does not limit the size or number of the subject.

To use a simplistic example, visualize a clown standing next to five dogs. One of them, a yellow one, barks. The clown says:

The dog that is yellow barks.

Here, the clown restricts the subject *the dog* by saying which one of the pack it was. Therefore the clown uses *that,* and does not surround the clause with commas. Now, imagine that clown standing with one dog, and it barks. The clown says:

The dog, which is yellow, barks.

Here, the clown does not try to clarify which dog barks since there is only one dog, after all. The clown is just handing out more information, and so the clause is nonrestrictive. Therefore, the clown would use *which* and would surround the clause (which, grammatically speaking, is a nonessential clause) with commas.

The distinctions created by *that* and *which* can make a crucial difference in newspaper stories. Think about the difference between the two examples below.

> The gun, which Lewis held, went off accidentally, according to Grooms.

Here the author is implying that only one person—Lewis—held a gun. Now look at the second example:

> The gun that Lewis held went off accidentally, according to Grooms.

The author is saying that others were also holding guns during the stickup. This might seem a minor distinction, but the others involved in the holdup, and their lawyers, might not find it a small distinction at all. The possibility for inferences that aren't what the writer intends is reason enough for exercising care.

Now compare another two examples:

> The class, which went to Pomona for the debate tournament last year, will travel to Chicago.

Here, *which* indicates that there is only one class in question. But consider:

> The class that went to Pomona for the debate tournament last year will travel to Chicago.

Here, the clause limits the discussion to the one class that went to Pomona. Unlike the previous example, a mistake probably would not end with snippy letters from lawyers. But a mistake could confuse readers.

A final example, and a situation guaranteed to get the unwary into hot water:

> Some 250 striking workers gathered at the north gate of the Kenyon plant. The group, which Norris led, began to pelt the security guards with rocks. The district attorney has filed assault charges against the group.

Here, the writer is saying that the whole group took part in the stoning, and that the D.A. will prosecute all 250 of them. But maybe what the writer meant to say was:

Some 250 striking workers gathered at the north gate of the Kenyon plant. The group led by Norris began to pelt the security guards with rocks. The district attorney has filed assault charges against the group.

The incorrect use of *which* is not only an error but a potential libel, since it implies that all the workers who were gathered at the plant had assault charges filed against them.

As these examples suggest, sometimes the choice of *that* or *which* is more than a picky rule of grammar.

SUMMARY

- Avoid colons, semicolons and dashes.
- Never use an exclamation point in a newspaper article.
- Commas must appear in five basic circumstances.
- Write short sentences, but include a few long ones and a few very brief ones for variety's sake.
- Vary sentence types.
- *That* and *which* have different uses. If a subordinate clause is essential to the meaning of a sentence, use *that*. If a clause is not essential, introduce it with *which*.

IN-CLASS EXERCISES

1. Find 10 instances of sentences that use dashes in a local or national newspaper. Rewrite the sentences without dashes.

2. Find 10 uses of colons and semicolons in lists in your local newspaper. Rewrite the sentences in which they appear, using neither colons nor semicolons.

3. For the following 10 sentences, determine whether *that* or *which* is correct.
   a. Blevins said the dog, _____ was yellow, was rabid.
   b. This led the State Bureau of Health representative to call for a measure _____ had not been implemented in Nebraska since 1942.
   c. In this measure, over 700 dogs were held for two weeks at a facility _____ had been specially prepared for the purpose.
   d. Any dog _____ displayed any symptoms was quarantined, and further tests were performed.
   e. Of the 200 dogs _____ had been impounded as of Jan. 1, 12 were found to be rabid.

f. "This is not the only way to deal with this problem," said a spokesperson of the group, _____ calls itself "People for the Pets."

g. The group, _____ was founded last fall, considers the state's plans unnecessary.

h. A boycott _____ was arranged by the group is to go into effect Tuesday.

i. "We won't say what it will target," said a spokesperson. The group, _____ is only one of three groups protesting the impounding, will hold a press conference next week to announce the target of the boycott.

j. "The dogs _____ are rabid need to be helped, but this just isn't the right way," said the spokesperson.

4. In the following 10 sentences, fix the use of commas.

a. Thorsett who was the man wanted by the police was taken into custody last night.

b. Smith leader of the band Tammy's Portion was interviewed by a local radio station.

c. Halliburton said that his work was not done but that someone else would have to carry on.

d. In fact Schering's pension plan is well-funded for the remainder of the century.

e. Only men over 40 women over 45 and people in high-risk groups need ever consider screening for Taylor's disease.

f. Tall dark and plump, Mr. Mulligan was the soul of intellectuality.

g. The taxi which had been waiting at the hotel door sped away as Lindsey Thompson and his entourage came down the stairs.

h. On 14 occasions, Lemmin was charged with minor traffic violations appearing in court for none.

i. Hammond said they would continue to manufacture switching gear but intended to phase out their consumer products division.

j. Wanting to meet people Nadia joined several civic organizations.

5. Correct the following sentences for punctuation and the use of *that* and *which*.

a. The products that were defective were returned for inspection but the rest were shipped to clients.

b. Renaldo said he did not understand that Milledgeville and Tacoma Heights were the cities which the document mentioned.

c. Hunting for an excuse Valipolicelli suggested that Gleason might have arranged the loss of the football game.

d. Those units which have serial numbers between 18K100 and

18K400 have been recalled but the rest of the units are working fine Snelling assured the group.

e. The process was acceptable to everyone but Framington who still felt more time was needed.

f. The menu for the next week is Monday, rice and beans, Tuesday, potato cakes turnips and squash, and Wednesday chicken pilaf pineapple, and breadsticks.

g. Lewis the world heavyweight champion, was unable to attend the ceremony which Halston staged, but did attend the one which was held later.

h. Merman's book *Possible Futures* was reviewed well in the *Times,* in the *Herald* and on television.

i. The performance was marred by continual coughing that disturbed everyone in the hall.

j. The airplanes that were at the maintenance center were examined further but the ones at other sites were not inspected.

6. Find a news story that uses a bulleted list. Rewrite the story to include the bulleted information in the body of the story. Which version do you prefer, and why?

7. In your campus newspaper, correct a story for comma mistakes. For each error, describe which comma rule was violated.

OUT-OF-CLASS EXERCISE

Conduct an interview, and write a story from it. In every case where you use *that* or *which,* include a note explaining why you chose the word you did. For every comma, explain which comma usage rule motivated its use.

CHAPTER 14

Advance Stories

Advance stories report events that have not yet happened. **Advances** include press releases, most announcements, weddings and obituaries (which are more funeral announcements than anything else), and many election, business, and political stories.

Most beginning reporters write a lot of advances. Reporters can expect good cooperation from sources on advances since these stories, by definition, announce planned events. Often, advance stories involve a lot of routine—political candidates, for example, will often distribute the text of a speech at a press conference before the event. Usually the people involved with the story have, as part of their jobs, publicized the event, and so advance stories usually concern well-promoted and well-planned events staged at a civilized hour. All these factors make advance stories an ideal place for beginning newspaper writers to start. Sources generally cooperate; the event involves enough routine to give a reporter ample time to prepare; and the event usually takes place at some central, pleasant location.

Advances usually come to the attention of the newspaper through press releases or news conferences. Usually, advance stories lack a straightforward **time peg** (the "when the story happened" element that must appear in the lead of every news story). One time peg tells the time of the announcement that the event will occur. Often, though, the time when somebody announced that something would happen has far less interest than the time the event will occur. A reporter has to focus on the event while getting into the lead both the true time peg (when the announcement was made) and the time peg of interest (when the event is going to happen). A lead could read:

> ABX Corporation this morning announced plans to build a 15-story office building within the next three years in the 1400 block of Broadway.

This lead includes both times.

Beginning writers tend to overload the leads on advance stories, making them so long or so complex that it becomes difficult to figure out what clause belongs to which predicate, as in:

> ABX Corporation announced plans to build a 15-story office building within the next three years in the 1400 block of Broadway in a press conference held this morning at the company's main offices in Tampa.

This lead is overloaded, with five different clauses.

Often, more complex tense structures (the past perfect tense, the use of words like *had* or *have*) will help simplify the leads of advance stories. These verbs show that an event occurred in the recent past, while leaving a hook for that information to show up in the paragraphs of backfill. For example:

> The De Bartolo Company has announced plans to build a 15-story office building in the 1400 block of Broadway.

✦ TRUE ADVANCES

Reporters do write real advance stories. Famous musicians come to town, the city holds elections, and the like. In such cases, background information and interviews provide the facts for the story. The time peg usually concerns the time of the future event.

> State Senator Marilyn Fugazy will address the West Town Republican Association Friday at 7 p.m. at Funk's Grill.

Often, as in the case presented here, the time when the newspaper learned of the event has little or no importance, and so that information is left for backfill, as in:

> The last surviving member of The ManTans, the popular rock-and-roll band of the 1970s, will speak at Howard Gap High School this Thursday on the dangers of narcotics.

"We were young and didn't know any better," Tommy (Taz) Johansen said during an interview at King Books, where he was autographing copies of his new book, *Life Without ManTans*. "I just hope that, by speaking next Thursday, I can convince somebody to avoid what happened to Leon and Jinx."

Leon Black and Jimmy (Jinx) Attenborough died of drug overdoses in separate incidents. Black died in 1980, and Attenborough died in 1990.

"We're just delighted that Johansen will come to speak to our students," said Howard Gap principal William James in a press conference held at the high school last night. "Sometimes the kids won't listen to us older squares, but maybe the message will come through if they hear it from someone hip."

Here, the time information about the announcement falls naturally into the fourth paragraph. Almost always, the time of the announcement has less importance than the time of the event. The time peg of the lead should be the time of the event.

✦ THE FUTURES FILE

As discussed in greater detail later in this book, a **futures file** can really help a reporter. Properly speaking, a futures file consists of a calendar and a file folder. When reporters hear about upcoming events, they note the date on their calendars and file any notes or comments about the event in a futures folder. At the beginning of every working day, the reporter checks the futures file, looking to see if anything noteworthy will come up that day or in the next few days.

Obviously, the futures file stores good story ideas for the day, but it also stores advance stories that look at the impact of some event. In this sort of story a reporter interviews people about what they expect from an event. An example might be:

Next Tuesday's reopening of the Cheyenne Parkway, closed for almost a year and a half after the San Mateo earthquake, may result in a vast increase in traffic through the San Miguel and Trackham neighborhoods, said local officials.

"We're anticipating it with dread," San Miguel Police Chief Darryl Banks said yesterday. "From 2,000 cars per day to 20,000 is a big increase, but our patrol budget hasn't gone up in a long time."

The change in traffic routing will help some firms.

"A fast-food franchise depends on passersby for its business," said Jerome Hudgins, manager of the Mello-Burger near Exit 4 on the Cheyenne Parkway. "The increase in traffic can only do us good."

Sometimes these stories contain real drama, as in a story describing the horror one neighborhood felt at the prospect of the release of a convicted murderer who planned to return to his old home.

✦ PRESS RELEASES

Public relations firms and public information officers generally construct press releases to announce some new service a firm wants to sell or promote. An employee or agent of the firm writes the press release and has it approved by an executive in the firm. The result poses as news but has a closer relationship with advertising. Running a press release as is not only gives away the advertising that newspapers sell, but also damages the credibility of the paper because it makes it look as though publicity agents have free run of the news pages.

Take, for example, this press release.

> Not every painter combines high levels of skill with a personal commitment to engineering change in our society. Skip Weber does, though, and the Alpha Gallery is proud and fortunate to feature his blown-glass sculpture for the next two months.
>
> "I believe that art has power, power to change the way people live and think and work. In my art, I try to showcase spiritual truths that could heal our world—if only our world would pay attention."
>
> The Gallery, which is at 94 Carmichael Street, charges no admission and is open from 9 to 5 every day but Sunday.
>
> "We're very happy that we can showcase the work of an artist of the level of skill that Skip possesses," said Trinh Nguyen, owner and curator of the gallery. "This is a real boon for our community, and we hope that the presence of Skip's healing art will help heal some of the wounds in our community."

Clearly, this lead contains editorial comments, as does the rest of the story. A good newspaper would not use this press release without a significant rewrite.

Beginners at newspapers usually draw the assignment of rewriting press releases because the rewriting gives a rookie practice with the news formula. A rewriter treats a press release as a tip about a possible story, not as a story in itself. A press release, after all, will never include a conflict angle. Is a firm announcing the construction of a new office building? Call the neighbors and see what they think about it. Will a crafts fair bring thousands to downtown sidewalks? How are the police going to cope with that? And even if no conflict angle surfaces, the press release still needs rewriting to eliminate editorial comment. A reporter might rewrite the press release shown on page 178 as follows:

> The blown-glass sculpture of Skip Weber goes on display today at Alpha Gallery, 94 Carmichael Street.
>
> The show will run for two months.
>
> "We're very happy that we can showcase the work of an artist of the level of skill that Skip possesses," said Trinh Nguyen, owner and curator of the gallery. "This is a real boon for our community."

A reporter should check the subject in the newspaper's library of back issues. Sometimes, that old information becomes the story. Spurred by a press release about construction plans, a reporter might check on the past activities of a firm that develops downtown shopping malls. The check might reveal that the developers had not finished seven of their nine preceding construction projects. A check of the clipping file enhances the art gallery story as follows:

> Alpha Gallery, 94 Carmichael Street, reopened today after an arsonist's fire last October.
>
> Two men await trial for the burning, which prosecutors described as "racially motivated."
>
> The gallery's new show displays the blown-glass sculpture of Skip Weber. "We're very happy that we can showcase the work of an artist of the level of skill that Skip possesses," said Trinh Nguyen, owner and curator of the gallery.
>
> "This is a real boon for our community, and we hope that the presence of Skip [Weber]'s healing art will help heal some of the wounds in our community."
>
> Weber said art has "power, power to change the way people live and think and work.
>
> "In my art, I try to showcase spiritual truths that could heal our world—if only our world would pay attention."

Most press releases, though, do not undergo such a dramatic change in focus. A reporter just rewrites them to cut all opinion words and to play up the most newsworthy item instead of the business's name. If the story seems to deserve more length, the reporter calls the contact person at the firm and gets more details. Rarely, though, does a press release story deserve more length. Generally, the task of rewriting a press release involves chopping the copy in half.

The story itself should carry all essential information, including the local name and place of business of the organizer of the event. Thus, there's no need for a summary paragraph giving names and phone numbers. For example:

> "We had one hell of a time getting permission for this fair," said Andy Jones, whose office at the Red Cross will handle ticket sales. "The city's officials just do not seem to understand the importance of this project."

Anybody who wants tickets knows where to get them. Avoid concluding with a paragraph like:

> For tickets or further information call 555-2399. The Gallery is open from 9 to 12, Monday through Saturday.

Businesses should buy advertising space to promote information like this.

✦ PSEUDO-EVENTS

Daniel Boorstin, in a perceptive book about the news, discusses what he calls the **pseudo-event.** Organizers stage pseudo-events like press conferences, marches, and rallies purely to draw reporters. In an announcement of a scientific breakthrough, for example, something newsworthy only appears to happen. The real discovery happened sometime earlier in the laboratory.

Often, pseudo-events turn out to be all puff and no substance. All the talk about limitless free energy from cold fusion, for example, turned out to be no more than talk. Many new business projects or construction projects announced with much fanfare never occur. The cheering crowd at a rally may consist of company employees with orders to cheer lustily or lose their jobs. Promises only promise, and intentions only intend. Writing about promises and intentions as if they will occur does not serve readers. Thus, a news story such as the following raises interesting ethical questions.

> Scientists at the Arkin Biochemical Laboratories announced today a major breakthrough in the medical treatment of obesity.
>
> "We have been able to achieve weight reduction of about 10 percent in our test subjects, and that weight loss has persisted after the treatments were completed," said James E. Kelley, associate professor of endocrinology. "That would correspond to about 20 pounds in the average overweight human."
>
> The research on rats used neurochemical treatments to turn off the hunger centers of the brain, Kelley said.
>
> The researchers plan to begin tests of the treatments on humans in five years. If those tests are successful, and if the Food and Drug Administration

(FDA) approves the drug used in the treatment, weight-loss medicines based on Kelley's research might go on sale as soon as the year 2009.

Because not all readers will make it to the critical point where the story reveals that the experiments involved rats, a better lead for this story would go:

> Scientists at the Arkin Biochemical Laboratories announced today a break-through in the medical treatment of obesity.
>
> Experiments involving neurochemical treatments of rats resulted in significant weight loss. Should the same procedure be applicable to humans, a weight-reduction pharmaceutical based on this research could go on sale as soon as 2009, researchers said.
>
> "We have been able to achieve weight reduction of about 10 percent in our test subjects . . ."

Unfortunately, announcements of pseudo-events do not immediately indicate the right way to lead a story. In the case of a product or research announcement, the firm making the announcement tends to emphasize the importance of its discovery. The more important the discovery, after all, the more positive an impact it has on the price of the stock of the firm. Sometimes these firms go to great lengths to disguise the drawbacks of their discoveries.

The good reporter, however, will seek to uncover those drawbacks. Much of the public cynicism toward media and the press, research suggests, stems from articles promising great boons to humanity that then vanish without a trace. Just because a treatment will cure obesity in rats does not mean that it will do the same in humans. A reporter must determine the real event behind the pseudo-event and then report on the real event.

✦ WEDDINGS

The prototypical advance story announces a wedding. Such stories are so formulaic that many papers provide skeletons for their construction. An engagement announcement skeleton taken from a local paper reads:

> <Woman's parent(s)> announce the upcoming wedding of (their)(his)(her) daughter, <Woman's name>, to <Man's name>, of <Man's place of residence>.
>
> The couple will wed <date of wedding> at <place of wedding>, <city of wedding>.

And so forth. The completed engagement announcement would then read:

> Mr. and Mrs. Julius Schwartz announce the upcoming wedding of their daughter, Esmelina, to Philippe Porteré, of Cayenne, Guyana.
> The couple will wed July 1 at St. Patrick's Cathedral in New York City.

Whatever skeleton the newspaper uses, a reporter should follow it slavishly. Nobody will applaud a precise approximation of the skeleton, but any errors will result in trouble. Readers do not appreciate originality in a wedding announcement any more than they like to see creativity in an obituary.

To write a wedding announcement, clip one out of an old newspaper and just change the names and places. That will make most editors happy. At some newspapers, reporters do not even write wedding announcements. Instead, someone called a "news clerk" or a "news secretary" writes them.

For wedding announcements that appear in the paper before the wedding, all descriptions go in the future tense; in wedding announcements that appear after the fact, the tense changes to past. More and more, papers are treating wedding stories as futures. They want to avoid running a story about an event that did not take place because the bride or groom skipped town. Always get the name and number of someone to contact after the wedding, but before the story appears, to confirm that the wedding actually took place.

Hoaxes haunt wedding stories. High school kids and drinking buddies often call newspapers to announce the marriage of some pair who despise each other. Careful checking and a call back to someone named in the story can insure against getting hoaxed. Such pranks are not very amusing, and they can also result in even less amusing lawsuits.

✦ OBITUARIES

Obituaries, or obits, are often routine stories that use an outline, just like wedding stories. The advance part of the story usually announces the time and place of the funeral, which serves as the time peg of the story. Some newspapers do not announce time and place, but the construction of the story is the same. Sometimes, though, the people dealt with in obituaries have sufficient fame to make their deaths newsworthy. In this case, the reporter provides sufficient background information to give the outlines of the life of the deceased.

> Harold (Hank) Sulzer, the first stock-car racer to win the Palmetto Prize three years in a row and one of the first African Americans to enter the sport, died in Columbia, S.C., yesterday at the age of 62.
> He died of heart failure, said his daughter, Eunice Sulzer.

Sulzer entered stock-car racing at the age of 15, working with the pit crew of well-known racer Tommy (Fireball) Parsons. After Parsons' death in 1968 at Bristol Speedway, Sulzer became lead driver for the Edmondton Cigarettes team, and later the Chiniaski Auto Parts team.

Between 1970 and 1980, Sulzer frequently won at Daytona, Charlotte, and the remainder of the Grand National circuit. More recently, Sulzer ran his own racing team, with Benny Mills as lead driver.

"Race doesn't enter into it," he said once about his status as one of the few African Americans to race stock cars. "A man who's not smart enough to know that race doesn't matter isn't smart enough to work on our team, anyway."

Sulzer is survived by a son, Edmond; a daughter, Eunice; and two grandchildren. Services are at Crossroads Baptist Church in Irmo, S.C., with interment at Forest Lawn Cemetery in Columbia.

Here, the third, fourth, and fifth paragraphs are backfill, giving a condensed biography of the life of the deceased. Otherwise, the story reads exactly like a standard obituary.

As with wedding stories, many newspapers no longer have reporters write obituaries. Some newspapers accept only paid obituaries; some will write an outline obituary, permitting family and friends to pay to print other materials if they wish. At other newspapers, obituary writing, because of its sameness, falls to the newest reporter.

Even though obituary writing carries little prestige, the writer must remember that accuracy and precision matter just as much in obituaries as in any other sort of news story. No surviving relative should need to nag a newspaper to correct some error of fact or spelling in an obituary.

SUMMARY

- Advances report events that have not yet happened.
- Rewrite press releases to cut all opinion words and to play up the most newsworthy item instead of the business's name.
- Groups stage pseudo-events like press conferences to get their names in the newspaper, not because any real news will emerge from the events.
- When writing wedding stories and obituaries, imitate the newspaper's prototypical story, but beware of hoaxes.

IN-CLASS EXERCISES

1. Find an advance story in your local newspaper. What is the time peg? Is the peg the time of the announcement or the time of the event? Does this matter in how the story is written?

2. Find a news story you think was motivated by a press release. How closely do you think the story stuck to the press release? Do you find the story credible? What do you conclude from this?

3. For the story you think was motivated by a press release, list 10 questions you would ask if you were rewriting the story so that it was a real news story.

4. Find a news story in your local newspaper that is based on a pseudo-event. Write a list of 10 questions you might pursue in order to turn the story into a real news story.

5. Why are wedding and obituary stories considered advance stories? Do some wedding and obituary stories have news values that could make them more than simple futures stories? Find such a story in your local newspaper, and explain why it has significant news values.

6. Interview a student in your class concerning something that is upcoming in his or her life, and write an advance story on it.

7. If you were going to interview your local representative to Congress about an upcoming election, what questions would you ask? How do the questions you prepared for this advance story differ from the questions you might have prepared for a regular news story?

OUT-OF-CLASS EXERCISE

Get a press release from a source such as your campus public information office. Rewrite the release, transforming it into a future-based news story. This will require additional research and interviews.

CHAPTER 15

Breaking News

Stories

Breaking news stories cover events that unfold while the reporter writes the story, or events that have just happened. These can include press conferences, on-scene crime reporting, final election coverage, and much of the gloomy destruction and mayhem that fills newspapers.

In some ways, a reporter has an easy time doing breaking news stories. The reporter has little trouble deciding on a lead, the backfill takes little space, and time angles are simple. In other ways, though, breaking news really challenges a reporter because gathering the information can be tough. In other types of stories, the clipping file or press releases provide much of the information, but with a breaking story, a reporter has to find out nearly everything. And, quite often, a reporter writes breaking stories under intense time pressure, with editors peering over the shoulder of the writer and presses sitting idle, waiting for copy to appear.

Most often, reporters enjoy covering breaking news. Besides, many judge the quality of a newspaper by the proportion and quality of its breaking news. Good newspapers do not rely much on routine stories and press releases, and instead fill their pages with breaking news. Reporters love breaking news because of the excitement such stories involve and the challenge to a journalist's reportorial skills. While much of reporting is routine, the breaking news story, by definition, involves an unusual event.

In addition, breaking news stories have played an important role in the development of the modern news story. Newspapers invented the inverted pyramid news formula to deal with the breaking news of battles during the American Civil War, and almost all great newspaper stories involve breaking stories.

Even though the inverted pyramid structure makes breaking stories easy to write, these stories can cause trouble for beginners. Often, new information comes in to the newsroom just as a writer has completed the article. The reporter has to stop and add a new lead, or new paragraphs. Sometimes, reporters writing breaking stories feel as though they must abandon their stories rather than finish them. Every seasoned reporter knows the queasiness of having some crucial piece of information arrive seconds after the story has gone to the composing room, beyond reach. Despite its apparent simplicity, the breaking news story can challenge even the best writer.

French chefs say the simple white sauce is the great test of the cook because no one can fake it or hide a mistake. Similarly, the breaking news story tests a news writer.

◆ LEADS

In a breaking story, lead with whatever event has most recently taken place. Avoid cluttering the lead with nonessential detail. The Associated Press calls cluttered leads **mumblers.** They happen when a writer tries to cram as much information as possible into the lead. Really, though, shorter and more direct leads carry more power. Take these two leads:

> Franklin D. Roosevelt, 26th president of the United States and grandnephew of President Theodore Roosevelt, died at 4:30 p.m. today at his Warm Springs retreat from a cerebral hemorrhage.

> President Franklin D. Roosevelt died at 4:30 p.m. today at his Warm Springs retreat.

The story must eventually report all the information in the first lead, but it does not all have to be crammed in that one sentence. The bigger the news story, the shorter the lead should be. The impact of the event itself will carry the lead.

To find mumblers, isolate the main event, and then look at the lead and take out the unnecessary details.

> Two masked men held up the Chun Yee convenience store on Ambrose Dr. this afternoon, then fled down Murphy Ave.

Robbers, at least those who get away, always flee after their crimes. Unless they leave in an unusual manner, the fact that they fled does not need notice in the lead.

Occasionally an extra detail can explain the newsworthiness of an event. If the detail explains the conflict or unusualness angle, it should stay.

> Two masked men held up the Chun Yee convenience store on Ambrose Dr. this afternoon, then fled down Murphy Ave. on skateboards.

Here, the "then fled on skateboards" explains why this story is of particular interest.

Mumblers also use **weasel words** like *alleged* and *supposedly*. People are innocent until proven guilty in court. The newspaper should not convict people in print, but a reporter can avoid this without using the awkward *allegedly*. Call people charged with a robbery "suspects" until their conviction or exoneration. Avoid leads like:

> Two masked men allegedly robbed the Chun Yee convenience store this afternoon. The suspects fled down Murphy Ave. on what appeared to be skateboards.

That "allegedly" makes little sense; after all, either the robbery happened or it did not. The masked men become suspects only when police name them. Until then, in police jargon they are perpetrators or bad guys. In newspaper jargon, they are thieves or robbers. Of course, "what appeared to be skateboards" is silly. What would a witness mistake for a skateboard?

Beginning reporters sometimes have trouble with the leads of breaking news stories because they try to avoid changing them. As a story develops, new information may merit going into the lead, but that means rewriting. Some unseasoned journalists try to stick with the lead they have already written and put new information in a new paragraph somewhere down in the story. The reporter ends up violating the principle of the inverted pyramid. A beginner might write:

> A jury found Anson (Andy) Harris, the last defendant in the New Salem murders, guilty today in Portsmouth Superior Court.
>
> After Harris' mother, Bethany Pinner, called the judge a "butcher," bailiffs escorted her from the courtroom.
>
> Judge Roy Todd later sentenced Harris to two life terms, citing the "unusual cold-bloodedness" of the crimes.
>
> Harris' attorney, Leon Vendermann, plans to appeal the case.

The most important angle of the story, the two life sentences, should lead the story.

> Anson (Andy) Harris, the last defendant in the New Salem murders, received two life terms from Judge Roy Todd in Portsmouth Superior Court this afternoon.
>
> After Harris' mother, Bethany Pinner, called the judge a "butcher," bailiffs escorted her from the courtroom.
>
> In announcing the sentence Judge Roy Todd cited the "unusual cold-bloodedness" of the crimes. Earlier this afternoon, after only three hours of deliberation, a jury had announced a guilty verdict for Harris.
>
> Harris' attorney, Leon Vendermann, plans to appeal.

Even though a lot of work goes into the construction of a lead, the reporter covering a breaking story must often discard a lead, or perhaps even several leads, as a story develops.

Sometimes, on a breaking story, time runs out and a reporter must use an incomplete lead:

> A verdict is expected soon in the first-degree murder trial of Anson (Andy) Harris, the last defendant in the New Salem murders, said his attorneys.
>
> "We're hoping the jury will realize that the inconsistencies in the testimony of prosecution witnesses lead to plausible doubt about Harris' involvement," said attorney Leon Vendermann.

Reporters and editors hate inconclusive leads, but sometimes deadlines demand them. In this situation editors use a command that terrifies beginners, "Go with what you've got." That means, "Finish the story in the next five minutes using available information."

✦ BACKFILL

Backfill tells of past events that tie in with the story. Even breaking news stories require some backfill, and effective journalists do not begin to write stories until they have checked the newspaper's files to get background.

A man arrested for stealing a car may have a long history of auto theft, or he may have been rushing a woman in labor to a hospital. Every story, no matter how straightforward, comes with some context that would make it more interesting. Previous criminal activity, extenuating circumstances, and other information add to the news.

The newspaper's **morgue, clip file,** or **backfile**—a library of previously published articles—can yield background information. So can other editors and reporters, almanacs, dictionaries, census reports, and even encyclopedias. Often the backfill makes the story, and even in stories written under the worst time pressure, good journalists find—and use— backfill.

The arrest of a couple for cruelty to animals would not normally make the front page of any newspaper. But if a reporter discovered that the pair had been officers of the local humane society, the story, through emphasis of the unusual, would become much more interesting and might make page one.

David Duke's initial run for office as a candidate for the Louisiana State Senate was not a big story until someone looked in the backfile and found out about the candidate's links to the Ku Klux Klan. Then the story made newspapers nationwide.

Presenting backfill in a story can be a challenge. Often reporters will try to interject it in dribs and drabs, and will end up confusing the reader.

> Allen, who spent seven years as a Navy commando, became a hostage when Stedman first entered the bank. Only when Allen, a native of Plattsburgh, started talking to his captor did he realize he might survive.

Placing the backfill all in one place keeps the reader from having to jump back and forth between past and present.

> Allen became a hostage when Stedman first entered the bank. Only when Allen started talking to his captor did he realize he might survive.
> Allen, a native of Plattsburgh, spent seven years as a Navy commando. That experience, he said, made him calm in dangerous situations . . .

Very few stories run without backfill, even if the backfill just provides context. Such contextual backfill could include:

> Judge Thomas Harriman ordered two reporters for the *Herald* to name the person who told them about upcoming court proceedings against Mayor Leon Trieber or face contempt of court charges.
> *Herald* reporters have faced similar situations in the past, and one *Herald* reporter spent two weeks in jail for defying court orders to reveal sources.

Here the backfill gives context from the past.

Sometimes, backfill helps set up a situation or explain some subtle aspect of the story.

> Judge Thomas Harriman ordered two reporters for the *Herald* to name the person who told them about upcoming court proceedings against Mayor Leon Trieber or face contempt of court charges.

State law requires reporters, when subpoenaed, to testify in court naming their sources of information. The law conflicts with the state reporters association's code of ethics, which describes the confidentiality between reporter and source as similar to that between doctor and patient.

These two stories, although they have identical leads, would differ markedly after the backfill paragraph, because the backfill paragraph would dictate the structure of the remainder of the story. Since the second story has played the conflict between law and ethics prominently, the quotation–summary segments to follow would begin with that angle.

State law requires reporters, when subpoenaed, to testify in court naming their sources of information. The law conflicts with the state reporters association's code of ethics, which describes the confidentiality between reporter and source as similar to that between doctor and patient.

"The code of ethics gives us a set of rules that have passed every constitutional test. If the law tells us to do something contrary to the code, then Dakota law is wrong," said Bill Potter, attorney for the *Herald*.

The first story, which plays up the angle of the other *Herald* reporters' experiences, would demand an entirely different use of quotations.

Judge Thomas Harriman ordered two reporters for the *Herald* to name the person who told them about upcoming court proceedings against Mayor Leon Trieber or face contempt of court charges.

Herald reporters have faced similar situations in the past, and one *Herald* reporter spent two weeks in jail for defying court orders to reveal sources.

"Those two weeks were the worst time of my life," said Tim Bullman, whose refusal to tell who had leaked confidential information about a scandal in the state Dakota Enterprise Agency resulted in a stay in the Long Butte jail. "But reporters have to uphold confidentiality. Otherwise no source with an ounce of sense would talk to a reporter at all."

Backfill not only gives readers enough information to make sense of stories; choice of backfill also determines what angle a story will play up.

◆ BACKFILL AND TENSE

Tense can be a problem with backfill. The writer is reporting a breaking story, a story happening now, yet the backfill concerns information from the past. The past perfect tense, the use of words like *had* or *have*, can help with this problem.

Manley, who had lost elections twice before, said he would avoid the name-calling and ill-will that characterized previous campaigns.

✦ ASK LOTS OF QUESTIONS

To get information for a breaking story, find the people who saw what happened and interview them. Most newspapers keep a police-band radio going in the newsroom. When they hear officers dispatched to an event, they go, too. A reporter who is on the scene when the event occurs or during the mopping up can easily find witnesses. Most breaking news, though, does not come from on-scene reporting because newspapers cannot afford to staff every police and fire call.

Usually, police officers or firefighters provide the information for breaking news stories. A reporter can find these officials by calling the police station or the firehouse. Officers make good sources because they keep written records of the events they were involved in. Ordinary citizens who witnessed an event are harder to find, although the incident report, available from police or fire departments, may contain the names of witnesses.

Try to get as much detail as possible. Listen to what people say—as raw information, for summary paragraphs and leads, and as quotable quotes. Listen for the unusual phrasing, the incongruous fact; probe repeatedly.

Never worry about asking a dumb question. If things are unclear, ask again, and again. Do not accept fudgy or fluffy quotes. Instead, ask sources to elaborate. Be persistent. Take notes quickly. Use a tape recorder. Do not lead sources as they speak; just continue to ask questions until they have explained everything clearly.

✦ AVOID CONFRONTATIONS

Beginning reporters often think that public officials such as police officers and politicians are always hiding something. These reporters adopt a confrontational, even belligerent attitude to try to wring information out of their sources. This does not work. Public officials, being human, react to antagonism the same way anyone else does. They adopt a fighting stance and stop talking. No one will reveal a secret to a rude reporter. Asking leading or obnoxious questions, or talking down to subjects, will only make them clam up—not just now but in the future. Public officials actively avoid obnoxious reporters. An exchange like this between a reporter and a source could drive the source away:

"Could you tell me what you know about the man who's holding those people hostage?"
"I need to finish getting these people moved out of the line of fire."

"Listen, the press has some rights in this country. If you don't talk to me, I'll talk to the chief about it."

"You do that. By the way, do you have written permission to be behind our police barrier?"

It's much better to say:

"Could you tell me what you know about the man who's holding those people hostage?"

"I need to finish getting these people moved out of the line of fire."

"OK, I'll wait."

"Make it ten minutes. I'll meet you right here, then."

At a crime scene, police and fire squads put up barrier tape to keep the public away from evidence and danger. Reporters have the privilege of crossing these barriers, but they should not abuse this privilege.

Reporters who pick up guns at murder sites to read their caliber may end up becoming murder victims themselves. When a fire squad has to haul a reporter out of a burning building, that reporter should expect to get no more new leads from the fire department. A pleasant attitude and sensible caution will always extract more information than a bellicose stance and foolhardy behavior.

As in any relationship, it takes time to build trust with police and firefighters. Do not expect a joyous welcome at first. But the reporter who treats public safety officials fairly will soon find open communications.

✦ SPELL NAMES CORRECTLY

People, even those accused of the most horrific crimes, complain bitterly if newspapers misspell their names. People also tell reporters, "Spell it just like it sounds." They have been writing down their names for years, so, of course, the spelling seems easy to them. Always make all interview subjects spell out their names. People spell the name Smith as Smythe, Smithe, Smith, or, like the comic strip character Snuffy, Smif. Take no chances with names. Also, reporters should always get addresses and phone numbers, in case they need to call back for more information later.

✦ CHECK EVERYTHING

The city directory, campus directory, or phone book lists names and addresses; check them all. Check the police roster for spellings; check the names of all public officials. Check the spelling of street names on a city map; business names in the Better Business Bureau guide or in the phone book; athletes' names in the team roster.

This checking serves two purposes. First, it helps avoid the embarrassment of misspelling a name; more important, it will help catch the occasional creep who gives a false name during an interview. Though rare, such jokers can destroy a story and a reporter's reputation.

People who lie about their names have proven that they are liars. That means they probably provided other false information. A reporter who cannot verify a name should drop that source and his or her information. Some larger papers have "dotters," checkers who scan all names for accuracy. Even in such a case, a reporter still should check all names. Better safe than fired, as the newsroom saying goes.

✦ WRITING THE BREAKING STORY

Ten minutes to deadline, Tom Sciara is wrapping up a story about a visit of the governor to town to dedicate the new terminal at Lincoln International. A dull story, with an unexciting lead.

> Governor Franklin Wilbur today dedicated the new TransGlobal Airlines terminal at Lincoln International Airport, saying that the terminal "reflected the commitment of the state to international business and cooperation."
>
> The state helped build the $250 million terminal after a bitter and controversial campaign spearheaded by Governor Wilbur.

It's about 4:45 p.m., and the state edition normally goes to bed at 5 p.m. to get late newsstand sales by 7 p.m. Sciara is just writing the last paragraph when the police scanner starts squawking. The first message sounds confusing, something about a 10-33.

"Gunshots," Sciara thinks. Light number four on the scanner has locked on. That's the State Trooper frequency.

The editor stands up. "Who did the governor story?"

"Me," Sciara says.

"Scan the Lincoln security frequency."

"It's jammed. Something's going on." The phone rings, and Sciara picks it up. It's a student Sciara met at a party.

"I'm covering this dedication for a journalism class," the student, Janine Reid, says. "Somebody took a shot at the governor as he was finishing his address."

Sciara is already typing.

> An unknown assailant fired shots at Governor Franklin Wilbur today during the dedication of the new TransGlobal Airlines terminal at Lincoln International Airport.

At press time, the *Bugle* had no information on the extent of the governor's injuries, if any, or the identity of his assailant.

Earlier, Governor Wilbur dedicated the terminal, saying that the building "reflected the commitment of the state to international business and cooperation."

The state helped build the $250 million terminal after a bitter and controversial campaign spearheaded by Governor Wilbur.

"Was he hurt?" Sciara asks.

"Couldn't tell," responds Reid. "About a dozen state troopers jumped on top of him."

Another reporter comes over to Sciara's desk. "I was listening to the State Trooper frequency. They called St. Jude to ask for an ambulance, and then called back to say they didn't need it, that Snowbird was OK. Snowbird must be today's code for Wilbur."

Sciara returns to the phone, hands poised over the keyboard. "What did you see, Janet?"

"It all happened so quickly. Wilbur was leaving the stage, shaking hands with somebody, and there was a shot. Then state troopers came from every direction. Three grabbed this little short man and hustled him out of the building, and four or five dove on Wilbur. One second it's a boring speech, and the next there are guns everywhere."

The story changes:

An unknown assailant fired shots at Governor Franklin Wilbur today during the dedication of the new TransGlobal Airlines terminal at Lincoln International Airport.

Initial reports indicated that the governor suffered no injuries. At press time the *Bugle* did not know the identity of his assailant.

"Wilbur was leaving the stage, shaking hands with somebody, and there was a shot," said Janine Reid, a student at Lincoln State. "Then state troopers came from every direction.

"Three grabbed this little short man and hustled him out of the building, and four or five dove on Wilbur. One second it's a boring speech, and the next there are guns everywhere."

Earlier, Governor Wilbur dedicated the terminal, saying that the building "reflected the commitment of the state to international business and cooperation."

"I got somebody at the State Troopers' office. A Pat McKinney. She says they've taken a Chester Allison into custody; no charges yet," shouts another reporter.

The editor, looking over Sciara's shoulder, says, "Let's not go with the name yet. It's five; have we got enough to go?"

Sciara nods. "I'll get down to the county jail and see if I can catch them booking this guy. I'll be back before the 7:15 edition goes out."

The state edition runs with the story. Additional information, gathered by 7:15 p.m., makes the final story read:

> A disgruntled former employee faces charges of shooting at Governor Franklin Wilbur today during the dedication of the new TransGlobal Airlines terminal at Lincoln International Airport.
>
> The governor received no injuries. Police have charged Chester Allison, 42, of Bloomberg Hills, with attempted homicide.
>
> State troopers escorted the governor from the building, but he returned to reassure the audience. "I'm just fine—not even nicked," he said.
>
> "Wilbur was leaving the stage, shaking hands with somebody, and there was a shot," said Janine Reid, a student at Lincoln State. "Then state troopers came from every direction.
>
> "Three grabbed this little short man and hustled him out of the building, and four or five dove on Wilbur. One second it's a boring speech, and the next there are guns everywhere."
>
> TransGlobal Airlines (TGA) had fired Allison two weeks ago, said TGA personnel officer Shelly Feingold.
>
> "He was moody, but quiet," Feingold said. "I would never have thought him capable of this."
>
> Earlier, Governor Wilbur dedicated the terminal, saying that the building "reflected the commitment of the state to international business and cooperation."

Almost always, everyone in the newsroom collaborates on breaking news, from a variety of sources. These stories can require more writing than any other type of story because the reporter has to repeatedly rewrite leads. But reporters have fun with breaking stories because they are working at the center of the action. That can generate a rush of adrenaline that many reporters find addictive.

SUMMARY

- Breaking news stories deal with events that happen as the reporter writes the story or with events that have just happened.
- Finding background detail can turn an ordinary story into an excellent one.
- Lead a breaking story with the event that has taken place.
- Avoid cluttering the lead with nonessential detail.
- To get information, ask lots of questions.
- Always verify the spelling of people's names.

IN-CLASS EXERCISES

1. Locate a story that uses extensive backfill. What purposes does the backfill serve? Would the story work without the backfill? Why or why not?

2. Find a story with a lead you think could be simplified for more impact. Rewrite the lead and the story, being sure that the information you remove from the lead is included elsewhere in the story.

3. Find a brief news story in your local newspaper. List 10 questions you might ask, and sources you might pursue, to increase the backfill in the story.

4. Find a story in your local paper, and check the spelling of every name in the story. What resources did you use? Did you find any errors or discrepancies?

5. Find a news story in a national newspaper, and attempt to find a local angle to the story. What sources did you use? What other sources might you have used? Rewrite the story so that the local angle is prominently played.

6. Locate a story in which the backfill seems insufficient for a good understanding of the events that are covered in the story. Devise a list of questions you would ask, and the sources you would locate, to make the backfill better.

7. Find a wire service story in your local newspaper that doesn't present a local angle. Attempt to find a local angle. What sources would you use? What questions would you ask these sources?

OUT-OF-CLASS EXERCISE

Write a breaking news story. This will involve finding a story, and then conducting interviews and research to complete the story. Remember to follow the news formula in your writing.

CHAPTER 16

Ongoing Stories

Ongoing stories, often called **second-cycle stories,** combine elements of the advance and a breaking story. The newspaper may have reported a robbery yesterday. Today, police have surrounded a house where the suspects have barricaded themselves. The ongoing story includes events from the past (the crime) and the future (the storming of the barricade).

In essence, the ongoing story follows a news story that is in the process of happening. Some parts of the story have already happened; some are happening now; and in the most complicated stories, some part of the story has still to happen. Such stories have a complex time peg and verb tense structure. The dynamics of the lead imply that the most timely element, the part of the story that most recently happened, takes precedence. Yet any sort of understanding of the story demands a description of past events, if only in a bare-bones form, very early in the story.

Reporters have to write ongoing stories while the event continues to unfold. Consider:

Police arson investigators continued to search the ruins of the Kramer Furniture Company today for evidence of arson.

"Fires don't often spread that rapidly without some sort of inflammable liquid being involved," Fire Chief Tami Kurzendorf said this morning. "We feel certain there was arson, yet we haven't found any physical evidence to support that theory."

The main showroom and warehouse of the Kramer Furniture Company, at 88 Nevada Road, burned to the ground yesterday afternoon. Fire companies from as far as Upper Gainesville helped keep the fire from spreading to neighboring buildings.

The big fire happened yesterday; today the arson squad tries to figure out how the fire started. The investigation rates an article, but not as elaborate a story as the fire itself earned. The background information, yesterday's events, must go in the summary paragraphs at the top of the story to avoid mystifying readers who missed yesterday's newspaper.

A similar situation appears in stories that, by definition, must unfold over time. Stories on elections and trials, by their nature, will in general involve a good deal of backfilling and providing background on previous events.

✦ THE ONGOING STORY, START TO FINISH

The section that follows presents a series of stories concerning one event. As the stories unfold, new sequencing becomes necessary for making sense of a story that becomes increasingly complex.

Marietta Halloran, Republican candidate for the U.S. House of Representatives for the 13th District, was charged today with driving under the influence, reckless driving, and creating a public hazard.

State Trooper Miguel Santos pulled Halloran over near the Shenandoah County Rest Stop on I-95, where she scored .10 on the new three-part intoxication test. The law considers any score above a .08 legal intoxication.

"I haven't talked to Halloran yet, but I can tell you that I'm sure this is politically motivated," said Brant Bittner, Halloran's campaign manager. "She's said that she'd like to see the State Trooper squad have new leadership, and suddenly they stop her. It sounds like revenge to me."

On the second day comes a comment from the candidate.

A candidate for Congress vows to continue her candidacy despite her arrest yesterday on charges of driving under the influence of alcoholic beverages.

"I won't let this sort of old-fashioned bullying get in the way of serving the public," Marietta Halloran told a group of supporters and well-wishers at a press conference today. "After the election, we'll see who is laughing."

Halloran's arrest came yesterday after an officer stopped her on Interstate 95. The state highway patrol said she scored a .10 on the three-part intoxication test. A score of .08 or higher legally defines intoxication.

A few days later, a poll appears, and so a story goes out as follows:

Marietta Halloran's commanding lead in the 13th Congressional District race has evaporated, according to a new poll. Ahead by 15 percentage points as of Oct. 1, she is now leading James (Jimmy) Franchetti by only two points.

"The decisive factor appears to have been her arrest for driving under the influence," poll director Harvey Kleinbaum said today. "Sixty-eight percent of those we polled said it had altered their opinion of Halloran."

The state highway patrol arrested Halloran Oct. 12 after she scored a .10 on the new three-part intoxication test. A score of .08 or higher legally defines intoxication. She goes to trial Nov. 12, a week after the election.

A separate, parallel story—often called a **sidebar**—might appear after the election to discuss the effects of the arrest.

Newly elected Congressman James (Jimmy) Franchetti said today that the arrest of Marietta Halloran for driving under the influence had "only an infinitesimal effect" on the outcome of the election.

Franchetti Tuesday won the 13th Congressional District seat by a slim margin of 1,200 votes of some 180,000 cast.

Polling results released early this month by a Washington firm, however, told a different story. Some 68 percent of those responding to the survey said that news of Halloran's arrest had had a significant effect on their evaluation of the candidate.

"We ran a good race, and it's a shame people are going to think she handed it to us by getting arrested," Franchetti said. "Our people worked hard, and they, not some fluke, deserve the credit."

Finally comes an article on the trial.

Marietta Halloran, a losing candidate in the recent 13th Congressional District election, pled guilty to a charge of driving under the influence today in County Court. The judge dismissed charges of reckless driving and creating a public hazard. Halloran declined comment.

"She doesn't want to talk to you," said Marcia Sternbergh, Halloran's daughter. "She just wants to be left alone."

The highway patrol arrested Halloran Oct. 12 after she scored .10 on the new three-part intoxication test. Any score above a .08 legally defines intoxication.

Her election opponent, James (Jimmy) Franchetti, has said that the arrest of Halloran had "only an infinitesimal effect" on the outcome of the election.

Franchetti won the 13th Congressional District seat by a slim margin of 1,200 votes of the 180,000 cast.

Ongoing stories often recapitulate previously reported material, using similar if not identical language.

✦ RETROS

Wrap-ups, or **retrospectives (retros),** can be the hardest to write. These stories about the first, 10th, or 50th anniversary of a big event have in common a preoccupation with the past. The big news—the important event—happened long ago, and some conclusion lies in the future. The writer must create an article from somewhere in the middle.

Do not solve this problem by having some public official (firefighter, police officer, federal investigator) examine (poke through, probe, sift) the historic site (still-smoldering wreckage, abandoned farm, twisted metal). In such clichéd pieces, public officials are usually grim-faced "in quest of why this happened," as in:

> In their search for answers, state inspectors continue to examine the data from flight recorders taken from the twin-engined plane that crashed near the Ellingburg airpark last month. Why did the plane radio that it had collided with another plane only two miles from the airpark, when radar showed no other plane for miles?

The question mark in the lead is a dead giveaway that the reporter does not have any answers. Another leaden approach:

> Little Jimmy's toys sit untouched. He stands by the door, waiting for the heavy sound of work boots on the porch, the hearty, "Hi, Jimmy," the hug as his father gets home from work.
> Big Jim Turner will not be home—today, or ever again.

Pathos works in news stories only if the writer does not have to force it. Report facts that will make a reader cry, but avoid commanding the reader to feel something. It just will not work.

To write second-cycle stories, find the best timely news angle possible, and make that the lead. Use the summary paragraphs for a quick synopsis of the previous events, and then stick Little Jimmy down where he belongs, in straight quotes, played straight. If Little Jimmy will not say he misses his father, do not surmise that he does.

> One year ago today, Deputy Jim Turner died in a courthouse shoot-out. Authorities never found his assailant.
> At his son Jimmy's high school graduation, Jimmy and his friends talked and thought about his dad.
> "Dad would have been proud," Jimmy said. "And I guess I'll go into law enforcement. Dad taught me that there was no better way to spend your life than helping others, and that's what I intend to do."

Straight quotes, played straight, can have an emotional impact far beyond that of hoked-up approaches. Readers have, by now, seen all the possible gimmicks; but the real article, delivered without fuss, can give even the most jaded readers pause.

A particular variant of the retro story, the business anniversary story, can cause trouble. Usually, the firm plans the anniversary in hopes of getting some favorable publicity. The reporter who attends the celebration, in whatever form it takes, will usually receive a packet of information about the firm, including a press release written in news story format but containing only favorable information on the firm.

Often the event will also include stiff drinks and high-calorie snacks. By the time the reporter gets back to the paper, head spinning from too much sugar and sherry, temptation says to give the press release a slight gloss and run it. These stories usually read something like:

> Chelmsford Print Works celebrated the 50th anniversary of its founding today, marking what President Fiona Barbers described as "a half-century of service to our beloved city."
>
> Chelmsford has some 2,400 employees, and pays approximately $2 million per year in taxes to Hart County.
>
> "We know we've given a lot to the community, but the community has given more, much more, in return," said Barbers.

And so forth.

The enterprising reporter would include events outside the celebration as well. Interesting facts would add a conflict angle to an otherwise dull story.

> Chelmsford Print Works celebrated the 50th anniversary of its founding today, marking what President Fiona Barbers described as "a half-century of service to our beloved city."
>
> Protesters outside, however, demonstrated against the environmental record of Chelmsford. "A Half Century of Toxic Waste," read one placard. "Chelmsford Pollutes Rheims Creek," read another.
>
> "We tried to get into their little party, but their security people barred us," said Tammy Agnew, head of a group called Stop Toxins Or Pollutants, or STOP. "I guess they don't want any version of the facts getting out but their doctored one."
>
> Chelmsford, which has some 2,400 employees, has been repeatedly sued by STOP. In 10 court cases, Chelmsford has paid out almost $1 million in damages.

The reporter who relies on press releases and official speeches at retrospective stories will get a prettified version of reality.

✦ SPORTS

The ongoing sports story not only describes the outcome of a single match; it also places the outcome in larger perspective by presenting a team's standings, chances of invitations to the league tournament, or past performances. Thus, the average sports story, by placing the outcome of the most recent event in perspective, classifies as an ongoing story.

> Carl Sandburg High School's Terrapins lost 7-14 to the Oakwood Lions in the 4-A football tournament game held in Forest City last night.
>
> "We played as well as we've ever played," said Jerry Schildt, coach of the Terrapins. "Getting to the tournament was a major thrill.
>
> "We always tell the boys that playing well is more important than winning, and by that standard, we're winners."
>
> The Terrapins won every game in regular-season play, with quarterback Jerome Chatham receiving the state's Most Valuable Quarterback award two weeks ago.
>
> Oakwood dominated the game throughout, with a defensive line Schildt described as "awesome."
>
> "They played like pros," Schildt said. "Their line was undefeatable."

Much of the interest of the story lies in the game as a capstone for the entire season.

Many beginning sportswriters find it tempting to trick up the lead by trying to write colorfully. The outcome can mumble like this:

> Bats blazing, the Memphis Blues slammed in four straight home runs against the Bulldogs in the sixth inning to clinch a playoff berth in the South Atlantic League's 2-A competition.

Playing it straight works better. Putting the outcome of the game in the first sentence and the significance of the outcome in the second, and losing the blazing bats—a repellent image—will improve the story.

Sportswriting, more than any other genre, lends itself to mumblers. Sportswriters must choose to lead with only one factor, either the outcome of the current match or the significance of that outcome. Also, sportswriting tends to rely on overheated language.

Tech Talk

Sportswriters also sin by using technical language and sports slang the average reader cannot understand.

Zenk looked at the lights after a German suplex, followed by a Thesz press, by Garvin. The crowd popped big for a chair shot ref Teddy Long took from Freeb Hayes.

German suplex? Thesz press? Chair shot? A popping crowd? A Freeb? Most readers would never understand these lines about professional wrestling. Equally incomprehensible is:

Ellen Warburg, a senior at West State and captain of the volleyball team, won the "Spiker of the Year" award from the state sportswriters association for her play in the regional semifinals. The sportswriters' citation described Warburg's spiking as "incendiary."

By this point, the writer has lost all but the hard-core volleyball fans. Most baseball stories read just as incomprehensibly to most of the newspaper audience.

Avoid tech talk and slang whenever possible, because newspapers should neither confuse nor mystify. Tech talk in sports stories confuses uninitiated readers.

Using a term like *Frankensteiner* in a wrestling trade journal makes sense. An article in an equestrian journal can call a jump a *Helsinki*. For general newspaper audiences, though, only use terms that most people would understand.

When quotes contain phrases that readers may not know, do not use brackets to include definitions. They talk down to the reader.

"Thoms was eliminated right after me," Green said. "That Helsinki [a jump with side panels] was the jump that decided who'll be in the Pan Am games."

Instead, paraphrase a quotation that includes technical jargon. Use a separate sentence to define the technical term.

Thoms lost her place in the Pan Am games at a Helsinki, a jump with side panels that often confuse horses, said Green.

Balance

Unfortunately, partisanship dominates the coverage in many sports pages. Some editors assume that all readers root for the hometown team. Cheering for any side in an athletic competition is editorializing. Avoid this. Readers do care about what happened, but favoritism for any one team represents, in some readers' eyes, support for the wrong team.

✦ TRIALS

Court reporting involves many of the difficulties of second-cycle stories. Jury selection, often dull, can go on for days; lengthy forensic testimony of a highly technical nature can drag on for weeks. Although court reporting involves tedium, trials can also offer high drama. The battle between two opposing sides inevitably provides a strong conflict angle.

To write a court story, use the first one or two paragraphs of the summary section to recap previous action:

> A University of Kansas student accused of stealing hundreds of valuable artifacts from an archaeological site today protested in court what he called "the clearly prejudiced nature" of his trial.
>
> "I want it known that I'm being mistreated," said Jerome K. Stallings, 31, of Poland City. "I've done nothing wrong, and yet I'm being kept in horrible conditions."
>
> Stallings was student director of an archaeological expedition to Venezuela. On this trip, 380 pottery shards and ceramic figures, worth about $400,000 on the black market, disappeared.
>
> The district attorney has charged that Stallings sold a figurine to an undercover agent of the Venezuelan government.
>
> Throughout the trial, Stallings has maintained his innocence.

SUMMARY

- An ongoing story combines events that happened yesterday with events that happened today.
- Avoid using clichés or pathos in retros.
- Sports stories combine the outcome of a single match with an analysis of the effect this match will have on the team's season standing.
- Avoid using technical language, including sports slang, in news stories.
- To write a court story, use the first one or two paragraphs of the summary section to recap events from previous days.

IN-CLASS EXERCISES

1. Find an ongoing story in your local newspaper. What is the backfill? What is the lead? What is the time peg in the lead, and what was the time of the actual event?

2. Locate an ongoing story in your local newspaper, and find the original story from the issue when the story in question first broke. How much of the new story is taken from the original breaking story? What are the time pegs in the respective stories? Which story do you find most interesting? Why?

3. Find a retrospective story in your local newspaper. What is the back-fill? What is the lead? What are the five Ws in the lead?

4. Find a wrap-up story that uses pathos. Does the story work? Why or why not? How might you rewrite the story in order to strengthen its impact? Why do you think that would work?

5. Find an ongoing court story in a local or national paper. What is the lead? What are the five Ws in the lead? What is the backfill? What is the time peg of the lead? Of the backfill? Does this story work? Why or why not?

6. Locate an ongoing story on a television news program. What is the backfill? What is the lead? What is the time peg in the lead, and what was the time of the actual event? Locate a newspaper story on the same event. Are the time peg, the backfill, and the lead the same? Why or why not?

7. Find an ongoing story in your local newspaper. When and if a retro-spective story is done on the event covered in the story, what questions will it seek to answer, and why?

OUT-OF-CLASS EXERCISE

Write an ongoing news story of some event on campus or in your community. This will involve finding an ongoing story, and then conducting interviews and research to complete the story. An important part of your research will be finding previously written stories about the topic to draw from. Remember to follow the news formula in your writing.

PART THREE

The News Business

CHAPTER 17

Professionalism

Professionalism, an attribute that everyone admires and respects, includes the concepts of preparedness, knowledgeability, willingness and ability to work with others, and expertise. Perceptions of professionalism are often derived from first impressions and snap judgments on the part of editors, sources, and the community. Even when wrong, these perceptions help people decide whether to cooperate with a reporter or to stonewall.

For example, think about customers in a restaurant. When they enter, they expect a staff member to seat them promptly at a clean table. Timeliness and cleanliness help define a good restaurant. Professionalism can also involve other less rational but no less important attributes. Given a choice between a physician in a loud Hawaiian shirt and one wearing a white lab smock, most people would prefer to receive care from the doctor in a smock, even though everyone knows that clothing makes no difference in the ability of a doctor to perform medicine. People expect professionals to have the tools they need at hand. They suspect a dentist who must go looking for his little mirror, and similarly, sources suspect reporters who have to fish in their pockets for pens or pencils.

Some things about a reporter's professionalism on the job have to do with ability, but others (like appearance) have more to do with overall impressions than with actual skills. Yet even these seemingly minor matters help create the overall impression that sources, editors, and the world at large have of a reporter, and it's those impressions that people use to decide whom to talk to and whom to freeze out.

✦ KNOW THE EQUIPMENT

Imagine the impression conveyed by reporters whose hands shake as they set up their tape recorders in front of sources, or who ask to borrow pens from sources. Since this looks like disorganization and inexperience, sources might well worry about how accurately such reporters will quote them in the resulting article. A source in an interview with such a reporter would quite rightly give out very little information.

A reporter has asked a source to set aside time for the interview—time the source could be spending elsewhere. Sources want to help, but reporters should help too by having their tools ready at hand and in working condition.

✦ KEEP THINGS NEAT

In the same way that having the tools of the trade handy makes a difference in the impression sources have of a reporter, keeping things orderly at work is important. Fairly or unfairly, many people believe the old adage: A cluttered desk means a cluttered mind. In contrast to many other professionals, reporters usually have desks that sit out in the open in newsrooms where any clutter displays itself not only to coworkers and editors but also to sources who come into the newsroom for interviews. A messy work area can decrease efficiency. Of course, editors and coworkers will overlook a messy desk, but a reporter would do better to avoid giving colleagues, employers, and sources something to overlook.

One situation demands neatness. At newspapers where separate morning and evening staffs share a newsroom, reporters for the morning and evening editions often share desks. In this case a mess at the end of the workday becomes somebody else's problem, too. Coffee-machine conversations at these newspapers often feature tales of fishing other reporters' half-eaten tacos out of desk drawers.

✦ BE PREPARED

Reporters need to have pencil, paper, and tape recorder ready when meeting a source, but they also need to prepare intellectually. The first question the reporter asks should be trenchant and to the point, and should cover new ground. The first question establishes important initial impressions that will determine how the remainder of the interview goes. A reporter who begins with a fumbling, general question—the sort of question that asks the source to explain the story—does not inspire trust. To avoid this, the reporter needs to acquire some background before going to the interview. Nothing puts off a source quite like having to answer the same questions another reporter from the same newspaper asked yesterday.

The first question carries particular weight for beginning reporters. Sources often think beginners will go easy on them, and sometimes they do not take these reporters seriously. A first question that is well-constructed, well-informed, to the point, and trenchant can tell sources they are working with professionals.

✦ DRESS PROFESSIONALLY

Clothing does help convey a first impression. Those dress-for-success books make the point that looking professional does not necessarily mean dressing stylishly, but it does mean more or less meeting the expectations of other people in the workplace. Sources, editors, and the myriad others with whom the reporter has contact expect men and women to wear clean, neat, comfortable clothes similar to those worn by other people attending the event they are covering. An interview with a diva after a concert will demand different dress from a day-in-the-life story about a landfill supervisor.

As students, many future reporters may have dressed in thrift-store grunge, but clothes that worked on the quad may not help a newsroom career. Quite often, a kindly senior reporter will take the new staffer on a trip to a local clothing store, pointing out items that might work well. The clever novice heeds such well-meant advice.

✦ AVOID WEIRDNESS

Since reporters depend on people's trust for their livelihood, they should play down things that might make them seem strange. A reporter may, for example, have an encyclopedic knowledge of professional wrestling, but a recent picture of the writer at Madison Square Garden with an arm around Chief Wahoo McDaniel may not impress the mayor. Such an interest is fine, but discussing it with a potential source while flashing the photo with pride may not convey just the right impression. When sources perceive weirdness, they worry about weird treatment in the article. Into this category, too, fall hair pulled over to cover a bald spot, tight clothing, dramatic fingernails, and exotic hairstyles.

Smoking clove cigarettes, carrying a copy of Chairman Mao's little red book, or wearing dramatic colognes may make interesting personal statements, but they do not earn the trust of sources. After a reporter has gained that trust, then maybe the time has arrived to share a clove cigarette or describe the ant farm in the living room at home.

✦ MAINTAIN A PROFESSIONAL DEMEANOR

Overly friendly or familiar approaches also have a tendency to turn sources into clams, because they seem so ungenuine. Hostile or confrontational stances work even less well. People will not confide in someone who threatens them.

Unfortunately, many novices, overestimating the power of the press, subconsciously think that they can command sources to tell everything. Reporters do have rights, and can indeed (on some occasions) force certain public officials to reveal some kinds of information. Yet constantly reminding a source of the rights of the press, or of the right of the public to know, or of the ace legal staff at the newspaper, merely antagonizes people. A professional approach, cordial without being familiar, respectful without being subservient, works best.

Many beginning reporters have trouble dealing with local police officers and sheriff's deputies. The deputy and the reporter at first seem to have very little in common. The police have important work to do at a crime site, as do reporters, but for the reporters to do their job, they have to convince officers to talk with them. Unfortunately, some police miss the fact that working with reporters is part of their job. When reporters suggest, by word or by general attitude, that police officers must talk to them, many will respond with irritation.

Often, even polite and understanding reporters get the brush-off from officers who have been burned by other reporters in the past. Sometimes a friendly call from an editor to a police chief can solve this problem, but the commonly used approach of telling an officer about the First Amendment rights of the reporter will always fail and will often increase animosity. When one source will not talk, try another, and avoid getting into arguments with the police about the press's rights versus theirs. Write a good, fair, accurate story. Over time, the police will evaluate a reporter and decide to become more chatty.

✦ SHOW TRUSTWORTHINESS

If a reporter says, "I never reveal the names of my sources," that had better mean not only "never have," but also "never will." If something is on the record, the reporter needs to say so. When something goes off the record, the reporter has an obligation to make sure that it stays that way. Word spreads in a community, and reporters who violate the confidence of one source will likely find several more who are uninterested in speaking with them.

In general, a reporter would do best to avoid off-the-record information. Start all interviews on the record by having a tape recorder in plain sight and running, and by writing in a notebook. If a source asks to keep information off the record, ask what the source means. Does the source mean that the newspaper can print the information, but not say who said it? In that case, of course, the information has little value. Does the source mean that the reporter can tell some other source about the information, and ask that source to confirm it? Or does the source mean that the newspaper cannot use it in any way? As a rule, accept information off the record only if it can be had in no other way. Off-the-record information tends to decrease the trust between reporter and source, because no matter how the newspaper uses it, sources may believe themselves compromised.

✦ SHOW AN INTEREST IN ACCURACY

Most sources worry mainly about the accuracy of the story in which they will appear. Since the source may not recall having read anything the reporter has written, the subject may well depend on subtle cues to evaluate the reliability of a reporter. The reporter who takes no notes at all, relying solely on a tape recorder, looks lazy. The reporter who takes no notes and uses no tape recorder looks scary. Reporters prepared with notebook, tape recorder, and questions, on the other hand, look trustworthy. These cues, minor as they may seem, often make the difference between getting the story and missing it.

Other cues go more directly to perceptions of self-confidence. In the United States, a weak handshake indicates weakness and fear. Looking a source directly in the eyes shows honesty. Confident body language matters.

✦ KNOW THE NEWSPAPER'S HISTORY

Longtime city and county employees will have talked to numerous reporters from a local newspaper over the years, and will know a good bit about the history of the newspaper. They will naturally view this as a good topic for conversational warming-up, and so a fairly standard opening comment the beginning reporter may hear is, "Gee, how's old Irv enjoying retirement?" Knowing that Irv likes fishing in Florida may seem trivial, but it indicates an interest in the newspaper and in one's prede-cessor. Subliminally, it indicates that sources can trust this reporter just as they trusted good ol' Irv. Beginning reporters should ask some questions about their predecessors, and should be familiar with the history of their newspaper. This little thing can make a difference in getting off to a good start.

✦ DON'T TAKE FREEBIES

Quite often, reporters will find themselves offered little things by sources. Although one might envision huge bribes of stacks of hundred-dollar bills, sources usually offer lunch, or a couple of free tickets to a ball game, or even something like a free brake job. To avoid bias, avoid accepting freebies. The $10,000 gift is an obvious bribe in exchange for a favor, but it differs from a doughnut only in size. Reporters have a hard enough time writing without bias under the best conditions, but there is a subtle but real psychological pressure on the reporter not to report unflattering information about a source who has done the reporter a favor, even of the smallest kind. Most newspapers' strict policies against freebies, even little things, make sense.

✦ AVOID TIME-KILLERS

Professional time-wasters are people who do not have enough to do, or have something to do but don't want to do it. Instead of doing whatever they ought to do, they hang out in the newspaper office, starting con-versations by chattering idly about how much work they have to do. An hour later, still there, they have not only not gotten their work done but have also kept the reporter from working. Similarly, some sources will keep a reporter in their offices for hours, jabbering about random sub-jects. Reporters who face such sources should try to exit quickly.

✦ START AT THE BOTTOM

Some people can give reporters the information they seek. Although a reporter naturally tends to go to the person highest on the organizational chart, usually that will not work.

The higher people sit in an organization, the more subjects they know about, but the less information they have on any single subject. The superintendent of schools for a county will know something about trouble with a single teacher, but the principal of the school where the teacher works will know the most. The right person to interview usually has the lowest rank in the organization—in this case, the principal. Further, sources lower in rank generally speak to fewer reporters and will cooperate more. The superintendent of schools in many counties may see a reporter every other day, but the average principal who talks to the press infrequently may well see an interview as a treat.

Start information-gathering at the lowest level. Secretaries, bailiffs, and housekeepers have lots of information. Many of these sources resent being overlooked by reporters who start at the top. It may be easy to dial the top person in an organization, but the people actually working with a problem know the most about it.

✦ KNOW HOW TO WORK WITH PHOTOGRAPHERS

Photographers and graphic artists—people who produce visual images—are as important to a newspaper's success as writers. Since striking photographs, snazzy graphics, and attractive layout make real differences not only in newsstand sales but in subscriber satisfaction, newspapers, in competing with more visual media like television, have begun to pay ever more attention to graphic images.

Some newspaper reporters who have been around since the days before serious competition from television treat photographers and artists with contempt, but the wise reporter knows that a striking and apt photograph or a telling chart can brighten a dull story and make a good story better.

The reporter who makes the effort to help set up photographs and graphics will receive appreciation from colleagues and bosses.

Understanding the Photographer

A reporter working with photographers needs to understand their limitations and their needs. Requesting shots that a camera cannot take antagonizes photographers. Photographs need light. Indoors, often not enough light exists for a photo. The human eye, far more sensitive than even the fastest lens, can pick up plenty that the camera cannot. In general, the lighting must be beyond standard room lighting for the camera to capture an image. Usually, that means flood or television lights, or a well-lit stage. Photographers can push their film, which means they develop it for a longer time than normal, or they can use a flash in situations with less light than flood or stage lighting.

Photographic flash units have their own limitations. Since the distance of the subject from the flash unit determines its brightness, all the important elements in the photograph must be more or less the same distance from the camera for the exposure to work out well. When some element of the photograph is too close to the flash unit, that object dissolves in white light. Photographers call this the "Casper effect," after the pale and washed-out form of the cartoon character Casper, the Friendly Ghost. Elements too far from the flash disappear into the shadows. The photographer will generally want to position all the important elements of a flash photograph at the same distance from the flash unit.

Outdoors, photographers have more flexibility. They particularly love cloudy days because on a sunny day they must fight deep shadows. Some sun and some shade make it extremely difficult to get a good photograph. For instance, if the photographer exposes for the sunlit parts, the shaded parts come out too dark. In particular, the head-and-shoulder shots that pepper modern newspapers have this malady. Overhead sun can create shadows on the face from hair, eyebrows, nose, and upper lip, giving the subject zebra stripes. Photographers particularly hate hats. A cowgirl may look great in person, but in her photo, her face will disappear into deep shade under the hat.

Up Close Is Better Than Far Away

Photographers must get as close to their subjects as possible. The reproduction of photographs in newspapers has improved vastly in the last 15 years, but it is still relatively poor. Small details in the original print vanish into grayness in the newspaper reproduction process. Newspapers print photographs by reducing them to a series of little dots of ink, called a halftone.

Good photographs involve a single dominant element, which fills the frame. Usually, photos emphasize faces because people make judgments of character by looking at the faces of newsmakers. A photo for a story about an architect and her creations, for instance, should emphasize the architect's face in the photograph more than the building she designed. The building might—and probably should—serve as a backdrop, but photographs should emphasize people.

Setting Up the Photograph

A photograph should support the article it accompanies. To communicate with photographers, a reporter should describe the lead of the story instead of the picture the story needs. Usually, the photographer will then set up the photograph, while the reporter gathers the final bits of information. If the photographer proposes several different photo ideas, the reporter should respond, "Gee, those all sound good. Why not take them all?"

Newspaper photographers have a saying: "Film is cheap." Be pleased with a photographer who gets as many shots as possible.

◆ WORKING WITH GRAPHICS

Increasingly, editors want reporters to return from assignments with data an artist can turn into graphics. Many stories involve numbers as well as other facts, and it makes good sense to utilize that information to create eye-catching pie charts and line graphs.

Most newspapers use three kinds of graphs. When the information involves percentages of some total, an artist will usually do a pie chart. When the information involves a trend over time, an artist usually does a line graph. When the information compares the size of several things, the newspaper often does a bar chart.

The type of information determines the type of chart that accompanies the article. To report percentages, the reporter needs to find that the percentages add up to 100. If the data runs over time, the reporter has to gather data for each and every time period from the beginning to the end. If the data compares sizes, incomes, or the like over time, the reporter must get a number for every relevant category.

Reporters have a significant role to play in the graphic appearance of the newspaper. Graphs and charts please readers as well as editors—and the clever reporter will not only collect information for graphs when ordered, but will seek out such information at every opportunity.

SUMMARY

- Professionalism helps a reporter succeed in the newspaper business.
- Keep things neat.
- Bring the right equipment, and be prepared.
- Dress appropriately.
- Avoid weirdness; maintain a professional demeanor.
- Show trustworthiness and an interest in accuracy.
- Avoid freebies and time-killers.
- Start at the bottom when seeking sources.

- Get out of the way and let photographers work.
- If the story involves numbers, collect enough data for a graph.

IN-CLASS EXERCISES

1. Select an article from your local newspaper. List all the possible sources you might approach to gain information for a follow-up story on the topic. For each potential source, list (a) how much information that source would be able to provide and (b) how likely that person would be to talk to a reporter. Can you draw any conclusions about which sort of source could provide information and would be willing to talk?

2. Working in pairs, interview another member of your class and take notes. At the same time, tape-record your interview. Now, working from your notes, prepare quotes as you would for an article. Now listen to your tape. How accurately did you reproduce the quotes?

3. Find a story in your local newspaper that presents numerical information. Write down the numerical information, and devise and sketch an appropriate graphic, chart, or illustration for the story. Why did you select the format you chose?

4. In your local newspaper, locate a news story that has no photograph with it. Write the instructions you would have given the photographer had you written that story. Who would you have the photographer photograph? How would you have the subject positioned? What item would you include in the photograph? Why? What news value would you seek to maximize?

5. What sort of behaviors do you associate with professionalism? Why? How would a reporter display those qualities?

6. Locate the unemployment statistics for your county for the last two years. Write a lead for a story about these statistics, and sketch a graphic using the statistics to illustrate the story.

7. In your local newspaper, locate a news story that has no graphics with it. What graphics could be added to enhance the story? Write the instructions you would have given the artist had you written the story. What would you have the graphics contain, and why?

OUT-OF-CLASS EXERCISE

Interview a campus or local official, taking notes and taping the interview. Pay particular attention to how you are treated, what is said, and the like.

Write a page or two on how your source responded to you. What things that you did seemed to work? What things didn't? What things would you do differently in the future?

Now, write your story in about three pages, using your notes. Then use your tapes to prepare a second, corrected version. In about a page, describe the differences between the two versions. What conclusions can you draw from this?

Working

Efficiently

A hidden factor (inefficient work habits) makes or breaks most journalism careers. To succeed, a journalist has to have writing ability, interviewing skills, and news judgment, but lots of reporters have these. Even though all reporters have the same number of hours in their working day, lack of time drives many reporters out of the news business.

Work habits that served very well in college can hurt a newspaper career. In college, many students spend a great deal of time stewing over a term paper, researching it very carefully over a long period. Slowly and painfully, they produce a first draft. Then they rework and rework their drafts.

One beginning reporter the authors know found himself working 60 hours a week for 40 hours of pay, and his editor nagged continuously for more copy. One day, the editor sat the reporter down for an in-depth discussion of the reporter's low productivity.

It turned out that the reporter had a serious time management problem. The reporter hated to use the telephone, arguing that personal interviews worked better. Consequently, he left the office and did an in-person interview for every story.

On top of that, when he returned to the office he spent an hour typing out his handwritten notes so they were easy to read. Only after this retyping did he begin to compose a news story. After some gentle hints from his editor, by doing more telephone interviews, and writing his articles directly from his notes without first transcribing them, he cut back to a 40-hour workweek—and began filing more copy, as well. He had to give up the slow and careful style that had earned him such success in college.

This chapter describes some strategies for using time efficiently in a newspaper job. For the student in college, they may sound counterintuitive—but college isn't always like the real world.

✦ THE DAILINESS OF NEWSPAPERING

Reporters love their jobs because daily a team of journalists can hold in their hands a final product—a copy of that day's edition of the newspaper. Journalists, like construction workers, build things.

An electrician will drive by a house and say, "See that house? I did all the wiring in there. The architect gave us some nonsense blueprints, but I managed to get the wiring together so circuit breakers don't pop all the time." A journalist says, "See this newspaper? Getting that front-page story in there was really tough. I had to pound those keys on deadline, but I did it and here's the story."

Only rare jobs allow workers regularly to hold finished products in their hands and say, "Look at this. I made it." Most people do routine tasks day after day. These tasks contribute to an end product, but the workers rarely see the product.

Department store managers lead their teams, fill out affirmative action reports, hire and fire. They can never really hold end products in their hands because department stores sell the things that others make.

Third-grade teachers give their students information on reading, writing, and arithmetic, but they rarely see the finished product—the educated young adults their pupils grow into. University fund-raisers spend most of their time meeting and greeting people, planting seeds about the worth of their institutions. Only in the fullness of time do these seeds mature into large bequests.

Every day, journalists hold in their hands newspapers they helped make. They work as craftsmen, daily building documents for people to hold in their hands and read. The dailiness of newspapering makes journalism a great job—but this dailiness, the necessity of producing an end product, also can make newspapering anguish for some people.

In journalism, ready or not, every day a newspaper must come off the presses. No journalist can say, "Well, today nothing really interesting happened, so let's just not publish an edition." Journalists have to publish, and a daily paper comes out once a day no matter what the interest of that day's events, no matter what sort of mood the newspaper's staffers are in. This necessity to gather information and get it written up in time to have something to fill the newspaper creates tremendous pressure.

✦ USE THE TELEPHONE FOR INTERVIEWS

The quickest time-saver in journalism is the telephone. Without question, reporters get more and better information during a person-to-person interview than over the telephone. In terms of time management, though, a telephone is a much more efficient way to gather information.

To do person-to-person interviews, reporters have to call and schedule meetings. Then they have to get in the car and drive to wherever they're to meet their sources. After the interview, reporters have to drive back, and, often enough, they take time out to drop by the convenience store to pick up a soda. Efficient reporters save this driving time by just using the telephone.

Also, when reporters do phone interviews, they can type notes directly into their computers. Then, when they write their stories, they can just move the quotes into their story files. They avoid having to type the quotes out from their handwritten notes.

An in-person interview runs longer than a telephone interview. To start a person-to-person interview, two people must go through the essential social niceties. "Nice weather today," they have to say to each other before getting down to business. In contrast, the rules for proper telephone behavior call for brevity. Telephone courtesy dispenses with the necessity to conduct a cordial discussion of the weather, sports, or current events before the two people can get to the purpose of their conversation.

Usually, over the telephone, a reporter can do the interview itself in about the time it takes to make an appointment to speak with a source in person. Of course, sometimes reporters must do person-to-person interviews; for information on this, see Chapter 8. But for many, if not most, of the standard situations reporters face, phone interviews are the norm.

✦ GATHER INFORMATION FOR SEVERAL STORIES AT ONCE

Chaos defines the news business, and a beginning reporter needs to learn how to move through this chaos. Experienced reporter Carolyn Feinstein has received a county planning board agenda in the mail. The county wants to cut down two ancient oak trees sitting on a traffic island in the middle of San Francisco Drive. The neighborhood loves its ancient oaks, and so a conflict angle—the heart of an interesting news story—presents itself.

To do a story, Feinstein needs to do two interviews: one with the county planning director and another with the president of the neighborhood association. Feinstein calls the planning director, but she is in conference. So the reporter leaves a message for her to call back. Then Feinstein tries the neighborhood association president, but he is in transit from home to office. So the reporter leaves another message. The threatened oak trees must wait until these two sources call back.

Feinstein would love to just concentrate on one story and only begin gathering information for a second when the first one has gone to the editor. While waiting for calls back about the oak tree, Feinstein could go get a cup of coffee or chat with a coworker. Then she could try again to get the two sources on the phone—but, as an experienced news writer, she knows she can use her time more efficiently. Thus, she starts to work on another story while she waits for the sources on the oak trees to call back.

Feinstein also has to write up the sheriff's calls for the day. After leaving messages about the oak trees, Feinstein calls the sheriff's office and gets information. Then, she can write up the sheriff's information while waiting for her other calls to come in.

Feinstein starts her workday by getting as many phone calls out as possible. Eventually, she will find a source to interview. In the meantime she has left callbacks for the other people. Then, Feinstein can start producing copy while waiting for other information to come in.

Every two or three hours, Feinstein takes stock of the day's assignments. Maybe she needs to try calling back the people who have not returned her calls. She can then stop writing and do another round of phone calls to harvest more information.

Reporter Feinstein tries to be flexible. She will jump from writing assignment to writing assignment, and gather information as she can find people to interview. In the slack times, when she can find no one she needs to interview, she writes.

Thus, as a general rule, the most productive reporters set up their days so that they attempt to arrange all their interviews at the very beginning of the day. If sources are unavailable—out of town, say—then they have all day to try to find someone else to talk to. If sources are out of the office, they learn early on when they will be available, and can then schedule the rest of their day around the availability of their sources. And the sources that are available get interviewed early, so the reporter has something to start writing about.

✦ WRITE ONLY ONE STORY AT A TIME

Gathering information on many stories at the same time improves efficiency, but Feinstein has learned that she should work on only one piece of writing at a time. The news formula shows a reporter how to write an article quickly. Because it should take less than an hour to write any but the most complex story, the reporter tries to concentrate on just one piece at a time. Trying to write two leads at once, or leaping back and forth between articles, muddles each piece of writing because changing from story to story interferes with a reporter's concentration.

While Feinstein waits for callbacks on the oak trees, she calls the sheriff and gets all the information she needs to write up the police calls. She is writing the third paragraph of her sheriff story when the phone rings. The neighborhood association president can now talk about the importance of saving those trees. She does the interview. Just as she hangs up, the county planning director calls her back. She does that interview too.

Now she has everything together to write the oak trees story, but she still waits to start that piece. First, she needs to complete the article about the sheriff. Since she has already written three paragraphs—including the most critical, the lead—she knows the direction the article will take. She has already decided what information she will bring up, and in what order.

If she writes another story or two before returning to the sheriff's calls, she may well lose her train of thought on the sheriff story. When she finally gets back to the sheriff, she will have to review her notes to remember just what she planned to say, and then reread her first three paragraphs and replan the story.

Even though she now has all the oak tree information amassed, Feinstein goes back and finishes the sheriff story. Even with the sheriff story done, she still does not start writing about oak trees. She wants to keep at least two stories working at once.

She also has an advance to do on a community theater production of *Hamlet*. Before starting to write up the oak trees, Feinstein calls the director to get some quotes about the production. She strikes pay dirt—the director answers the phone.

After talking with the drama director, she can now begin writing about the oak trees. When she gets that piece done, she will start gathering information on a fourth story and then turn to writing up the play.

Feinstein tries to finish writing one story before beginning to write a second, but she also always has feelers out. While she writes up one story, she also starts gathering information for her next one.

Our best advice for beginning news writers, then, is to write only one story at a time. The reporter is gathering information for several stories at one time, but writing only one. Trying to write more than one story at once introduces confusion; a reporter who doesn't know which story a quote belongs to is in serious trouble.

✦ CONTROL INTERRUPTIONS

During her workday Feinstein tries to perform an orderly little dance: interview, then write, interview, then write. Unexpected interruptions can keep her from sticking to this dance.

The phone rings. An angry reader wants to discuss a story from last week's paper. Another reporter sits down on the edge of the desk to talk about the new music club in town. The editor wants to talk about a problem with a story. Someone is making a sandwich run, and wants to know what Feinstein wants to eat.

The electricity goes off and all the computers die. A plane crashes, an earthquake strikes, a tornado roars through a neighboring town, and the entire newsroom empties, with everyone rushing out to cover the event.

Peace and order do not reign in journalism. In newsrooms, some people write away while others do interviews and others take breaks to joke around. There's always some reporter who believes that creativity is enhanced by country music, one who hums tunelessly while writing, others who write so quickly that they spend most of their mornings just wandering around the newsroom, distracting the other staffers. People are talking, the building shakes when the presses roll, phones ring, terminals beep, and the police scanner squalls and toots. All reporters learn to concentrate despite the normal newsroom chaos.

In terms of time management, reporters have to learn to discourage people who interrupt. Feinstein has learned to say no.

To the phone caller Feinstein says, "I cannot talk to you right now. Can I call you back?"

To the music fan she says, "I'm right in the middle of this piece. You want to go get coffee in half an hour?"

To the editor she says, "I'm right in the middle of this story; can I talk to you in 15 minutes?"

In general, if Feinstein is in the middle of a piece of writing, she explains this to her visitor and tries to set up another time to chat. Other professional writers will understand this; professional interrupters will think it rude, but at least they'll bother somebody else.

A reporter must heed some interruptions, though, when they happen. If the electricity goes off, writing on a computer stops. Then Feinstein has to figure out something else to do. She makes a phone call, she gets some coffee, or she sits back and curses the gods of electricity who have just eaten her brilliant piece of writing. In the worst case, she reverts to a legal pad.

When someone interrupts to offer to make a sandwich run, she does not snarl. She blesses him.

To the sandwich buyer Feinstein says, "Oh, thank you. Thank you. I'll take a ham on rye with mustard and an iced tea. Here is a five-dollar bill."

If a major disaster strikes, Feinstein gives up the oak trees, grabs her notebook, and joins everyone else in the scramble to cover the event.

The routine day, though, features lots of casual incidents and no natural disasters. To the interrupters the reporter needs to say, "It's not convenient for me to talk now. Can we talk in 15 minutes or half an hour or an hour?"

In general, then, reporters have to guard their time carefully. Writing is hard work, and there are thousands of possible distractions in a newsroom. Part of being a successful reporter is learning how to ignore the distractions and keep working. Every editor knows that there are reporters who get twice as much work done in half the time as their coworkers. Try to be one of them.

◆ EVADE GAMES OF PASS THE POTATO

Frequently when a reporter calls for information, the source responds, "I don't really know much about that. You need to call Fred Jones." So the reporter calls Jones, who says, "I don't really know much about that. You need to call Sally Rivera." So the reporter calls Rivera, who says, "I don't really know much about that. You need to call Mamie Grueber." And guess who Grueber is? The first person the reporter talked to.

People often try to evade interviews with this device. Some people fear reporters. Others want to avoid seeing their names associated in print with a particular issue. Others just do not want to take the time. In actuality, most sources who play pass the potato really do know something about the topic and could give a reporter enough information for a brief story on it.

Reporters should prevent sources from sending them on pointless chases, by trying to get sources to talk with them rather than referring them to someone else.

When reporter Feinstein calls and a source says, "I don't know much about that. You'll have to call someone else," the reporter does not answer, "OK." Instead Feinstein says, "OK, but tell me what you do know." Then she asks a specific question. "Is it true the neighbors are angry about the plans to cut down the oak trees?"

Usually the person will answer a specific question. Once a source has started talking, the ice is broken, and the person will usually continue answering questions.

At the end of the interview, Feinstein says, "You seem to have given me the information I needed. Should I still call Fred Jones? Is there another aspect of this he could tell me about?"

✦ ORGANIZE YOUR DESK

Having an organized day's work is much easier when a working space is organized. Some people claim to be able to work well in a cluttered work area, but one wonders how much more effective they might be if their working space were better organized.

Through the course of a day, documents seem to come flooding in to an office. Standard advice given to beginning executives, but equally applicable to beginning reporters, is that one should pick up each piece of paper only once. After reading the piece of paper, take action on it, throw it away, or file it. One system advocates keeping one file in the desk for pieces of paper about pending stories, and putting notes about finished stories into a file cabinet.

Under this system, after writing up an advance story on a school board meeting, the reporter keeps the agenda for the meeting itself. This piece of paper needs a temporary home where it will not clutter up the desk-top. So she throws it in the pending file. When she leaves for the school board meeting, she gets it out.

The reporter keeps a second drawer for old notebooks and documents on stories she has already written up. When she finishes a piece, she puts all the documents in that drawer. When the drawer gets so stuffed she cannot shut it anymore (about once every three months), she takes an hour and goes through the drawer. A few things have value; these go into a file cabinet. The rest go in the trash (or, at a more enlightened newspaper, into the recycling bin).

In general, a reporter will find it easier to concentrate on one project if she keeps information on all other projects off her desk. The reporter spends her last five minutes at work each day taking everything off her desk. She puts papers either in the file cabinet or in her pending drawer. Then, she picks the documents for one project and sets these on her desk.

In the morning when she comes to work, she can start right in on that project. On occasional evenings she has to rush out of the office leaving a desk that, to her, feels chaotic. When this happens, she finds her next day also in chaos. The papers she can sort and get rid of in five minutes after the workday will take her an hour to process when she first gets to work the next morning.

The upshot of this is that the reporter will develop a style of maintaining his or her personal space. If a cluttered style works, that's fine. There's no need to justify it. But if clutter gets in the way, seek to control it.

✦ PICK UP A PIECE OF PAPER ONLY ONCE

No matter what a desk looks like—compulsively neat or appallingly messy—a reporter should handle each sheet of paper as few times as possible. Every time reporter Feinstein picks up a piece of paper, she has to read it and decide what to do with it. She tries to go through the process only once.

She picks up the piece of paper and begins making the calls necessary to turn it into a news story, or picks up the piece of paper and finds no news. In that case, she throws the piece of paper in the trash or puts it in a file cabinet.

All reporters should keep at least one file, a file of phone numbers. Feinstein avoids spending time typing up numbers on Rolodex cards. She keeps a file folder for addresses. When she has written a story, she throws all business cards, notebook pages, and slips of paper with addresses and phone numbers in the folder. The information in this file folder may take a while to pay off, but eventually it becomes invaluable.

"Say, you remember that piece you did on sexual harassment at the university two years ago?" the editor asks Feinstein. "I heard a rumor a complaint's been filed against the sheriff. Do you know anyone at the Equal Employment Opportunity Commission?"

"Let me look in my files. I talked with a really outspoken lawyer there. I think I kept her phone number," Feinstein answers.

Eventually, a reporter has to decide the fate of every piece of paper. Most should provide the basis for a story, then go into a temporary file and then go into the trash. A few, most particularly those with addresses and phone numbers, should go into a permanent file. No matter the eventual fate of a particular piece of paper, reporters can fight snowstorms of paper efficiently by deciding the fate of each sheet immediately. Feinstein forces every piece of paper to justify its existence or she tosses it into the trash.

✦ VISIT THE COFFEE POT AND THE WATER FOUNTAIN

Thus far, this chapter has portrayed reporters as robots. Positioned in front of computers, they type away at 80 words a minute, telephone sources with diligence, and efficiently sort and process blizzards of paper.

When someone interrupts them, these robots say, "Please wait. Processing. Processing. Processing."

Reporters must resort to this robotic behavior to some extent, but all reporters should remember that human beings, unlike robots, need breaks. Continuous efficiency leads to exhaustion and burnout. Visits to the coffee pot, the water fountain, and the photocopy machine help create a successful reporter.

When writer's block strikes, a little stroll down to the water fountain with a stop for a chat with another reporter about the future of hemlines or the fate of the Braves often brings inspiration. Somehow, the unconscious part of the brain continues to write while the conscious part of the brain takes a break. After a break, the words will leap onto the computer screen.

Breaks do more than provide story inspiration. They also produce invaluable information for survival at a newspaper. Like any other bureaucracy, an individual newspaper has its own internal rules of behavior. Some editors and reporters are always rising in prestige while others are falling. Office politics can make or break a career.

When Feinstein finds a line at the copy machine, she sees not an inconvenience, but an opportunity. Instead of waiting in line pacing irritably, she chats with the others on line.

For instance, she asks, "What's going on with the editor? Why was she so happy yesterday? Is it really true she is about to be promoted to the home office?"

For survival in a bureaucracy, a reporter needs to keep up with information like this. Strolls through the newsroom for a coffee refill can provide such data.

✦ TAKE A DRIVE IN THE COUNTRY

Some days a reporter just cannot find the energy to work with robot-like efficiency. On these days it becomes crucial to avoid over-the-telephone interviews.

The school board in a small town just at the county line has hired a new superintendent of schools, who moved to town about a month ago. Ever since, reporter Feinstein has known she really needs to drop by in person for a chat, but she has been avoiding spending the half day it will take to drive out there, do the interview, and come back to the office.

On a burn-out day, Feinstein calls and sets up a personal interview with the superintendent. On a robot day, the 45-minute drive out looks like a big waste of time. On a burn-out day, especially with bright, warm sunshine and a mild temperature, a little drive in the country looks lovely.

These little journeys out into the real world help a reporter. Yes, they take time and interfere with the efficiency of story production, but they also can revitalize a reporter. On these little jaunts, Feinstein tries to avoid obsessing about work at the office. When she gets back to the office refreshed from her drive, she finds she can handle her work better. After a couple of years at a newspaper, the reporter will notice that the necessity for on-site interviews increases on nice days, and decreases on grim, rainy days.

◆ LEAVE WORK AT WORK

The reporters who last in the newspaper business may work like robots, but they remember that the newspaper owns them for only 40 hours a week. They use all this efficiency to get the work done in 40 instead of 60 hours a week.

The reporters who fail in journalism are usually those who work diligently and then use the time they free up to take on more story assignments. For them, all sorts of dire psychological collapses loom in the future. Burnout, alcoholism, or a physical collapse eventually nails workaholics.

While a business may benefit from its employees' workaholic habits, the employee loses out. Eventually, the employee collapses and loses her job. The business survives this crisis just fine. It hires a new worker, but the burned-out ex-employee has no job and no energy to look for another one.

A job works like a bell. Either it can ring the employee or the employee can ring it. Either way, the job gets done. The bell rings. Employees who wrap their hands around the bell handle find happier lives than workers who hang onto the clapper banging around inside the bell's bowl.

For this reason, reporters should avoid making their jobs into their lives. Reporters should maintain separate personal lives. Keep and nurture friends who have nothing to do with the news business, who only occasionally read the newspaper. Take up bird-watching, gardening, target shooting, or toy soldier collecting. Follow World-Wide Professional Wrestling, ride horses, go hiking, knit. Take a break. Avoid doing news business all the time, and the news business will get better.

SUMMARY

- Efficient work habits can help you meet deadlines.
- Use the telephone for as many interviews as possible.

- Research several stories at once.
- Write only one story at a time.
- Control interruptions.
- Avoid letting sources run you in circles.
- Know how to find things quickly amid the pile of papers on your desk.
- Touch each piece of paper only once.
- Chat with other people in the office.
- Enjoy the occasional drives in the country that are a part of a reporter's work.
- Leave work at work.

IN-CLASS EXERCISES

1. In what ways, during your day, is your time wasted? List the things that waste your time. What can you do about these things? Will any of these time-wasters persist when you become a full-time reporter?

2. Do you have a personal filing system, a day organizer, an address book? How often do you use these items? What changes will you need to make in them when you are a full-time reporter?

OUT-OF-CLASS EXERCISE

Interview a reporter for a local newspaper; if possible, spend at least part of a day watching the reporter's activities, logging how this person spends his or her time. How did the reporter spend most of the day? What sorts of activities predominated? How does the reporter arrange his or her time and work space? Do you think this system would work for you?

CHAPTER 19

Cultivating

Sources

People think the work of journalism consists of writing articles in a newspaper. Yet the work of journalism involves much more than sitting at a computer and writing. The film *All the President's Men* gives a good picture of the job. Journalists spend most of their time on the telephone or out calling on people. Only a small part of their time goes to writing. Most of a journalist's time at work is spent gathering information. Writing up the information, while crucial, takes only a small part of a journalist's day. Mostly, journalists talk to people. They use the term "cultivating sources" to describe the work of finding people to interview and convincing those people to trust interviewers.

✦ WRITERS VERSUS REPORTERS

Most newspaper staffs have two kinds of journalists—the writers and the reporters. The writers, the wordsmiths, have just the right touch with the English language. When their fingers hit a computer keyboard, magic pops up on the screen. These people build careers writing columns on the editorial page or doing feature stories for an inside section. They write the think pieces while others do the breaking, hard news stories.

Reporters, on the other hand, excel at digging up information. The great reporters can get a blank wall to talk to them. Like the private detectives in crime novels, they see the important implications of one small bit of information, and they can figure out where to go looking for another fact that will dovetail with that first bit of information.

Good reporters all have a baseline skill in writing. They can all use the news formula to put together a competent news story. They don't bury their leads. They use grammatically correct English. They can write quickly on deadline. But their pieces dominate the front page not because of their brilliant word choice, but because of the compelling facts they have found.

People become really great reporters through on-the-job experience. Most journalists begin their careers with college degrees, basic writing skills, and a general interest in news. Only after they go to work at a newspaper do they begin to make a career as either a reporter or a wordsmith. (Of course, the most awesomely talented both gather news and write really well.)

◆ STARTING WITH THE COPS

Most beginning reporters draw the **cop shop**—the police beat—for a first assignment. Wise editors send their beginners to the cops for basic training in the trench warfare of journalism. At the cop shop a journalist either learns how to cultivate sources or selects a new career.

The police can either tip a journalist to really good stories or refuse to talk at all. Reporters have to prove their trustworthiness to the cops.

Because of the basic nature of their job, many police officers do not readily trust people. The police spend their lives working with people who steal, murder, and commit other mayhem. Because they work daily with crooks, some cops develop a siege mentality. In their job, they only see criminals, victims, other police, and the press.

Many American policing agencies divide the world into two groups of people, the Good Guys and the Bad Guys. In house, they use the term Bad Guy to refer to suspects and to perpetrators of crimes. They call criminals Bad Guys and they call cops and victims Good Guys. They see journalists as either Good Guys or Bad Guys. Individual journalists must convince the cops that they belong in the category of Good Guy journalists.

Bad Guy journalists interfere directly with the cops' work. At a fire, they don't identify themselves. Instead, they duck under a barricade and run right up to the inferno. This can start a stampede of people through a fire line. It also can place a journalist in danger of injury from the fire. Bad Guy journalists who leap barricades without permission can find themselves spending a pleasant night in jail waiting for the editor to come up with bail.

Good Guy journalists go up to the cop standing at the barricade, identify themselves as journalists, and ask to cross the barricade.

"Hi. I'm from *The Daily*. Can I go over and talk to the fire chief?" the reporter asks. The Good Guy journalist acknowledges the police officer's authority and asks permission to enter the dangerous situation.

A Good Guy cop will say, "Sure, come on through. The chief is over there by that Fire Department pickup truck. But don't walk too close to that wall. They're expecting it to fall in at any minute."

The Bad Guy cop says, "Get out of my face. The firefighters don't need the press in here underfoot." The same cop will behave like a Good Guy for some journalists and a Bad Guy for others. Some reporters will get through the fire line and others won't.

Cops only let reporters they know and trust get close to stories.

Covering the cop shop successfully, then, means getting to know the police officers. Ideally, journalists do this in noncrisis situations. While covering routine news, the journalists prove themselves trustworthy. Then, when the big story breaks, those journalists can trade on reputations as Good Guys.

Every day someone from every daily newspaper, radio station, and television station in America talks with local cops. The reporter wants to know what calls the cops responded to in the last 24 hours. The information the reporter collects—the break-ins, armed robberies, and auto accidents—form the bread and butter of journalism. Reports of police activity help fill a newspaper with local news.

Not only does the cop shop offer lots of good news stories; the cops also must by law share information on their activities with reporters. Local taxpayers fund the police. The cops work for the public, and the boss, the public, has a legal right to know how the police department spends citizen tax dollars. Beyond this, Americans have an abhorrence of secret police. Americans prevent secret policing by making police activities a matter of public record. By law, then, the cops cannot refuse to share information with the press. The public, including the press, can, by law, read police reports. The police honor this law, but they tend to keep the really valuable information out of their written reports.

Almost all police officers have at some time dealt with an unscrupulous reporter. For instance, an officer tells a reporter the police may soon make an arrest in a murder case. The officer asks the newspaper to withhold the name of the suspect. The newspaper runs the name anyway. The suspect reads about the impending arrest and leaves town.

Because police officers fear that news coverage can destroy an investigation, they grow secretive around a reporter they don't trust. That reporter's questions get lots of answers like, "Yep," or "Nope," or "Maybe," or "No comment."

Effective police reporters, then, must cultivate some sources. That means reporters must get to know police officers: Hang around the cop shop and drink coffee with them. Talk shop with them and don't print everything they tell. Write very accurate, reliable pieces on all the little stories. Reveal a sense of decency and ethics. Then, when the big story hits, the cops will happily share information.

College newspaper staffers have an excellent opportunity to learn to cultivate sources. While administrators and faculty members practically plead for the opportunity to pontificate for the student newspaper, campus police often stonewall the student newspaper.

City police and county sheriff's departments report to elected officials, the city council, the county commissioners, and the sheriff. These elected officials want to read only good press about their police department. City police who refuse to discuss their activities with the public bring very negative coverage and angry politicians down on themselves. Campus police, in contrast, work within a huge bureaucracy that gets little supervision from the public. Private colleges have no obligation to talk to the press because they do not depend on the taxpayers for funds. At a state institution, the nearest elected official, a state legislator or the governor, has far bigger responsibilities than merely watching over the local campus police. The campus police, then, have little to fear by refusing to give out information. Since they generally withhold information, they can teach a beginner a lot about cultivating sources.

✦ TOO MUCH CLOSENESS

A reporter can become too friendly with sources—a phenomenon called **getting married.** Writing a negative news story about a close friend creates a real conflict of interest. The reporter who dates a police officer will find it difficult to write up a story about that officer rigging bids to have all city autos cleaned at her brother's car wash.

As part of cultivating sources, a reporter must teach them about journalism. Explain to them that a reporter has to ask the tough questions and has to write the tough stories even if it hurts friends. From the beginning, a reporter has to tell people frankly about this part of the job.

Over coffee, the reporter can confide, "You know, it was really tough last week. A guy I really like, his kid was driving the car in that fatal auto accident. His kid is fine, but two others died. The guy's really upset because we reported the story, but there was no choice. Even though he's a good friend, we couldn't sit on that story."

Because of this problem of conflict of interest, many reporters avoid intimate friendships with sources. They form close friendships only with people unlikely to take part in a major news story. The people they expect to come to their aid when a personal tragedy strikes work as teachers, artists, or accountants. Reporters maintain cordial but more distant relationships with lawyers, politicians, and police officers—the people who appear regularly in the newspaper.

✦ SEXUAL HARASSMENT

Sexual harassment can come in two forms:

1. *Quid pro quo* sexual harassment happens when one person asks another to trade sex for a favor. For instance, a publisher offers to promote a reporter from an obituary writer to city hall reporter if she will sleep with him.
2. *Hostile environment* sexual harassment occurs when coworkers constantly make comments about women as sex objects. Their comments create a hostile working environment for women. For instance, printers festoon the pressroom with nudie pictures. A woman has a tough time doing an effective job when her coworkers see a woman's only purpose as sexual.

Within the newspaper office, handling the problem of sexual harassment is straightforward. Sexual harassment is against the law. The newspaper can lose a lot of money if an employee sues. Most newspapers have sexual harassment policies and procedures. If someone is sexually harassing a woman at the office, she should file a complaint.

Reporters face a more difficult kind of sexual harassment outside the office: harassment by a source. Working with sources is akin to working as an outside salesperson. A drug company saleswoman who goes from doctor's office to doctor's office has fewer ways to complain if a doctor makes advances to her.

A reporter the authors know had a problem with the local sheriff. The sheriff was always most anxious to talk with her, in his office with the door closed. She would ask, "What about the arrest on J Street last night?"

"Your eyes are especially beautiful today. You should wear that color more often," he would answer.

When she tried to talk to her editor about the problem, he did not get it. He would say things like, "Hmm. So old Sam thinks you're cute."

A newspaper editor will resist attacking a sheriff for praising a reporter's beauty. The editor sees it as part of the reporter's job to establish a working relationship with her sources, just as the medical supply salesperson has to establish enough rapport to get a doctor to consider buying her products.

Unfortunately, the reporter has to solve this problem herself. She can talk to the sheriff about her disgust when he says something offensive. When the sheriff begins the harassment, the woman can stop the conversation and tell him he's being rude.

For example, the sheriff says, "Your eyes are especially beautiful today. You should wear that color more often."

"Look, I'm trying to get a news story. Cut out the compliments," she can respond.

Most harassers will get the message and become businesslike at this point. A few jerks will come back with, "Oh, but you're so beautiful."

"I don't like that. Stop it," will usually work.

If that doesn't work, the reporter can try nuclear war with the harasser. The reporter could say, "If you don't stop doing this to me, I'm going to start taping all of our interviews. Then I'm going to write an article about you and sexual harassment, and I'm going to quote from the tape recording the things that you say to me."

Unlike many women workers, newspaper reporters do have a particular power. They don't have to resort to the courts for redress. They can instead write articles. If the sheriff harasses a woman reporter, he probably also harasses women on his staff. The threat of public disclosure of his problem may well convince him to stop the behavior. This would be a service to all the women who work with him.

✦ SOME TRUE STORIES

When students graduate from college and go to work as reporters, they quickly discover that they are expected to establish business relationships with people who are nothing like them. Most sources are much older than beginning reporters. Many sources also have either a lot less or a lot more education than beginning reporters. To be successful, all reporters have to learn to deal with differences of age, gender, race, and class.

Most reporters have a story to tell about the moment on the job when they learned an important lesson about cultivating sources. The rest of this chapter tells some of these stories from friends and former students of the authors.

The Silent City Council

A young, beginning reporter of the authors' acquaintance drew for his first job the task of covering city government for a daily newspaper. He dutifully went down to city hall and made the rounds, introducing himself to secretaries and to city administrators. He attended the weekly city council meetings, took very accurate notes, and competently wrote up stories.

He loved writing about city policy issues, but he had not warmed to the people he covered. He was young, just out of college, and they were all 40, 50, and 60 years old. He saw them as dull, middle-aged people, boring and over the hill. Still, no one had snubbed him and he got a chance to write interesting stuff.

He thought things were going along really well until his second week on the job, when the city workers walked out on strike, and he had had no idea it was going to happen. A major event had occurred on his beat and he had missed it. Since the city council agenda did not include the strike, the only way he had to find out about it was if someone told him, but no one at city hall had confided in him.

His editor was not pleased. "You've got to make friends with these people. They have to like and trust you," the editor roared.

The reporter went back to his beat, interviewed the strikers and the mayor, and wrote his stories. The strike ended quickly and things settled back into a routine.

Two weeks later, the editor asked the reporter, "How's it going? Are they warming up to you?"

"Not too well," answered the reporter. "I don't know what I'm doing wrong. I go to city hall every day. I go to all the offices. Everyone is always very nice, but they're sort of cold. They seem really busy and don't take much time with me."

"OK, son," said the editor. "The city council meets next Tuesday, right? What time is the meeting over?"

"Well, they start around 7 p.m., and they're usually out about 10 p.m.," he answered.

"Your job, my boy, does not end until 11:30 p.m. next Tuesday," said the editor. Then he pulled a 20-dollar bill out of his wallet. "After that meeting is over, I want you to go up to one of the councillors, it doesn't matter to me which one. I want you to ask the councillor to go out with you for a pizza and a beer, and you use my $20 to pay for it. While you're having pizza and beer, don't say a word about the city or city government. Just talk. You gotta make friends with these people or you're never gonna get anywhere."

The reporter was dubious. What would he say to one of those dull councillors for an hour and a half? Most of them were older than his parents. But the reporter followed orders. He picked a councillor, approached him after the meeting, and asked him to go for a pizza and a beer.

To his shock, the councillor said yes. At first, their conversation went roughly. The councillor talked about his kids and his mortgage—but then they hit on a topic of mutual interest. By the end of the hour and a half, the beginning reporter decided, "This old guy is OK." The next week after the council meeting he approached a different councillor and took her for pizza and a beer. Soon, he was good buddies with all the members of the city council and began filing great copy.

Most new reporters have to deal with age differences when they start out on newspaper jobs. Beginners are usually noticeably younger than the people they interview.

Most beginners have more education than many of their sources. Reporters at the top ranks of journalism in Washington, D.C., or on major metropolitan dailies may spend their time interviewing brilliant Ph.D.s, but beginners talk with small-town police officers. Most officers have, at most, a two-year college degree. Reporters, on the other hand, have four-year degrees. Journalism-school writing classes have drilled upper-middle-class English into their brains. Like the young city council reporter, beginning reporters want to write up the news, but they don't know how to make human contact with their sources.

Cultivate sources by sharing food and drink. Talk about family, gardening, politics, sports, hobbies, and general interests. Soon the source becomes a human being, not just a thing to milk for information. Once the two people form a human bond, the source will trust the reporter with information.

The Stonewalling Cops

Cathy Mitchell, an author of this book, began her journalism career covering the police department in a small Southern town. She was 24 years old, with a fresh new master's degree from a prestigious university. She probably radiated a certain youthful disdain for the tired old men in that small-town police department.

The police chief probably saw an inexperienced girl he did not trust. At any rate, when she began covering the cops, the chief announced, "We're instituting a new policy. We're not giving out any information about crime in our town except that a crime happened and the place it happened."

She went to her editor. "What do I do?"

He called the chief, who stood firm on his new policy.

"Write it up," the editor said. "If the chief's not going to talk about crime in our city, that's news."

Every morning Mitchell would go down to the cops and check out the police log. Then she would come back and write something like:

Armed robbers hit a grocery on Wilson St. yesterday at 8:15 p.m. City police refused to provide any more information on the incident.

After about a week of this, the editor wrote an editorial attacking the police chief's refusal to share information with the public. He sent copies of the editorial to newspapers and television stations around the South. They all published editorials attacking the police chief, and they sent him copies. Finding himself depicted throughout the region as a press-hating thug, the police chief eventually gave in.

One morning during the news blackout, Mitchell duly went down to the police station. As always, she greeted the receptionist politely and asked for the police log—a brief summary of police activities in the last 24 hours. One older cop was hanging out in the reception area watching her. He had spoken kindly to her in the past.

She looked over the police log and everything looked pretty boring. The list of police calls included the usual missing persons, two phone calls asking the police to check on elderly relatives, an angry neighbor complaining about a barking dog. Only one mildly interesting story appeared on the log. Two pink plastic flamingos were missing from a lawn on Orlando Road. As usual, she asked to speak to the police chief. The receptionist, as usual, answered, "Sorry, he's still not talking to the press."

Mitchell got up to leave. The older cop came over and took the log from her. "See this?" he roared, pointing to a missing person item. "I've been ORDERED not to tell you ANYTHING about IT."

"Huh? You mean this missing person?" she asked. "Usually missing persons are just people who have run away from their spouses. Is there something more about this one?"

"I ABSOLUTELY cannot give you ANY information on THIS ITEM," he roared.

She took the information back to the newspaper and called other sources. It turned out that the missing person was a lawyer's secretary. An angry client had kidnapped and murdered her. This tragic and important story made national news.

Even when a reporter's relationships with a source are truly horrible, persistence pays. One Good Guy will always want to see that the truth reaches the public. Most Americans believe in the rule of law. Most Americans, and most sources, also believe in freedom of the press.

That cop wasn't going to risk his job to get information into the newspaper, but he knew this important story should see print. He tipped Mitchell even though he barely knew her and probably mistrusted her. Even if a reporter lacks strong sources, someone will often come forward with a tip.

The Bereaved Family

An African American reporter the authors know got his first job out of college with a daily serving a small town with almost no African American population. His college degree and his race made him different from the working-class white people he covered, yet he almost immediately began to get good scoops.

For instance, when a little girl was kidnapped and sexually molested by a family acquaintance, a media horde descended on the family, demanding interviews, but the family turned everyone away. The young reporter knocked on the front door.

"I'm from the local newspaper and I would like to talk to you about your daughter. I'm just really appalled about what happened to her," he said.

The family gave him the interview and let him talk with the daughter. They told him they wanted the story in the newspaper because they wanted people to know how horrible child molestation is. They told him they were giving him the story because he had human compassion for the child.

Basic decency and compassion can cross barriers of race, class, and gender. Reporters who go for the jugular in every interview miss good stories. They get a reputation as people to avoid. Hurried reporters who define their work by deadlines miss stories. The people they interview know that these journalists see their sources only as quotations in a news story. The sources see reporters tied down by deadline pressures with no concern for the people in the story. Seeing this attitude, potential sources try to avoid becoming a part of these journalists' stories.

To cultivate sources, then, make a human bridge to the people who will appear in news stories. Establish some commonality. See the real person, have compassion and show an interest in that person.

The Advantage of Youth

Here is one last true story about a reporter and a source. A young reporter got his first job out of college covering county government in the Midwest. On his first day on the job he did what new reporters do. He went around city hall from office to office introducing himself to all the clerks and administrators. They gave him the usual response: "Nice to meet you, kid. I've got to run to a meeting." Everyone spoke kindly to him, but no one wanted to spend any time with him.

Then he got to the county tax collector's office. Something clicked. He and the tax collector, a guy in his 50s, really got along. The reporter found himself telling the county official all about his life. He had dreamed of a career in journalism. He had majored in journalism in college, and now, today, he was starting the work he had always wanted to do.

They chatted for 45 minutes, and then the tax collector said to him:

"Look, you're such a nice young man. It's good to see idealistic young people like you. I'm going to help your career. It's going to come out soon anyway, and I would just as soon let you be the one to break the story.

"I've been embezzling from the county for 20 years."

The tax collector gave the young reporter the details and the reporter went back to the newspaper and wrote the story. The tax collector went to jail. The tax collector had wanted some good to come from his crime, so he helped out a beginner.

Beginners do sometimes have an edge over seasoned reporters. People like to encourage a youth who shows promise. They'll bend things to throw the advantage to an enthusiastic novice.

SUMMARY

- Reporters must excel at talking with people.
- Covering the police is the best way for beginning reporters to learn how to cultivate sources.
- Avoid becoming too friendly with sources.
- Don't tolerate sexual harassment.
- Share food and drink with sources.
- In chilly situations, be pleasant but persistent.
- Be genuinely caring and friendly.
- Beginners have an advantage in cultivating sources because people like to boost the career of an enthusiastic novice.
- A reporter can overcome differences of age, race, class, and gender by making human and compassionate contact with sources.

IN-CLASS EXERCISES

1. Examine the news section of your local newspaper. For each story, list the source that provided the primary information for the story. Describe whether or not the reporter would have had contact with the source as a result of that reporter's beat.

2. Imagine yourself having to interview your uncle for a newspaper story. How would you explain to him about the journalistic ethic that might demand that you report on him without favoritism?

3. Using the list of news sources in Exercise 1, list the institutional affiliation of each source. What percentage of them are police, firefighters, public officials, or other public employees? What percentage of these people deal with the public as an integral part of their jobs? What does this imply about the sorts of information reporters usually encounter? What can a reporter do to counterbalance this tendency?

4. Describe the two types of sexual harassment. Which do you think would be harder to deal with? Why? Whose responsibility is it to reduce harassment in the newsroom? When interviewing sources?

5. Choose a story from your local newspaper. Call the reporter, and find out where and when that reporter was educated. Find out the educational level of a source in that story. Are the educational levels of the source and the reporter similar, or different? What sorts of difficulties could arise from this? Why?

6. Pick a story from your local newspaper. Call the reporter who wrote it, and find out whether or not sources seemed cooperative. Ask the reporter to assess why the sources were or were not cooperative. Would you agree with the reporter's assessment?

7. What sorts of difficulties could arise from angering news sources, particularly those with whom a reporter works on a beat? Telephone a local official who deals with the press, and ask the official what qualities make him or her want to work with a given reporter. What are those qualities?

OUT-OF-CLASS EXERCISE

Interview a campus police official about crime rates on campus. After writing the news story, write a page or two concerning how the interview went. Was the official forthcoming and candid, or guarded? Did the official give you information willingly, or did you have to probe? Why do you think the interview went as it did? What avenue would you have pursued had the official been unwilling to talk with you? Why?

CHAPTER 20

The Reporter

and the Law

American laws protect the rights of journalists to get information. The law also protects individuals and groups from damage caused by the media. Reporters must know when they stand on firm ground, and when they are on shaky territory.

Unfortunately, the law is not always clear on the rights of reporters. Laws concerning libel are in a state of flux, and consequently reporters are well advised to check with their editor whenever they find themselves in a position that's the least bit questionable. Most newspapers have a lawyer on retainer, meaning that the lawyer is paid a set sum to be available to the editor when questions come up. In questions of law, the best resource is a lawyer.

✦ THE THREAT OF LIBEL

Anyone who plans a career in news must clearly understand libel law. Reporters do not want to lose all their assets in a libel lawsuit. Damages for libel can run into the millions. The newspaper absorbs most of these losses, but people who sue for libel also sue the author of the libelous piece. If the newspaper loses the suit, the court will order the author as well as the newspaper to pay damages. In addition, the hassle of depositions and court appearances drains a person emotionally. The mere existence of a libel suit can damage a reporter's reputation.

Most journalists, at some time in their career, face at least one libel suit, but very few lose those suits. Journalists need to know and understand libel law for a second reason. People know that reporters justifiably fear libel suits. Routinely, people try to stop the publication of an article by threatening to sue for libel. Almost every journalist has received such a threat. Reporters who lack a thorough knowledge of their rights under the law may well let these threats frighten them away from good stories. Many libel-suit threats stem from interviews during which subjects say something they later deny. Since second thoughts are common, defend against them by taping the conversation or taking very thorough notes. A detailed recounting of the conversation usually settles the matter.

With beginning reporters, though, editors worry not so much about the good story lost as about a lost lawsuit.

◆ THE DEFINITION OF LIBEL

Libel is the publication of false information that hurts a person's reputation. To win in court, private citizens must prove defamation (that is, that the article held them up to contempt, ridicule, or hatred). Any falsehood that a newspaper publishes about a person that makes readers think less of that person could cause the newspaper to lose a libel suit, but one should examine especially closely stories that do any of the following:

- accuse someone of being incompetent to do a job
- allege that someone has a disease that implies moral misconduct
- charge that someone has participated in sexual activities that the most conservative members of a community would consider immoral

Every day, newspaper articles do damage people's reputations. Police news, by definition, hurts someone's reputation. A story reporting the arrest of a neighbor on burglary charges makes adjoining property owners think less highly of that person, but truth shields a newspaper in a libel suit. The newspaper that can prove the truth of a damaging item will win the libel suit. A reporter who has strong documents and witnesses who are willing to appear in court to prove the truth of an allegation can proceed with publication with some confidence.

Even if the false and damaging item appears in a joke, or in a direct quote, or in an advertisement, or in a letter to the editor, the newspaper can still lose a libel suit. The reporter who quotes, directly and in quotation marks, a libelous statement may be guilty of libel. A newspaper must establish the truth of everything it publishes and distributes to readers.

✦ LIBEL PER SE

Some words and ideas, if false, are libelous on their face, and to use them is to commit a defamation. Among these cases of libel per se have traditionally been:

- the suggestion that someone is unchaste or sexually promiscuous
- the suggestion that someone has a venereal disease
- the suggestion that someone has committed criminal conduct punishable by imprisonment
- the suggestion that someone is unfit in the conduct of his or her profession

In the modern world, the first two items listed above are very seldom mentioned as defamatory statements. The third and fourth, however, are often the crux of libel suits. Saying that someone has committed a crime punishable by imprisonment, when they have not, is libel per se in most states. Similarly, the suggestion that someone is unfit to hold a job—not bad at it, but actually unfit—is libel per se.

The best defense against libel per se is to be able to prove in court that the contention is correct. To be able to prove that a person is incompetent at his or her job, to a jury and a judge, can be a difficult matter.

✦ LIBEL AND PUBLIC FIGURES

The law of libel hinges on a legally defined distinction between private and public individuals. Public figures have a much harder time winning a libel suit than do private individuals. Public individuals (people who have sought publicity) include political figures, entertainment figures, and sports figures. These citizens must prove both the publication of a damaging falsehood and actual malice by the newspaper. Actual malice means a reckless disregard of the falsity of the material—that the reporter did not check the accuracy of charges in the article using normal journalistic procedures. The courts still struggle over the definition of normal journalistic procedures.

Additionally, not only people can be libeled. Dead people cannot be libeled, but corporations and other organized groups can sue for defamation. The government, however, appears corporately to be unable to sue for libel.

The good news about libel law is that truth is an absolute defense against prosecution. Better news yet is that, after the Supreme Court decision in the case of *New York Times Co. v. Sullivan*, the burden of proof lies with the plaintiff if the plaintiff is a public figure. Reporters do not need to prove in court that the statements about a public figure were true; the plaintiff must prove them false. And, since the good reporter deals only in truth, most reporters never find themselves being sued for libel, and most of the suits that are brought are merely nuisance suits. At least in theory, reporters who publish fair and balanced stories and carefully check out the truth of information included in them are probably safe from losing libel suits to public figures.

✦ LIBEL AND PRIVATE CITIZENS

The danger of losing a libel suit rests in the publication of false information about a private individual. When private citizens sue, newspapers face a much tougher standard of proof. In these cases the newspaper must prove, not that its editors thought the information was true, but that the information was really true. Many losing libel suits stem from mistakes at the newspaper. If the newspaper says police are about to charge John Smith of 321 Jones Street with murder, and it turns out that police charge Joan Smith of 322 Jones Street with the crime, John Smith has a winning lawsuit.

If a situation contains even the hint that it might materialize into a lawsuit, do not hide from the editor. Most newspapers keep a lawyer on retainer to answer legal questions from editors. Talk with editors about the situation. They may have a ready answer, or they might refer the question to the lawyer. Asking is cheap; guessing can lose a job plus a lot of a reporter's money. Further, it is important to remember that libel suits are almost always brought against everyone who had anything whatsoever to do with the publication of the material in question. This can include editors, publishers, corporations, news writers, and, for that matter, the truck drivers who delivered the paper. There's no getting into a libel suit without everyone at the newspaper knowing about it, because they'll probably be directly involved in it.

The law of libel in the United States is much more complicated than this brief summary suggests. Anyone contemplating staying in the news business should take a course in libel law from the journalism or mass communications department at the local college.

✦ COLLEGE PUBLICATIONS

The writer for a student paper should follow a similarly cautious path. When any doubt exists, tell the editor. The courts have ruled that publications produced by universities that receive state funding have the same

First Amendment rights and responsibilities as commercial newspapers. The First Amendment rights mean that the student newspaper at a state-supported school can run articles without prior interference from college authorities. With this right, however, comes responsibility. College reporters and editors can be sued for libel just like their counterparts at commercial papers—and the university does not have to supply a lawyer.

✦ PUBLIC MEETING LAWS

Most states have **sunshine laws** that guarantee public access to the documents and meetings of any agency funded by tax monies. Occasionally, a small-town official, unaware of these laws, will eject a reporter from a meeting or will refuse to let the reporter copy a document. When this happens, a reporter should not demand instant access.

Sunshine laws do allow officials to meet in secret under some circumstances. For instance, they can usually hold closed meetings to discuss hiring and firing or plans to buy property. Reporters need to know the sunshine laws in their states and should consult with their editors before taking any action about a closed meeting. If officials do hold an illegal meeting, an editor may embarrass the officials in an editorial or may arm a reporter with information about the law in that state. When a reporter returns to confront an official with a copy of the law and the threat of a lawyer, the problem usually vanishes.

In the 1972 *Branzburg* case, the U.S. Supreme Court determined that the First Amendment not only protects the right of reporters to report the news without prior restraint; it also protects the right of newspaper reporters to gather the news. The police cannot arbitrarily deny access to a crime scene to a reporter, nor can they arbitrarily deny a press pass to a reporter. Reporters can't be denied access to open meetings or open courtroom sessions, although they can be prevented from using tape recorders, still cameras, or video cameras. Reporters have some rights of access to prisons, mental institutions, and migrant camps, although the courts are still exploring these areas.

Another question that often arises is the extent of a reporter's liability if he or she comes into the possession of stolen documents. A common tactic for whistle-blowers is to duplicate incriminating documents and then slip them to reporters on the sly. The person who duplicated the documents is often committing a crime; but courts are unclear concerning whether or not a reporter who receives them is also committing a crime. U.S. statutes prohibit the theft of government documents and the receipt of such stolen goods; this law is often invoked in cases involving purloined documents. But if the document is duplicated, and then the original is replaced, the status of the duplicate as stolen goods becomes unclear. At the state level, similar confusion reigns.

Officially, the policy of many newspapers is to avoid the use of such duplicated documents. Unofficially, many newspapers use them, attributing the information they contain to unnamed sources or "a document obtained by the *Times*." In cases of doubt, ask the editor, who will probably check with the newspaper's lawyer.

And, in this day of desktop publishing, it is important to bear in mind that the creation of phony government documents is a simple matter. A series of allegedly stolen documents describing the operations of a supposedly top-secret government group called MJ-12 was circulated widely, and caused quite a stir before it was revealed through careful textual analysis that the documents were forged by unknown hoaxsters. To the untrained eye, the MJ-12 documents appeared real, but with scanners, font libraries, and the like, making impressive but false documents is a snap. The good reporter is wary of anonymous secret documents that arrive unannounced.

✦ PROTECTING SOURCES

In trade for exclusive information, newspaper reporters can promise to protect the anonymity of a source. Many people want to see information in print, but do not want their names printed as the source of the information. Many beginning journalists think that reporters have a guaranteed right to refuse to name their sources. This is untrue. Every year, some reporter goes to jail for refusing to name a source. Also, the U.S. Supreme Court has ruled that reporters enter a binding contract when they agree to honor a promise not to reveal a source's name. If they reveal the name, they can lose a lawsuit.

Agreeing to protect a source's name helps get good information for a story, but all reporters should think carefully before making such a deal. These agreements include a commitment to go to jail if necessary to keep the source's name a secret. Some stories rate making such a promise, but most do not.

SUMMARY

- Many libel suits are frivolous.
- Libel is the publication of false information that hurts a person's reputation.

- The best defense in a libel suit is to have documents that will prove in court that the published statement is true.
- To win a libel suit, a public figure must prove in court that the newspaper knowingly published a falsehood.
- When in doubt, check with the editor.
- Being a careful reporter will usually keep a writer out of trouble with the law.
- Because the law is much more complex and subtle than this brief summary might indicate, you should take a college-level course in libel law before starting to work as a reporter.
- Meetings of government agencies and the documents they produce are by law open to the public.
- If you agree not to use a source's name, know that you are contracting to go to jail rather than reveal that name.

IN-CLASS EXERCISES

1. Examine a story in your local newspaper. What potential might it have for libel action? Who might sue? What would be the likelihood of their success?

2. Locate the text of *New York Times Co. v. Sullivan*. What are the implications of this court case for the reporter? Does *Sullivan* help or undermine the abilities of reporters?

3. Find a story in the local paper in which a meeting was covered. In the case at hand, what scenario might make a reporter need to use a sunshine law? Who would the reporter have talked to about the problem, and why? Who would the reporter have confronted, and why?

4. Locate a story in your local newspaper that uses a veiled source. How is the veiled source identified? Why did the source choose to remain unnamed? Was the news the source revealed worth going to jail to protect? Why or why not?

5. Examine a local college newspaper. Are there any articles in the newspaper that might be considered libelous by someone? Why?

6. Watch a story on the local news. What potential might it have for libel action? Who might sue, and would they win?

7. April Fool's issues of campus newspapers are often called the most dangerous issues of the year from the standpoint of libel. Why might that be so? Telephone the editor of your campus newspaper, and ask him or her whether the paper does an April Fool's issue, and why or why not.

OUT-OF-CLASS EXERCISE

Get a copy of your state's sunshine law. What sorts of rights and responsibilities does it give to reporters? Call a local reporter, and inquire
whether that reporter has ever had to make use of a sunshine law. If the
answer is yes, when, and why? Did it work? Why or why not?

CHAPTER 21

Ethics, or
the Problem With
Journalists

Poll after poll shows that the American people dislike and distrust journalists. Routinely, people say they respect journalists about as much as they respect used car salespeople and politicians. The public sees journalists as heartless people who bend the news to fit their personal biases.

Anyone considering a career in journalism should watch "Journalists' Round Table," a morning show on the C-SPAN cable television network. In this show two or three journalists answer questions phoned in by ordinary folks. The network puts callers on the air on a first-come, first-served basis, without screening. The callers include some nuts, some left-wing zealots, and some right-wing zealots, but most are just people interested in and concerned about American politics and government.

The callers have one thing in common. They almost all hate the press. In general, the public despises the callousness of journalists.

✦ HOW DID YOU FEEL?

An obsessed ex-husband guns down his estranged wife as she comes out of church. Television covers the funeral. The audience sees a reporter thrust a microphone into the grieving mother's face. "How did you feel when you found out your daughter was dead?"

From a reporter's point of view, this question works. A person has to give a strong and emotional response. The public, though, sees the question as cruel and heartless, and dumb besides. "How does she feel? Her daughter's just been murdered, you idiot. How do you expect her to feel?" viewers yell at their TV sets.

This heartlessness really glares when ordinary citizens get caught in a national story. Anyone who has worked for long at a small-town newspaper can tell harrowing stories of what happens when the national news media invade a town.

In the late '70s, the Trail Side Murderer waylaid women hikers in the Point Reyes National Seashore, pulling them off hiking trails and killing them. When the story broke, hordes of press, both print and television, invaded by car and helicopter. Suddenly, rude, pushy, fast-talking, on-deadline reporters crowded the sleepy town's main street, grabbing passersby for interviews. "How did you feel when you found out your hiking trails aren't safe?" the reporters asked anyone who didn't run away from them. When they had enough local reaction quotes to make a good story, they all climbed back into their cars and helicopters and departed, leaving an angry and exhausted town behind them. The reporters offered no thank-yous, no kindness, no compassion, and very little politeness.

✦ THE ETHIC OF "GET THE STORY AND GET IT FIRST"

This book has emphasized the importance of understanding readers and what they want. While giving the readers—the public—everything they have a right to know, journalists often forget another group: the people named in newspaper articles. Too often, interview subjects look like pathetic victims of a ravening press out to stomp on individuals in pursuit of a broader, and therefore more abstract, right of the public to know.

Unfortunately, too often the prevailing ethic in most newsrooms is: Get the Story and Get It First. Journalism is highly competitive. Even in one-newspaper towns, nobody wants to get scooped. When a local radio station, television station, or regional newspaper beats the local paper to a story, it hurts. Newspapers stay in business by being the first, best source of information. E. W. Scripps, a turn-of-the-century publisher, said, "A newspaper's first job is to make a profit so that it can continue to survive." Many journalists have rationalized all their actions in terms of this need to attract readers. They defend all their actions with the argument that in a free, democratic society the public has a right to know everything.

Clearly, though, much of what professional journalists do in their day-to-day news gathering is wrong. Much of the public detestation of reporters comes from their unethical behavior.

In the last 20 years, journalists, and particularly journalism educators, have begun to recognize this problem. They are now creating a new ethic for the profession of journalism. This chapter outlines some issues in journalism ethics, but anyone contemplating working in journalism should think about ethical issues in much more depth than provided here. Every journalism student should take a semester-long course in ethics.

✦ A WORD OF WARNING

Most of this book describes traditions and attitudes in practice at American newspapers today. This chapter on ethics breaks that rule. What follows are the authors' ideas about ethics. Many newspaper editors and journalism professors will agree with the authors' ideas, but others will disagree.

Groping for Ethics in Journalism, the title of an excellent book in this growing field, indicates the current state of journalism ethics. People in the newspaper business and journalism education are now trying to develop a completely well-rounded journalism ethic. The profession is still searching for definitive answers to some very difficult ethical questions, and some newspaper editors will argue with the answers this chapter provides.

✦ THE NEWS HURTS PEOPLE

Newspapers hurt people every day. If the newspaper reports the arrest of a prominent Realtor for running a major drug ring, that Realtor and his family will be hurt. To the agony of the arrest, the newspaper adds the pain of public humiliation and censure. Almost all crime news causes someone pain.

Victims also suffer. Newspapers traditionally withhold the names of rape victims, but many other victims do see their names in print. Some victims feel renewed pain when they relive the crime through the news pages.

Almost everyone, though, would argue that the press should cover crime news. People need to know about crime and how to avoid it. Readers want to know how safe their cities are. They want to know where robberies and beatings occur.

Readers want to know the circumstances of a murder. Yes, they want to gawk at the crime. They also want to know why the crime occurred. They want to learn how to avoid death.

For example, many women are murdered by their estranged husbands. Reports of the circumstances often suggest that the murderers have been following and threatening the women for weeks and months beforehand. Once this pattern emerged in newspaper reports, it started a movement to classify stalking as a crime.

Many states have now passed laws forbidding one person to trail and threaten another. The press coverage helped change the law. Authorities have begun intervening before the situation can develop to the stage of murder. The coverage of these stalking murders created new laws that will prevent similar deaths in the future.

✦ SHOULD A NEWSPAPER REPORT SUICIDES?

The public does have a need and a right to know much news that may hurt and embarrass the people named in a news story. Other stories, though, should not see print. The First Amendment gives newspapers the right to print almost anything as long as the information is true. Having that right, though, does not mean newspapers should always exercise it.

Suicide always hurts survivors. Guilt and shame compound their grief. When the coroner rules the death a suicide, must a newspaper print it? The newspaper does not name the causes of most other deaths. Why name suicide?

One can argue that the public has a right to know. If a newspaper reported every suicide death in a community, these stories would make the public more aware of the extent of the problem. If that newspaper also wrote a series of articles on the warning signs of suicide and preventive measures to take, the newspaper might save lives.

Naming every suicide victim in the city in the past year would be compelling, but is it compelling enough to balance the pain to families? The newspaper could still print a series on suicide prevention. Statistics could describe the extent of the problem. Names and faces would do a better job, but is the public's right to know really worth the pain to families?

✦ SHOULD A NEWSPAPER NAME TEENAGE CRIMINALS?

A weekly newspaper editor the authors know once decided to make war on teenage crime. He decided he would start printing the name of every child arrested for a crime. In most states the courts keep the names of juvenile criminals confidential. The idea is that a child should have a chance to make a new start and not have to go through life with this blot on the record. If a newspaper can find out the children's names, it is not against the law to print those names. The editor had good sources and got the names.

This editor soon abandoned his new policy of printing juveniles' names because it got so he dreaded Thursday mornings. The paper came out Wednesday afternoon. Every Thursday morning when he got to the office, there sat a row of angry, weeping parents. He would have to spend his Thursdays listening to their pain and ire.

Police had arrested their children. That was horrible. To have their friends and neighbors see it in the newspaper—that just compounded the pain. That just added to their difficulties.

The editor had moral righteousness on his side. After all, he was trying to prevent crime and encourage other teenagers to avoid the embarrassment of seeing their arrests featured on the front page of the hometown newspaper. But at the same time he was adding to many people's pain.

◆ BALANCING PUBLIC NEED AGAINST PRIVATE PAIN

Newspaper people can easily get carried away with the moral righteousness of a cause. Powerful pressures, like the need to scoop the competition and the need to interest readers, push toward publication. Deadline pressure makes it hard to pull back and remember the potential pain a story will cause. Yet reporters must remember that pain. Good news judgment includes weighing the pain a story will cause against the public good the story will create. Too often, American journalism today lacks that simple compassion.

American society allows people to cause pain when it seems needed. Police officers can manacle prisoners. Doctors can take knives to patients. Lawyers can reduce witnesses to tears. But American society disapproves of needless pain. We punish police officers who beat manacled prisoners, doctors who amputate the wrong leg, and lawyers who badger witnesses.

The public good clearly demands much of the pain that journalism causes. Crime news and investigations of public officials are necessary. Gratuitous pain, though, really bothers readers. The same reader who takes a vicarious interest in the close-up picture of a grieving widow also thinks, "I sure wouldn't want that camera in my face."

Journalism needs to change. Newspaper people need to temper their moral righteousness with more compassion for the people whose names and faces they put in the newspaper. A reporter should always try to identify with the subject of the story. A journalist should ask, "Would I want to be in the newspaper in this circumstance?" An answer of "No" does not mean the reporter should kill the story. It does mean asking a further question: "Is the good that publication of the story will bring to my readers worth the pain I'm going to cause these particular people?"

✦ SHOULD THE MEDIA PHOTOGRAPH FUNERALS?

Many stories, such as media invasions of funerals, just won't pass this test. Journalists who defend this practice argue that their newspaper should present a complete picture of life. Death and dying are a part of life and should be in the newspaper. Covering the funeral lets the public see and feel the deep grief of the mourners.

Really, who wants a camera in her face at such a time? The public already knows about death and dying. Is showing readers the anguished details of an interment really worth the pain the news coverage will give the grieving survivors? In ordinary deaths, the answer is, "Certainly not."

Compassion should rule even in extraordinary deaths. The bombing in Oklahoma City, a mining accident, a devastating hurricane, tornado, or earthquake—these extraordinary events demand coverage. Even in such events reporters should temper their enthusiasm with compassion for the survivors. They should consider whether the survivors want the media present at the funeral. Good newspapers can find other ways to cover a disaster besides taking close-up pictures of the mourners.

✦ ASKING PERMISSION

Interestingly enough, survivors don't all hate the press. Many, particularly those involved in an extraordinary tragedy, want coverage, want to talk about their pain.

A reporter assigned to cover the destruction of Korean Airlines Flight 007 dreaded interviewing grieving relatives who lived in her town. She worried about invading their pain. When she contacted the relatives, she found them anxious to talk. They wanted to share their pain with the public. They wanted people to know how this tragedy had affected them personally. They wanted steps taken to keep others from having to endure such pain.

Journalists can solve the problem of balancing the public's right to know against the subject's pain. They can ask the person who is suffering to give them permission to do the story, to photograph the funeral, to publish the interview. Then in the story or the picture caption or the television voice-over, reporters can tell the public that the subjects gave permission for the coverage. The story can explain why the subjects wanted the coverage.

In other words, journalists can show compassion for people caught up in a painful news story. They can show that compassion not only privately to the individual during the interview, but also in the news coverage itself, where they can tell readers why a person decided to go public with his or her pain.

✦ SOME STORIES SHOULD NOT SEE PRINT

Following these ethical principles means that some stories will not see print. Some people will refuse permission. In many, many cases, the public's need to know is not as compelling as the individual pain that publication of the story would cause.

Take the case of the tennis star Arthur Ashe. For two years, many news organizations knew Arthur Ashe had AIDS, but they sat on the story because that's what Ashe wanted. Various reporters heard rumors that Ashe had AIDS and tried to convince him to go public. They argued that the knowledge that a man of Ashe's integrity had AIDS would help fight the prejudice against AIDS victims.

Ashe had not yet told his young daughter he had the illness. He wanted her to mature before he told her. For these personal family reasons, he wanted to keep the fact of his disease private.

Finally, the editors of *USA Today* learned that the tennis star had the disease. The definition of news offered earlier in this book calls this a good story. It had strong human interest about a famous person. It showed AIDS as a disease of heterosexuals as well as homosexuals. *USA Today* decided to publish.

The editors did tell Ashe ahead of time that they were going with the story. Ashe told his daughter he had the disease and then held an angry press conference to attack *USA Today* and announce his illness to all the media. In the process, he eliminated *USA Today*'s scoop. Frank DeFord, a highly respected sports reporter, wrote a column in *Newsweek* explaining that he sat on the story out of compassion for Ashe and his family.

Without doubt, public knowledge of Ashe's illness helped fight the prejudice against people with AIDS. Should *USA Today* have drafted the unwilling Ashe as a foot soldier in this fight against prejudice? No. Only willing volunteers should fight such wars. The very fact that AIDS is an epidemic and is widespread means that lots of troops are available to volunteer. At about the time of the Ashe incident, another highly respected sports figure, Magic Johnson, tested HIV positive. Johnson volunteered for the war and went public with his illness.

Sometimes even the most compelling story should not see print. Even if the story will draw lots of readers and even though the competition may well run the story, sometimes a newspaper should refrain from publishing. Why not take Frank DeFord's high road with a story like Arthur Ashe and AIDS? DeFord sat on the story. When he got scooped, he published a think piece explaining why he had refrained from publishing. He ended up seeming compassionate while *USA Today* looked heartless.

✦ HEARTLESSNESS IS A DEFENSE MECHANISM

Some journalists grow heartless for a good reason. Writing about the evils of the world can become really depressing. Many journalists try to avoid this depression by dehumanizing the people they write about. This can result in a kind of journalism that creates new pain while fighting other evils.

Other journalists sin in the opposite direction. They become too involved with the people and the issues they write about. They become obsessed with righting wrongs and eliminating evil.

Cathy Mitchell, one author of this book, shared in a Pulitzer Prize in 1979. After winning the Pulitzer, she spent a year flying around the country giving talks to press clubs and newspaper publishers' associations. At one of these events, another Pulitzer winner asked her, "Did anything much come of your stories?" She answered, "No, not really. How about you?" He said, "Same with me. Nobody went to jail. Nothing much was done."

Journalists see themselves as the small guy at the parade, pointing at the emperor and screaming, "He's not wearing any clothes! He's naked!" It's really frustrating when no one seems to listen to this scream of truth. There's a real temptation to do more, to take a more active role—but that route leads, at best, to a change in careers from journalism to public relations, and, at worst, to acute depression.

✦ DON'T TAKE SIDES

The film *Under Fire* features Nick Nolte as a photojournalist covering a revolution in a Central American country. At first, he sees the people of the country only as elements in a photo composition—just shapes that join other shapes to create strong pictures.

Then he meets a young revolutionary who really likes American baseball. This human quality reaches through the photographer's protective shell. The turning point in the movie comes when a sniper kills this baseball-loving revolutionary. The photojournalist drops his camera momentarily and picks up a rifle. Later, he fakes a picture that helps the revolutionaries win their war but also causes a close friend to die.

The revolutionaries, romantic and compelling people, are fighting a venal, corrupt dictator. Many news stories look this way to a reporter. In many news stories one side seems clearly right to a reporter while the other seems obviously wrong. Reporters strive to be fair, but they come to the news with a complete set of personal ideas.

The essence of good reporting, though, is preserving a professional distance from the subject of the story. The reporter's only job is screaming a very detailed description of the emperor's clothing. Reporters who do more become active participants and lose their objectivity. At that point they have lost their status as trusted reporters of the truth. They have become publicists lobbying for only one side.

✦ DON'T TRY TO FIX THINGS PERSONALLY

The classic novella "Miss Lonelyhearts" illustrates the other problem with failing to maintain a professional distance from a news story. A young man, whose name the reader never learns, writes an advice column for the newspaper. The trouble is, he cannot handle the pain of the people who write to him. He wants to save them all. He wants to think of good, strong advice to help each of these troubled people find peace.

He can't find the answers. No one could find solutions for these people's problems. Miss Lonelyhearts can do no more than give advice to the troubled people who write him. Only those troubled people, themselves, can solve their problems.

The turning point for Miss Lonelyhearts comes when he agrees to meet one of his correspondents in person. This unleashes a chain of events that leaves Miss Lonelyhearts shot and perhaps dead.

The press describes all the problems of the world, but the press cannot fix those problems. The young boy who screams about the emperor's clothes cannot dress the emperor. Someone else has to do that.

✦ THE SIN OF COUNTERTRANSFERENCE

Psychotherapists have a word for the phenomenon of the therapist who takes an active role in a patient's personal life. They call it **countertransference.**

Successful therapy needs transference. Patients have to identify with and trust their therapists. When therapists become emotionally involved with their patients, however, countertransference occurs. Therapists abandon their positions as concerned advocates for patients. Instead, they begin using their patients to help them handle their own psychological problems. The treatment of patients takes a back seat to therapists' personal needs.

When a journalist begins to take an active role in a cause, that journalist does something similar. Miss Lonelyhearts knew about writing and publishing. When he began to deal personally with his correspondents, he tried to take on the role of psychotherapist, for which he lacked training.

A reporter who becomes part of a story loses the ability to cover the story fairly.

✦ PRESERVE BASIC HUMAN DECENCY

The job of being an ethical journalist, then, involves maintaining a careful balance between too much involvement with the subject of a story and too much neutrality.

A journalist must feel compassion for people caught in the news. This compassion must extend to the point of refusing to write some stories because the pain they would cause would be too great.

Simultaneously, though, a journalist must see the limitations of the news. The press has only limited powers. It can only point out the truth. It can scream, "The emperor has no clothes!" Others in society—the lawyers, the police, the politicians—must work together to clothe the emperor. The newspaper, alone, cannot do this.

SUMMARY

- The public hates the heartlessness of journalists.
- Reporters who ask "How did you feel?" when a tragedy has occurred almost always look callous.
- Pressures of deadlines and competition help create this insensitivity.
- Journalists and journalism professors are now groping toward creating a journalism ethic.
- Some very necessary news must hurt people.
- Stories about suicide often look coldhearted.
- Photo coverage of funerals almost always looks insensitive.
- In painful circumstances, ask permission to do the story.
- Don't take sides.
- Don't get personally involved in a news story.
- Feel for people in the news.
- Know that the press can do only what it can do.
- Preserve basic human decency.

IN-CLASS EXERCISES

1. Find a story in your local newspaper in which the "How do you feel?" question is asked of someone who has undergone some tragedy. Does the question seem to have been asked with compassion? Why does it seem that way? Was the question appropriate, considering the time, place, and situation under which it was posed? Why?

2. Conduct a straw poll by asking the first 10 people you meet how they feel about the ethics of the news media. What were their answers? What does this unscientific poll say about perceptions of the media?

3. Find a story in the local paper in which the reporting of the events in the story would be bound to cause pain and suffering for someone. Who is affected by the story, and how? Was this suffering outweighed by the importance of the story?

4. Call your local newspaper, and ask a reporter the paper's policy on reporting the names of teenage criminals. Does the reporter agree with this policy, and why? Do you agree with this policy, and why?

5. Find an article in your local newspaper about a newsworthy funeral. Watch the local television news coverage of the funeral. Do either the paper or the news show use pictures of the funeral? Were those decisions good ones?

6. At some point in your career, it may be necessary for you to ask the "How do you feel?" question of someone who has just undergone a tragedy. How will you handle it?

7. What attribute of the American press do you think is the most questionable in an ethical sense? How will you deal with that issue when you become a reporter?

OUT-OF-CLASS EXERCISE

Get a copy of the ethical code of your local newspaper. Interview one of the reporters about that code of ethics. How does this reporter feel about the code? Does he or she believe it safeguards the rights of both reporters and sources? How did the reporter learn of the newspaper's code—in formal training or orientation, by word-of-mouth, or what? Do you think the newspaper's code of ethics is sufficient and appropriate? Why or why not?

CHAPTER 22

Newsroom

Organization

When beginning news writers walk into newspaper offices, they receive confusing and conflicting advice from the staffers. The following brief guide explains who those newspaper staffers are and which ones to pay attention to. Many newspapers use a military type of command structure. Lowly employees have little to do with the exalted generals at the top of the command structure. Generally speaking, the person with the one-word title "editor" can exercise the most power over a reporter. All reporters want to please this editor, who is the person who sits at the top of the newsroom pyramid. Beyond that, though, newsroom structure depends on the size of the newspaper.

This chapter also discusses how to work with editors. Editors may seem intimidating at first, but once the reporter gets to know them better, they're still intimidating. But there are ways to work with editors that benefit everyone involved. This chapter concludes by discussing a new phenomenon, the writing coach.

✦ THE PUBLISHER

Very small weekly newspapers often have only one writer, usually a beginner. As the only writer, this person rates the title "editor." In this situation, the beginning reporter/editor should heed the **publisher** (the owner) of the newspaper. On slightly larger weeklies, the publisher retains the title of editor and has direct managerial control of the news-room.

On all other newspapers, the beginner should worry about the views of the editor, and forget the publisher. The publisher runs the entire newspaper operation, including the advertising department, the printing shop, the people in charge of distribution and circulation of the newspaper. The publisher worries about earnings, and whether the newspaper makes a profit. Although publishers care about their newspaper's content, they very rarely concern themselves with the day-to-day activities of news writers. A publisher who wants to give input on the content of the newspaper will do so through the editor. The editor rules the news department.

✦ EDITORS

On larger weeklies and smaller dailies, the person with the one-word title "editor" directly supervises reporters. The **editor** oversees the beginning writer. Large daily newspapers, though, have vast newsroom staffs and hordes of people with the word *editor* somewhere after their names. There are copy editors, news editors, state editors, sports editors, feature editors, managing editors, editorial page editors, associate editors, assistant editors, and city editors. In general, people with the word *editor* after their names seldom leave the newspaper office during working hours. They work internally, managing and directing the vast flow of words and pictures that make up a newspaper. People with the word *reporter* included in their title leave the newspaper office to gather and write the news. Editors edit the copy, lay out pages, and write headlines.

✦ EDITORS ON LARGE DAILIES

On a big paper, the person with the one-word title "editor" runs the entire newsroom. All the subeditors report to this one editor, but this one editor has a much bigger task than merely supervising the production of the newspaper. The editor has an external job representing the newspaper to the community. The editor makes speeches to local groups and talks with readers who have complaints or suggestions about the newspaper.

On a big paper, the **managing editor** handles the day-to-day operation of the newsroom. The managing editor, or **ME,** rarely serves as an external spokesperson for the newspaper. Instead, this editor has hands-on control of the newspaper office. The ME controls the budget and gives out the paychecks.

A **section editor** oversees the individual reporter on a large daily. This person assigns and reads a reporter's work. A reporter writes for a specific section—the regional section, the city section, the features section, or the sports section.

✦ ADVERTISING

Newspapers sell news to their readers, but newspapers also sell readers to advertisers. Subscription sales usually provide only a small percentage of a newspaper's total income. The bulk of the income comes from display advertising. As a result, the display advertising salespeople generally earn the highest salaries on the paper. Tradition in American newspapers keeps a strict separation between advertising space sellers and news writers. An elegantly dressed, mature, and affable advertising space seller may ask a young reporter to write a positive story on a business that spends money with the newspaper, but a beginning writer should not necessarily heed this request. Beginners would be wise to pass these requests on to their immediate editors.

Display advertising determines the economic survival of the newspaper. American newspapers, though, insulate the advertising department from the news department to preserve the editorial freedom of the news department. This tradition came about because of the general belief that a newspaper that puffs its advertisers will be dull to read. A dull newspaper has no readers. A newspaper with no readers cannot sell advertising and cannot survive.

✦ THE BACK SHOP

No such insulation protects reporters from the **back shop** or production section of the newspaper. Beginning reporters often have an inflated sense of the importance of the news department on a newspaper. After all, only skilled and talented people can gather the news and create interesting stories under intense deadline pressure. However, it is a major mistake for a newsroom employee to disdain the back-shop employees who handle the mechanical operation of printing the paper. Newsroom employees and the back shop must talk. Writers and editors have to check to see that the paper comes out as they planned.

Reporters and editors normally do not stay at one newspaper for long. They move up to bigger papers or out to jobs in public relations, but back-shop staffers often work at the newspaper for life. Over time, back-shop employees devise insidious ways to punish arrogant writers. All sorts of mysterious errors tend to crop up in the stories of rude and pompous writers. The paragraphs can be shuffled to make the story unrecognizable. At the last minute, the copy can disappear entirely, or four-letter words can mysteriously blossom in articles. Making friends with the back shop can decide a writer's survival.

Another whole set of employees work in the circulation department carrying the newspaper to readers' homes. These employees get furious when the newsroom misses its deadline. Carriers cannot do their work until the paper comes off the presses. No matter the importance of the breaking story, don't stop the presses. An army of back-shop and circulation employees will be sitting on their hands generating anger and overtime while they wait for the newsroom to finish its work. The later the paper gets, the more that printers and delivery people come crowding into the newsroom demanding that everybody stop writing so they can do their jobs.

✦ HOW TO TELL A GOOD NEWSPAPER

Unfortunately, not all American newspapers are good newspapers. The publishers of many papers worry much more about profits than about producing a product that reports the news independently and fairly. These poor newspapers have the highest turnover, and therefore have the most openings for beginners. A really good newspaper is a delight to read. It includes much soft news. Well-written features and sports sections generate subscriptions because they entertain readers—but the test of a really good newspaper comes on the city side. The reporters who staff the city desk do the hard news reporting about local people. Gutless newspaper editors frustrate their employees by killing really good stories that reporters dig up on their own enterprise. Ask these questions about a newspaper: Does it give fair and compassionate coverage to hard news that concerns all segments of the community? Or does the paper do fluff pieces about the moneyed segments of the community and harsh pieces about the community's poorest residents?

There are two traditional tests of the quality of a newspaper. First, when police arrest a prominent citizen, does the newspaper play the story up or down? If the mayor's arrest on charges of drunk driving makes the front page, it's a good newspaper. If the story goes unreported or appears in only three short paragraphs on the obituary page, it's a bad newspaper. Second, does the newspaper routinely publish puff pieces about its advertisers? If so, it's a bad newspaper.

A reporter on a bad newspaper should start looking for another job. The frustrations of having good stories buried for political considerations will, over time, become unbearable.

✦ ON A JOB INTERVIEW

Beginners on job interviews always worry about whether they can please interviewers, but a job applicant should worry as much about whether the newspaper will be a good place to work. The job seeker should ask questions to find out whether the newspaper does a good job.

Most editors know the two tests for a good newspaper mentioned in the previous section. To ask one of these questions would be an insult to the editor's integrity. Anyway, the editor of a bad newspaper may well lie. Instead ask the editor: Which of the pieces you've published in the last year are you proudest of? If the editor describes a gutsy, hard news story, it's probably a good newspaper. Ask the editor: What do you expect from a new reporter? How much copy will you want in a day? What will the hours be like?

Also, on a job interview look around the newsroom. If only people in their 20s sit in the newsroom, it's a bad sign. It may mean that some unpleasantness in the corporate culture makes staffers move on to other jobs as quickly as they can. Observe the interactions between the editor and other staffers. Do the interactions seem cordial and collegial? Or do staffers kowtow whenever they approach the editor? Do staffers seem harassed and stressed? Or are they relaxed and cheerful? Assess whether you think this editor will be a patient and cooperative teacher of the news business. A beginning reporter does not need a rude, impatient dictator for a first boss.

✦ WORKING WITH EDITORS

American companies, including newspapers, have decided to try to change the way managers expect employees to work and behave within organizations. Many American businesses are moving away from an office setting in which underlings take orders from bosses. In the new office setting, all employees make comments and suggest ways to improve the product. Many businesses have decided to move to this new management style, called **consensus management,** because it improves employee morale and improves the overall quality of the product that the business manufactures.

Under the old **authoritarian management** system, reporters did what editors asked them to do and gave very little feedback to higher-ups. Under the newer approach, editors expect all reporters, even the youngest and greenest, to speak up and give their opinions about the running of the organization. In this setting an editor expects all reporters to suggest ways to improve the product. This evolution in standards of organizational behavior creates a dilemma for a junior reporter.

Because even the most curmudgeonly editors know they should seek dialogue and discussion with their staffs, most editors will say that they use consensus management techniques in the operation of their newsrooms. Unfortunately, many editors will say that they believe in management by consensus, when in reality they expect obedience from their reporters without very much back talk.

Meanwhile, editors who use a true consensus model for managing their staffs want employees who will speak up. They expect reporters to make detailed comments, suggestions, and complaints about the organization. They want employees who will make contributions to the group effort to produce a newspaper of high quality.

This presents a new employee with a dilemma. The behavior expected by a consensus manager will get a reporter in trouble with an authoritarian manager. And the behavior expected by an authoritarian manager will cause problems for an employee working for a consensus manager. A junior reporter's survival on the job may rest on the ability to figure out whether the editor really uses the consensus approach to managing the newsroom, or if the editor only gives lip service to the idea of consensus while continuing to use an authoritarian management style.

◆ AUTHORITARIAN MANAGEMENT

The traditional organizational structure within American business and in American newsrooms is derived from the chain-of-command structure used in the military. One person at the top gives orders and sets the direction of the organization, and the rest of the staff executes these orders, creating the product visualized by the leader. In the army the general gives the orders; in the newsroom the editor takes command.

Under this authoritarian model the editor says, "I want you to cover the City Council meeting," and the reporter grabs her notebook and runs out the door to cover the City Council. Of course, editors who use the authoritarian approach to management do not expect blind obedience. They expect reporters to give some feedback about an assignment. They want their reporters to tell them if some obstacle blocks an assignment.

A reporter might tell her editor, "I've got an interview scheduled with the new superintendent of schools. We're supposed to get together at the same time the City Council meets. Shall I cancel the interview or can someone else go to the City Council?" All editors want reporters to warn them of potential problems with a particular policy or direction. They do not want an unknown factor to blindside them.

In the authoritarian approach, however, once a reporter has told an editor about the problem, the editor decides how to handle the problem and expects the reporter to accept that solution. For example, the editor might say to the reporter who already had an interview scheduled, "Everyone else is already working on other stuff. Call the superintendent and see if you can reschedule your interview for another time."

✦ CONSENSUS MANAGEMENT

The consensus approach gets away from this top-down approach to decision making. Instead, all the employees meet in a group to talk out a particular problem and try to find a way to solve it. Once everyone has explained how the problem affects them, the group discusses it until they can reach agreement about how to deal with the problem. Under this approach the editor works more as a discussion leader than as a military general.

A consensus manager might still ask the reporter to cancel the meeting with the superintendent and go to the City Council meeting, but the consensus manager would add, "Sally's surgery has really left us short-staffed. Maybe we'd better have a staff meeting to find a way to solve this problem."

One clear marker of a newsroom run on the consensus model is frequent staff meetings at which a group of employees makes many major decisions about how the organization will function. At these staff meetings the editor serves as a facilitator of discussion instead of a deliverer of policy.

For instance, the editor might begin the discussion with, "We've had a lot of problems lately with having reporters available to get to events. Sally's surgery is going to keep her out for at least three more weeks. How can we change things to be sure that the necessary stories get covered?" Then, reporters make suggestions.

John might say, "I think we should cut back on features so we can get all of Sally's local government beat covered." Mary might respond, "But features are important to the newspaper. If we just run a lot of meeting stories, we'll be putting out a dull product. I think we should use more syndicated copy to fill up the paper until Sally gets back."

At this point, an authoritarian editor might interrupt and say: "I like John's idea. We'll cut back on features." However, a consensus editor would say: "So we could cut back on features or we could run more syndicated copy. What do you think? Anne, how do you think we should deal with this situation?"

The discussion will continue, with the editor occasionally summarizing the discussion and seeking more comments from staff. Eventually, the meeting will end with a summary from the editor: "So, let me see if we've worked out a solution. Since it's summer and sports news is slow, we've decided Shalanda will move from sports to city government until Sally gets back. Meanwhile we'll fill the sports page with more wire service copy. Does everyone agree with this?"

✦ CONSENSUS OR AUTHORITARIAN?

A new reporter can figure out whether a particular editor functions as a consensus manager or an authoritarian manager by watching the way staff meetings function. Who does the most talking—the editor or the reporters? When they talk, what do they say?

At some newspapers the editor spends most of the staff meeting describing new goals and policies to reporters. The reporters talk very little, and when they do talk, they mostly ask questions. They ask the editor to clarify and give more explanation, but they make few suggestions for changing or improving the policy. A staff meeting where the editor gives instructions and the reporters seek clarification of these instructions is usually an indication of an authoritarian structure.

At the staff meeting about scheduling, an authoritarian editor would say, "Sally's surgery has really left us short-staffed. I've thought a lot about these scheduling conflicts we're having, and I've talked with each of you individually. Here's what I think we should do about it." Then the editor will outline the solution.

The editor will explain the steps she wants the staff to take to solve the scheduling dilemma. "Since it's summer and sports news is light, we're going to pull Shalanda out of sports and assign her to local government until Sally gets back."

A few reporters may point out problems they see with the new approach, but the authoritarian manager will answer, "I've thought about that, and here's what we're going to do." Mostly, during this kind of staff meeting the reporters will talk briefly and then only to ask for clarification.

Frequency of staff meetings also can tell a new reporter something about the editor's management style. An editor who has individual chats with reporters but rarely meets with the newsroom staff as a group probably uses the authoritarian approach. On the other hand, if the reporters do most of the talking during frequent meetings and the editor speaks only occasionally to summarize the discussion and keep it on point, then the newspaper functions on the consensus model.

In both cases, the problem and the solution may remain the same. The difference between the authoritarian and the consensus approaches lies in the way the group goes about defining the problem and reaching a solution.

In an authoritarian structure, the staff meeting exists to serve efficiency. The editor can save time by explaining a new policy to the entire staff at once instead of going around and talking with each reporter individually. In the consensus model the staff meeting exists to find a solution that all staff members can agree to live with.

Some American companies have decided to switch to the consensus approach because it improves employee morale. When workers feel that they have participated in solving problems in the office they feel more committed to and more invested in their work. They like their work more and they also pay more attention to quality because they know they can participate in improving quality.

✦ I TEAMS

Almost always, consensus management is the model in the newsroom for at least one group—the **I Team,** or **investigative team.** Most reporters file stories daily, but this group of reporters works on long-term projects. They may spend a month or more gathering information on a specific piece of news. Then, they write an in-depth series on the topic.

For example, the regular news staff may have written a heartbreaking story about a child beaten to death by his parents. The story might include an interview with a neighbor. "I called Social Services 22 times and told them what those people were doing to Sammy. Here's my record of the phone calls, but those bureaucrats didn't do a thing."

The I Team might decide to take an in-depth look at why Sammy died. Such a story would involve talking to friends and neighbors of the family, interviewing medical authorities, talking to the police, talking to the Social Services Department, talking with state regulators of the Social Services Department, and examining as many public records as the reporters can find on the case. After they have gathered the information, the I Team, as a group, will write up the story of Sammy's death. The resulting investigative series will appear in the newspaper every day for a week.

An I Team series like this represents a huge undertaking. It would take one person far too long to complete. So several reporters attack different aspects of the story. Since they all have equal status at the newspaper, they decide how to cover the story through a process of negotiation and consensus. They meet regularly to report to one another on what they've found out. Then, they decide what to search out next and when to stop researching and start writing. Often an I Team will work with an editor. This editor facilitates decision making by the investigative reporters instead of just directing their work.

✦ WORKING WITH WRITING COACHES

Perfecting one's writing craftsmanship is a lifelong task. Many new college graduates start newspaper jobs thinking that their learning about writing is complete. After all, they have mastered the news formula in their college classes. But after a year of writing steadily on deadline pressure on the job, they discover that they have settled into a fluid and efficient writing voice that makes their earlier college work look stilted.

A cliché about writing is that the best way to learn to write is to write. It is writing daily for pay that finally allows a beginning reporter to produce such a huge volume of copy that the process of writing, itself, becomes second nature.

However, this same writing under deadline pressure can also force a reporter to produce really poor stories. Many seasoned reporters would say they are proud of the writing in maybe only one third of the pieces they produce.

Deadlines can kill good writing. When a reporter runs the two blocks from City Hall down the street to the newspaper office and has only 15 minutes before deadline to write up the City Council meeting, there will be no time to pay attention to careful word choice. While running down the street, the reporter thinks up the lead. When he gets to his computer, he starts typing the five Ws. The rest of the story just follows.

This reporter is writing by instinct, relying on pure craftsmanship to beat the deadline. Because the newspaper must go to press, neither the reporter nor the editor can take time to craft the article into a more polished work. The story goes to the back shop, the public is informed—but the reporter knows that if he just had more time, he could have done a better job. A reality imposed by the deadline is that much newspaper writing cannot be of high quality.

For far too many newspaper reporters, however, the deadline pressure becomes an excuse never to worry about the art of writing. Whenever they sit down to write, they fall into deadline mode, quickly typing out a news formula piece and turning it in. There are always far more stories that need covering than there is time to gather the information and write it up. These folks get their stuff in quickly so they can return to the field and get more stories.

Often the pressure of deadlines and the desire to pursue more stories come to dominate the ethic in a particular newsroom. The entire newsroom staff, both reporters and editors, emphasize getting the news and getting it in the newspaper. In the process, they pay little attention to the quality of the writing that they are publishing. Over time, a newspaper produced by such a newsroom can become a very dull read.

To combat this tendency, newspapers have begun hiring **writing coaches.** These outside consultants come into the newsroom and work with individual writers on improving their writing style. They try to help writers improve the way the newspaper is giving the news to its readers.

Often the writing coach is a college professor from a department of journalism or English. Some newspaper chains maintain a circuit-riding writing coach on the home office staff. During the course of a year, the coach visits all the newspapers in the chain.

How do writing coaches operate? Different coaches use different techniques, but many of them are bringing some of the latest psychological insights into writing and creativity to the newsroom. Newspaper reporters good enough to have kept their jobs long enough to see a writing coach already know grammar and the basics of the news formula. Most of them probably know alternative structures for news stories, like the *Wall Street Journal* formula discussed in chapter 10. What most writing coaches focus on is new ways to get a story on paper in a hurry, while retaining that creative spark.

One insight that writing coaches often discuss is the nature of writer's block, or freezing. Every seasoned newspaper reporter knows that there are times when a story just won't come, when the reporter feels frozen at the keys. Psychological research has shown that this often happens because writers attempt to edit and plan entire stories in their heads before putting anything on paper, and so a common technique used by coaches is to encourage prewriting of various sorts. They encourage writers to jot down four or five different leads, to purposely write trick leads, in order to separate the creative part of writing from the mechanical part. Such techniques are usually initially met with a good bit of skepticism, but by the time the coach leaves the newspaper, often even the most hardened journalists will be trying a few of the tricks.

Each writing coach has a different method; some approaches will work for a given reporter, some won't. Burn out is a major occupational hazard of reporters, though, and so it makes sense to try whatever a coach suggests, no matter how odd. It may work—and if a coach is using a particular technique, it probably has worked for other reporters.

SUMMARY

- Always heed the words of your immediate editor. That person can have you fired or promoted.
- Always ignore advice from the advertising department. They have their own agenda.
- Always treat the back shop with consideration. A production employee can easily sabotage your work.
- Always meet your deadline.
- A good newspaper highlights bad news about prominent citizens and refuses to run puff pieces for advertisers.
- On a job interview, try to assess whether the editor will be a patient and cooperative teacher of the news business.
- A beginning reporter needs to figure out whether the editor is a consensus manager or an authoritarian manager.
- The authoritarian manager gives orders and expects them to be followed.
- The consensus manager expects reporters to speak up and make suggestions for improving the running of the organization.
- If the editor does most of the talking at staff meetings or if there are no staff meetings, the editor is likely to be an authoritarian manager.
- If reporters do most of the talking at staff meetings, the editor is likely to be a consensus manager.
- Most investigative reporting teams use a consensus approach to decision making.
- Writing coaches can be of real help, even to seasoned reporters.

Outline for a
News Formula
Story

Each line in this fill-in-the-blank outline represents a newspaper paragraph. Each item headed by a Roman numeral represents one of the sections of the inverted pyramid story as described in Chapters 3 and 4.

I. Lead sentence. Must include Who, What, and When elements.
   A. Follow paragraph. Tell Where and Why.
   B. Optional second follow paragraph to round out lead.
II. Summary or So What section explains significance of story. "_____," said John Doe.
   A. "_____," said Doe.
   B. _____, said Doe.
   C. "_____," said Doe.
III. First, and most important, topical section. Include a transition. Begin with a paraphrase of an important idea: _____, said Doe.
   A. Back up the idea with evidence: "_____," said Doe.
   B. More evidence: _____, said Doe.
   C. More evidence: "_____," said Doe.
IV. Second topical section. Include a transition. Begin with a paraphrase of an important idea: _____, said Doe.
   A. Back up the idea with evidence: "_____," said Doe.

     B.   More evidence: _____, said Doe.

     C.   More evidence: "_____," said Doe.

V. Third topical section. Include a transition. Begin with a paraphrase of an important idea: _____, said Doe.

     A.   Back up the idea with evidence: "_____," said Doe.

     B.   More evidence: _____, said Doe.

     C.   More evidence: "_____," said Doe.

VI. Fourth, and least important, topical section. Include a transition. Begin with a paraphrase of an important idea: _____, said Doe.

     A.   Back up the idea with evidence: "_____," said Doe.

     B.   More evidence: _____, said Doe.

     C.   More evidence: "_____," said Doe.

Recommended Reading

Baker, Bob. *Newsthinking: The Secret of Great Newswriting* (Cincinnati, Ohio: Writer's Digest Books, 1981). Describes the prewriting process—the analysis a reporter does before beginning to write.

Biagi, Shirley. *Interviews That Work* (Belmont, Calif.: Wadsworth, 1992). An excellent guide to interviewing techniques.

Clark, Roy Peter, and Don Fry. *Coaching Writers: Editors and Reporters Working Together* (New York: St. Martin's Press, 1992). One could consider Roy Peter Clark of the Poynter Institute in St. Petersburg, Fla., the dean of American writing coaches. In this brief book he outlines the process of coaching writers and working with coaches.

Gans, Herbert. *Deciding What's News* (New York: Vintage, 1980). This study of CBS News identifies the news values used in deciding what stories to air.

Goodwin, H. Eugene. *Groping for Ethics in Journalism* (Ames, Iowa: Iowa State University Press, 1987). A landmark examination of ethical problems journalists face.

Harragan, Betty Lehan. *Games Mother Never Taught You* (New York: Warner, 1981). A humorous but truthful guide to survival in American corporate hierarchies.

Hulteng, John L. *Playing It Straight* (Chester, Conn.: Globe Pequot, 1981). A short ethics handbook for reporters, published under the auspices of the American Society of Newspaper Editors.

Kessler, Lauren, and Duncan McDonald. *When Words Collide: A Journalist's Guide to Grammar and Style* (Belmont, Calif.: Wadsworth, 1988). An excellent reference guide that explains grammar in ordinary language using journalism examples.

Lewis, Anthony. *Make No Law* (New York: Vintage, 1991). A readable history of American libel law.

Literacy Committee of the American Society of Newspaper Editors, "Ways with Words" (Washington, D.C.: ASNE, 1993). This pamphlet describes an experiment conducted by the Poynter Institute in conjunction with the St. Petersburg (Fla.) *Times* concerning reader perceptions of four different ways to lead a news story.

Manoff, Robert Karl, and Michael Schudson, eds. *Reading the News* (New York:

Pantheon, 1986). A readable series of essays written from a sociological perspective describing how the media define news.

Missouri Group: Brian S. Brooks, George Kennedy, Daryl R. Moen, and Don Ranly. *News Reporting and Writing,* Fifth Edition (New York: St. Martin's Press, 1995). The best of the long, comprehensive news writing texts.

Ryan, Buck. "The Maestro Concept: A New Approach to Writing and Editing for the Newspaper of the Future," Report Prepared for the Annual Convention of the American Society of Newspaper Editors, March 30–April 2, 1993; copies available from American Society of Newspaper Editors. The pamphlet describes a Midwestern newspaper's experiment with consensus management of its newsroom.

Strunk, William, and E. B. White. *The Elements of Style* (New York: Macmillan, 1979). Most newspaper people consider this little book, first published in 1959, to be the classic description of the effective news voice.

Ullmann, John, and Steve Honeyman. *The Reporter's Handbook: An Investigator's Guide to Documents and Techniques* (New York: St. Martin's Press, 1983). Prepared under the auspices of the Association of Investigative Reporters and Editors, this essential guide to news gathering should sit on every reporter's desk.

Zinsser, William. *On Writing Well* (New York: HarperCollins, 1990). The modern classic on developing an effective news voice.

Glossary

action–reaction A method for organizing the body of the story in which summary and quotation paragraphs are presented for an action or event, and then summary and quotation paragraphs are presented for the reaction of someone or something to that action or event.

advance Information or a completed news story that discusses an event that has not yet happened.

advance copy Information a reporter receives before an event (usually a speech) takes place, in which the text of the speech is released before the speech itself is made.

advance stories Stories reporting events that have not yet happened. Advances include press releases, most announcements, weddings, obituaries (which are more funeral announcements than anything else), and many election, business, and political stories.

attribution The presentation of information that makes it clear who is providing the information in a paragraph. Unattributed information is assumed to be provided by the author of the story.

authoritarian management The traditional organizational structure within American business and in American newsrooms, derived from the chain-of-command structure used in the military. One person at the top gives orders and sets the direction of the organization, and the rest of the staff executes these orders, creating the product visualized by the leader.

backfile A collection of articles that the newspaper has already published; once called the morgue. Also known as the clip file.

backfill Material, presented in the body of the story, that presents information about events that happened before the time of the lead event—information that is essential to understanding the story.

back shop Printers, paste-up people, and other employees who handle the mechanical tasks of printing the newspaper.

body The summary and quotation material appearing after the lead, follow paragraph, summary paragraphs, and backfill, usually comprising the largest part of the story.

breaking news story A story covering an event that is unfolding while the reporter is writing the story, or an event that has just happened. Breaking news stories can include press conferences, on-scene crime reporting, final election coverage, and disasters like earthquakes, floods, and hurricanes.

bright quote A quote that succinctly expresses the conflict or unusualness angle of a story; it is usually used in the follow paragraph.

bullets Graphic devices used to make specific items in a list stand out.

buried lead A lead paragraph (the paragraph summarizing the most important angle of a news story) that appears somewhere other than at the very beginning of the story.

clip file A library of already published articles; also known as the backfile.

conflict The opposition and struggle between a person and some other person, thing, or situation. Conflict is the main driving force of news.

consensus management A team-building approach to running a newsroom. Editors who use this management style expect reporters to make detailed comments, suggestions, and complaints about the organization.

cop shop Reporters' slang for the local police department. Usually, beginning reporters draw the cop shop as one of their first regular story assignments.

countertransference A term from psychotherapy that describes what happens when therapists become emotionally involved with their patients. Therapists abandon their positions as concerned advocates for patients, and the treatment of patients takes a back seat to therapists' personal needs. Reporters can make the same mistake in covering news stories.

database A set of computerized files on a specific topic, often available to a reporter through the Internet.

double-decker A follow paragraph that conveys exactly the same information as the lead.

editor A supervisor of reporters.

five Ws Who, what, where, when, and why; the information that is used in the construction of a news formula lead.

follow paragraph The second (or, occasionally, third) paragraph of a news story, in which the brightest quote appears.

Fourth Estate A nickname for the U.S. press, emphasizing its importance in the governance of the nation. The first three estates—the presidency, Congress, and the judiciary—are, it is argued, so dependent on the press to inform the public of their activities that the press has become an unofficial fourth branch of government.

functionalism A sociological theory that describes every human social structure as serving some function.

futures file A calendar and a file folder where a reporter notes information for stories coming up in the future.

getting married A slang term for becoming so friendly with sources that one can no longer write negative articles about them.

grammar checker A computer program that lists possible grammatical errors in a draft of a news story.

idea, then evidence Another name for the summary–quotation structure used in the body of a news formula story.

impact A measure of the direct effect a news event will have on the lives of the readers of a publication. In general, the greater the impact of an event, the greater its news value.

Internet, the A system of fiber-optic cables that allow one personal computer to link up with individual computers and computer databases worldwide.

inverted pyramid A description of the news formula method of organizing material in a story; the most important information goes first, with the other information appearing in order of importance from most to least important.

I Team (or investigative team) A group of reporters doing in-depth investigative reporting.

lead The first, and most critical, paragraph of a news formula story; here, the five Ws appear in a sentence of 40 words or less.

leading a quote Preceding a quote with attribution. Leading a quote is usually to be avoided; attribution should almost always follow at least the first sentence of a quotation.

libel The publication of material that holds an identifiable person or group up for contempt, ridicule, or hatred.

managing editor (ME) The person who supervises the day-to-day operation of a newsroom.

morgue A somewhat antiquated term for a collection of articles that the newspaper has already published; also known as the clip file or backfile.

mumblers Cluttered leads that try to cram too much information into the first sentence of a news story.

narrative structure Beginning an article with a five- to eight-paragraph chronological story about a particular person involved in a news event.

news formula, the A method for writing and organizing information that generates a standard news story.

newsworthiness A measure of how interesting and important a timely report of an event would be to the average reader of a publication.

nice-nellyisms Pleasant euphemisms used in news articles to substitute for blunter words and phrases.

novelty A measure of how unusual and interesting an event is to the average reader of a publication.

nut paragraph (nut graph) The paragraph, sometimes also called the "so what" graph, in a narrative structure news story that summarizes the basic newsworthiness of the story.

off the record A term used to describe an agreement between a source and a reporter that the information the source provides will not be used in a news story.

ongoing story A story that follows a news event that is in the process of happening. Some parts of the story have already been reported; some are happening now; and more will happen in the future. Also called second-cycle stories.

orphan quote A one-word or one-phrase quotation inserted into a summary paragraph, as in: *Schiller said he would "fend off" any attempts at a buy-out.* Also called a quote-out.

press release An article written by an advocate of a position or group and submitted to a newspaper for publication.

prominence A measure of how well-known and significant a figure in a news story is to the average reader of a publication.

proximity A measure of how near an event is to the average reader of a publication.

pseudo-event An event like a press conference, march, or rally staged purely to draw reporters.

publisher The person who runs the entire newspaper operation, including the advertising department, the printing shop, and the circulation department.

quote-out Another term for an orphan quote.

retrospective (retro) A story that discusses an important event from the past—for example, the 50th anniversary of the end of World War II or the 30th anniversary of the Reverend Martin Luther King Jr.'s "I Have a Dream" speech.

saidism A nickname for the unwillingness to use the word "said," and for the attempt to come up with varied synonyms for "said" in news copy.

second-cycle story A story that follows a news event that is in the process of happening. Some parts of the story have already been reported; some are happening now; and more will happen in the future. Also called ongoing stories.

section editor An editor who supervises writers working on a certain section of the newspaper—for instance, the state, sports, features, editorial page, or city sections.

sidebar A companion piece to a main story, appearing on the same page, set off with some separating graphic treatment (usually a ruled box).

source book A directory of experts who work for a university, non-profit organization, or business and are willing to grant newspaper interviews in their areas of expertise.

so what graph The paragraph, sometimes also called a nut paragraph, in a narrative structure news story that summarizes the basic news-worthiness of the story.

spelling checker A computer program that lists possible spelling errors in a draft of a news story.

stylebook A reporter's reference listing proper formats for spelling, cap-italization, and abbreviation in news stories.

summary lead A lead that summarizes the information contained in the story; a news formula lead.

summary paragraphs The first five to eight paragraphs after the lead paragraph. These establish the main facts of the story in a summary format.

sunshine laws State and federal laws that guarantee public access to the documents and meetings of any agency funded by tax monies.

surveillance A function served by news; keeping tabs on what is hap-pening in one's surroundings.

timeliness A measure of how recent a given piece of information is.

time peg The "when" element in a five Ws lead; the time when an event happened.

topical section A group of action–reaction paragraphs that deal with a given topic; these usually consist of four to six paragraphs presenting opposing viewpoints or events concerning a single topic.

topical sentence The first sentence of a topical section, in which the conflict angle of the following topical section is described.

trick lead A lead in which the most important angle of the story does not appear, and is replaced by some clever or arresting phrase. Trick leads are, in general, disliked by editors.

unusualness A measure of news value based on the fact that unusual events have greater interest than events that aren't unusual, as in the traditional "man bites dog" story.

***Wall Street Journal* lead** Beginning an article with a five- to eight-para-graph chronological story about a particular person involved in a news event.

weasel words Words such as *allegedly, perhaps,* and *recently* that enable reporters to make assertions without ascertaining their accu-racy. Weasel words are sometimes relied on by reporters when specific facts and information are missing.

wrap-up A story which summarizes an important event which is now over.

writing coach An employee (or contract worker) for a newspaper whose job it is to help writers improve their writing skills.

yellow journalism Journalistic practices that emphasize emotion, horror, or pathos. Yellow journalism got its name from turn-of-the-century newspapers that depended on sensationalism to sell copy, and that used yellow paper in some of their sections. In general, "yellow journalism" is a derogatory term.

Index

About the Authors

Catherine C. Mitchell is professor of mass communication and department chair at the University of North Carolina, Asheville. She holds a Ph.D. in communications from the University of Tennessee–Knoxville. From 1975 to 1981, she was co-publisher of the *Point Reyes Light* in Point Reyes Station, Calif. After the newspaper's investigative reports on the Synanon Foundation won a Pulitzer Prize in 1979, Mitchell co-authored *The Light on Synanon*, a book about that coverage and its aftermath. She is also the author of *Margaret Fuller's New York Journalism: A Biographical Essay and Key Writings* (1995).

Mark D. West is assistant professor of mass communication at the University of North Carolina, Asheville. He holds a Ph.D. in mass communication research from the University of North Carolina at Chapel Hill. His dissertation on press coverage of the Vietnam War won both the ICA International Division and the AEJMC Nafziger-White awards. West has published two co-authored book chapters on continuous audience research methods and has presented numerous refereed papers on that topic. Before attending graduate school, he was a reporter for the Asheville (N.C.) *Citizen-Times* and co-authored several successful computer games.